**Embers of Emp
Brexit Britain**

Embers of Empire in Brexit Britain

Edited by
Stuart Ward and Astrid Rasch

BLOOMSBURY ACADEMIC
LONDON • NEW YORK • OXFORD • NEW DELHI • SYDNEY

BLOOMSBURY ACADEMIC
Bloomsbury Publishing Plc
50 Bedford Square, London, WC1B 3DP, UK
1385 Broadway, New York, NY 10018, USA

BLOOMSBURY, BLOOMSBURY ACADEMIC and the Diana logo are trademarks of Bloomsbury Publishing Plc

First published in Great Britain 2019

Copyright © Stuart Ward and Astrid Rasch 2019

Stuart Ward and Astrid Rasch have asserted their right under the Copyright, Designs and Patents Act, 1988, to be identified as Editors of this work.

This book was produced with the invaluable assistance of the Velux Foundation.

Cover design by Tjasa Krivec
Cover illustration by Miles Cole

All rights reserved. No part of this publication may be reproduced or transmitted in any form or by any means, electronic or mechanical, including photocopying, recording, or any information storage or retrieval system, without prior permission in writing from the publishers.

Bloomsbury Publishing Plc does not have any control over, or responsibility for, any third-party websites referred to or in this book. All internet addresses given in this book were correct at the time of going to press. The author and publisher regret any inconvenience caused if addresses have changed or sites have ceased to exist, but can accept no responsibility for any such changes.

A catalogue record for this book is available from the British Library.

A catalog record for this book is available from the Library of Congress.

ISBN: HB: 978-1-3501-1380-0
PB: 978-1-3501-1379-4
ePDF: 978-1-3501-1381-7
eBook: 978-1-3501-1382-4

Typeset by RefineCatch Limited, Bungay, Suffolk
Printed and bound in Great Britain

To find out more about our authors and books visit www.bloomsbury.com and sign up for our newsletters.

Contents

Notes on Contributors   vii

1 Introduction: Greater Britain, Global Britain   1
   Stuart Ward and Astrid Rasch

2 Debating Empire 2.0   15
   David Thackeray and Richard Toye

3 Brexit and the Anglosphere   25
   Michael Kenny and Nick Pearce

4 How Unique is Britain's Empire Complex?   37
   Elizabeth Buettner

5 Forgetfulness: England's Discontinuous Histories   49
   Bill Schwarz

6 Ireland and the English Question   59
   Fintan O'Toole

7 Scotland, Brexit and the Persistence of Empire   71
   Neal Ascherson

8 Gibraltar: Brexit's Silent Partner   79
   Jennifer Ballantine Perera

9 Brexit and the Other Special Relationship   87
   Camilla Schofield

10 Refugees, Migrants, Windrush and Brexit   101

Yasmin Khan

11 Rhodes Must Fall, Brexit, and Circuits of Knowledge and Influence   111

Saul Dubow

12 Relics of Empire? Colonialism and the Culture Wars   121

Katie Donington

13 The Guerrilla Arts in Brexit Bristol   133

Olivette Otele

14 Biggar vs Little Britain   143

Richard Drayton

15 Visions of China   157

Robert Bickers

16 Afterword: The Ongoing Imperial History Wars   169

Dane Kennedy

Index   175

Contributors

Neal Ascherson is a Scottish journalist and writer. Over a long career in journalism, he has written for the *Observer* (1960–90) and the *Independent on Sunday* (1990–98). He contributed scripts for the 1974 television documentary series *World at War* and the 1998 series *The Cold War*. More recently, he has been a regular contributor to the *London Review of Books*. His books include *Polish August* (Penguin, 1981), *Black Sea* (Cape, 1995) and *Stone Voices* (Granta, 2002). He is the Honorary Professor at the Institute of Archaeology, University College London. He is an Honorary Fellow of the Society of Antiquaries of Scotland.

Jennifer Ballantine Perera has, since 2011, held the post of Director of the Gibraltar Garrison Library. She is affiliated to the University of Gibraltar as the Director of the Institute for Gibraltar and Mediterranean Studies. Dr Ballantine Perera has worked on a number of research projects, including the AHRC funded project, 'Gibraltar Community and Identity' (2003–06); the ESRC funded oral history project on Gibraltar, 'Bordering on Britishness, (2013–17) with focus on border identities; and an EU funded project 'The Encyclopedia of Migrants' (2015–17) together with partnering European institutions. She founded Calpe Press, a publishing house dedicated to promoting Gibraltar writings, in 2009.

Robert Bickers is a Professor of History at the University of Bristol. His most recent books include *Getting Stuck in for Shanghai, or, Putting the Kibosh on the Kaiser from the Bund* (2014), and the 2018 Wolfson-Prize for History shortlisted *Out of China: How the Chinese Ended the Era of Western Domination* (2017). Currently working on a history of the British firm John Swire & Sons, he directs the 'Historical Photographs of China' and 'Hong Kong History' projects at Bristol.

Elizabeth Buettner has been Professor of Modern History at the University of Amsterdam since 2014. Her recent work focuses on decolonization, postcolonial migration, multiculturalism, and memories of empire in Britain and other Western European countries. Since her book *Europe after Empire: Decolonization, Society, and Culture* was published by Cambridge University Press in 2016, her research has extended further into the overlapping histories of post-colonial Europe and European integration.

Katie Donington is a Lecturer in History at London South Bank University. Her research focuses on the history, legacies and representation of British transatlantic slavery. She is a co-author of *Legacies of British Slave-ownership: Colonial slavery and the formation of Victorian Britain* (Cambridge: Cambridge University Press, 2014). She is the co-editor of *Britain's history and memory of transatlantic slavery: The local nuances of a 'national sin'* (Liverpool: Liverpool University Press, 2016). Her monograph *The Bonds of Family: Slavery, commerce and culture in the British Atlantic world* will be published by Manchester University Press in 2019.

Richard Drayton is Rhodes Professor of Imperial History at King's College London. His most recent book is *Whose Constitution? Law, Justice and History in the Caribbean* (2016).

Saul Dubow is a historian of modern South Africa with particular interests in empire, science and intellectual history. He is the Smuts Professor of Commonwealth history at Cambridge and a fellow of Magdalene College. His most recent book is *Apartheid 1948–1994* (Oxford, 2014). He is currently completing a book on the history of science in South Africa from 1750 to the present with William Beinart.

Dane Kennedy is the Elmer Louis Kayser Professor of History and International Affairs at George Washington University in Washington D.C. and the Director of the National History Center. He is a historian of the British imperial world whose latest book is *The Imperial History Wars: Debating the British Empire* (Bloomsbury, 2018).

Michael Kenny is Professor of Public Policy at the University of Cambridge and the Director of the Bennett Institute for Public Policy. He has published extensively on British politics and political history, and is the author of *The Politics of English Nationhood* (Oxford University Press, 2014), which won the WJM Mackenzie prize for best book in political studies in the UK in 2015.

Yasmin Khan is an Associate Professor of British History at the University of Oxford. She has published on the decolonization of South Asia including refugees, war and the Partition of 1947. Her most recent book is *The Raj at War* (Bodley Head, 2015). In 2018 she presented a short series, *A Passage to Britain* on BBC2.

Olivette Otele is Professor of Colonial History, Memory and Politics at Bath Spa University. Vice President of the Royal Historical Society, she is also an advisory board member of the UK's Arts and Humanities Research Council and a European Commission research grant evaluator. She is the author of several articles and volumes. Her forthcoming and latest publications include: *Post-conflict Memorialization: Missing memorials, absent bodies* (Palgrave Macmillan, 2019); *African-Europeans: a Hidden History* (Hurst, 2019); *Histoire de l'esclavage britannique: des origines de la traite aux premisses de la colonisation* (Houdiard, 2008). Professor Otele is also a broadcaster (BBC, Sky News, *The Guardian*, the *Daily Telegraph*, Radio France, Jeune Afrique, etc.).

Fintan O'Toole is a columnist with *The Irish Times* and Leonard L. Milberg lecturer in Irish Letters at Princeton University, USA. He is a regular contributor to the *New York Review of Books* and *The Guardian*. He has published over a dozen books on cultural, historical and political matters, the latest of which is *Heroic Failure: Brexit and the Politics of Pain* (Head of Zeus, 2018).

Nick Pearce is Professor of Public Policy and Director of the Institute for Policy Research at the University of Bath. He was formerly Head of the No. 10 Policy Unit and the IPPR think-tank. He is co-author, with Michael Kenny, of *Shadows of Empire: The Anglosphere in British Politics* (Polity Press, 2018).

Astrid Rasch is Associate Professor of English at the Norwegian University of Science and Technology. Her research centres on memory culture at the end of the British Empire with a particular focus on memoirs from Zimbabwe, Australia and the Caribbean, and the memory of Empire in Brexit Britain. She has published on autobiography, decolonization and nostalgia and edited the anthology *Life Writing After Empire* (Routledge, 2016). She is the founder and leader of the Decolonial Research Group in Norway and heads the Scandinavian network initiative Literatures of Change: Culture and Politics in Southern Africa.

Camilla Schofield is a Senior Lecturer in History at the University of East Anglia. Her research focuses on the history of decolonization, migration and racism in post-war Britain. She wrote *Enoch Powell and the Making of Postcolonial Britain* (Cambridge, 2013) and is now editing a forthcoming volume on the global history of white nationalism in the post-war period.

Bill Schwarz teaches in the School of English and Drama at Queen Mary University of London. He is currently engaged in completing his three-volume *Memories of Empire*. With Catherine Hall, he co-edits the Duke University Press series 'The Writings of Stuart Hall'.

David Thackeray is Associate Professor in History at the University of Exeter. He has published widely in the fields of British political history and the history of the British Empire-Commonwealth. His most recent book is *Forging a British World of Trade: Culture, Ethnicity and Market in the Empire-Commonwealth, 1880–1975* (Oxford University Press, 2019).

Richard Toye is Professor of Modern History at the University of Exeter, and is a specialist in the history of rhetoric. He is the author of numerous articles and several books, including *Rhetoric: A Very Short Introduction* (Oxford University Press, 2013) and *The Roar of the Lion: The Untold Story of Churchill's World War II Speeches* (Oxford University Press, 2013).

Stuart Ward is Professor and Head of the Saxo Institute for History, Ethnology, Archaeology and Classics at the University of Copenhagen, specializing in imperial history, particularly the political and social consequences of decolonization and its aftermath. His forthcoming monograph *Untied Kingdom: A World History of the End of Britain* will be published by Cambridge University Press. Between 2013 and 2018 he directed the collaborative research project 'Embers of Empire: the Receding Frontiers of Post-Imperial Britain'.

Chapter 1
Introduction: Greater Britain, Global Britain

Stuart Ward and Astrid Rasch

The Long Room, Lancaster House – scene of many an instalment in Britain's fall from imperial eminence since the Second World War. It was here in 1956 that Tunku Abdul Rahman staked a claim for Malayan Independence, insisting that his people were 'entirely capable of running their country happily and efficiently'.[1] The following year, the first of a series of conferences was staged at the same venue, culminating in an independent Nigerian constitution in 1960. Uganda and Kenya were next, their terms of independence thrashed out in the stately ambience of Lancaster's rococo halls between 1960 and 1963. Most famously of all, it was at Lancaster House that a peace settlement was brokered to end the bloody civil war in Rhodesia-Zimbabwe, finally discharging the last vestiges of Britain's colonial obligations in Africa.

In January 2017, the stage was set for an entirely new break with the past, one that brought its own complex constitutional conundrums. 'Plan for Britain' was emblazoned on the screen as journalists crushed into the Long Room's narrow press enclosure. Three additional words, etched in smaller print on the front of the lectern provided more than an inkling of what was to come: 'A Global Britain' – purposely divulged to media outlets even before a word had been uttered. When Prime Minister Theresa May finally entered to deliver her long-awaited Lancaster House speech, it was only left to flesh out her expansive vision for post-Brexit Britain. Echoing her Asian and African predecessors, she unfurled a grand design for an 'independent, self-governing' Britain – a country free to 'leave the European Union and embrace the world'. This, she said, was something the British people felt 'instinctively', impelled by the unanswerable dictates of 'history and culture' and the urge to 'get out into the world and rediscover its role as a great, global, trading nation'.[2]

It was here that the Prime Minister broke with convention, her bid for freedom veering sharply from the historic protocols of Lancaster House. The British people were not merely pressing for self-determination but embarking on a voyage of *rediscovery* – back into a world too hastily abandoned in 1973; a return to open vistas where the spirit of a lost vocation might be restored. The Prime Minister's lengthy peroration at Lancaster House was long on aspiration and conspicuously scant on procedure – less a 'plan for Britain' than a string of extravagant prophecies. Ample helpings of the adjective 'global' (recurring eighteen times in the speech, surpassed only by 'world' which tallied an extraordinary twenty-six utterances) jostled alongside questing verbs like 'reach', 'embrace', 'seek' and 'build' to beguile listeners into buying the destination before surveying the roadworks. Indeed, May herself repeatedly depicted Global Britain as 'the great prize for this country – the opportunity ahead ... the destination at which we arrive'.[3]

In calling for a 'bolder embrace' of 'truly' global nationhood, 'more outward-looking *than ever before*', the Prime Minister was surely setting the bar on the high side. Unspoken throughout was Britain's long history of imperial endeavour; of centuries plying and peopling the globe under the banner of civilizing benevolence that no post-Brexit programme of outward expansion could possibly match. Yet it remains remarkable, despite the passage of more than half a century since the Empire finally dipped beneath the billows, how its underlying élan could furnish such motivational force. The sheer audacity of borrowing the garb of independence movements that the British had doggedly suppressed for centuries has been gaped at by any number of observers. For Fintan O'Toole, it marks 'the fundamental contradiction of Brexit' – a reassertion of imperial self-confidence and an anti-colonial insurgency all at once.[4]

It was not Theresa May who gave us Global Britain but Boris Johnson, who began touting it in his *Daily Telegraph* column within weeks of the Brexit referendum of 23 June 2016.[5] He went on to road-test it a few more times in the autumn of that year before it was deemed a serviceable vehicle for the Prime Minister's big picture. Displaying none of May's signature self-discipline, the then Foreign Secretary had no qualms about appealing directly to the ingenuity of a people who 'used to run the biggest empire the world has ever seen'.[6] He would later conclude his Tory party conference speech that year with a similarly romantic flourish: 'Though we never can take our position for granted, Churchill was right when he said that the empires of the future will be empires of the mind'.[7]

This was but an early instance of what soon became a coherent strategy – invoking Britain's historical track record to instil confidence in a post-Brexit future, beckoning a divided nation back into the world. Such rhetoric could be skilfully deployed to stir latent imperial sensibilities while simultaneously disavowing them. Upon his resignation as Foreign Secretary in July 2018, Johnson would single it out as one of his main achievements in office:

It was almost exactly two years ago that I went into the Durbar Court in the Foreign Office. It was my first day as Foreign Secretary . . . and I announced a vision. It wasn't a policy. It wasn't much more than a slogan. It was the way we needed to think of ourselves in the wake of the referendum. It was time . . . for Global Britain. And by Global Britain I meant a country that was more open, more outward-looking, more engaged with the world than ever before. It meant taking the referendum and using it as an opportunity to rediscover some of the dynamism of these bearded Victorians; not to build a new empire, heaven forfend.[8]

'Heaven forfend'? Yet surely the reason for protesting so much was the weight of Johnson's own words, seemingly calibrated to conjure the very object he abjured. Whether invoking Global Britain in the same breath as 'empires of the mind', or drawing more coded comparisons with the bearded dynamism of the Victorian age, it seems evident that he was indulging his self-professed predilection for 'cake' (both the having and the eating of it). Leading Brexiteer Jacob Rees-Mogg deployed a variation on the technique, casting back to the nineteenth century for 'good historic precedent for what we are trying to do' while simultaneously insisting that there was no 'neo-imperial vision' (the Empire, after all, was but one aspect of Britain's traditional 'international and global approach').[9] Such disclaimers arguably served to enhance the effect, simply by bringing Global Britain into semantic proximity with its imperial antecedents.

More to the point, the May government's advocacy of Global Britain only exacerbated widely-held suspicions about the family resemblance between the ghost of empires past and the first rumblings of Brexit futures. Long before referendum day itself, critics of the Leave campaign had become convinced that the imperial past had much to answer for – deriding Brexit variously as a 'pining for empire'; the 'Last Gasp of Empire', and an 'Empire-era trick' (amid suggestions that the additional 'e' in 'Brexiteer' was a tactical ploy to conjure the 'buccaneers' and 'privateers' of the sixteenth century).[10] Ever since the fateful 23 June outcome, this line of reasoning has sustained a profusion of headlines, bylines and op-ed columns characterizing the British – or more typically the English – as a people 'wandering . . . through the imperial debris that litters their homeland, unable to say who they are'.[11]

More elaborately, pundits and experts have been quick to diagnose the push for Brexit as a collective neurological affliction, ranging from a 'visceral post-imperial retreat into narcissism', to 'post-imperial stress disorder' or simply a species of 'rage against the dying of colonial light'.[12] As if to lend credence to the armchair psychiatry, Tory MP Heather Wheeler tweeted up a storm with her celebration of the British Empire triumph at the 2016 Rio Olympics, with a combined haul of 396 medals easily outstripping the paltry EU (post-Brexit) tally of 258.[13] She tried feebly to pass it off as 'a joke', though one could only wonder what compelled her to enumerate such a meaningless medal count. 'Behind Brexit stalks the ghost of imperial exception', ventured Neal Ascherson on the eve of the 2016 vote, and such musings have only multiplied as the much-vaunted material benefits of Brexit have conspicuously failed to materialize.[14]

These impulses seem to derive, in turn, from a more deeply rooted readiness to attribute all manner of contemporary ills to the 'shadow', 'hangover' or 'blowback' of empire. The austerity measures of 2010, the London riots of 2011, or the recurring ructions over Gibraltar and the Falkland Islands have all been explained by one metaphor or another of this type. Controversies ranging from the Mau Mau High Court case or the fate of Trident to the Rhodes Must Fall movement have invited speculation about the lingering presence of the imperial past, while the problem of Scottish independence has long been associated (rightly or wrongly) with a species of unfinished colonial business, pointing to a deeper process of national disintegration. In education curricula, the arts, immigration policy and overseas military deployments, Britain's perceived failure to divest itself of worldly delusions is frequently cited, through rarely established beyond vague gesturing to 'ghosts', 'hangovers' and periodic bouts of 'nostalgia'. In this scheme of things, Brexit is merely the latest in a succession of mishaps where the dead hand of empire is said to dictate the terms of a dysfunctional post-imperial politics.

Much of this line of critique can presumably be dismissed as easy political point-scoring, saddling Brexit with as much odious historical baggage as its enemies can muster. But by no means all of it. Recent studies have brought the afterlives of empire to the fore, assessing the myriad ways in which fallen empires retain a present-day political and popular purchase.[15] The first serious critical analyses of the imperial mystique lurking beneath the Brexit clamour have begun to appear, suggesting that there is more than mere superficial logic to the Brexit-empire analogy.[16] Meanwhile, dissenting voices remain critical of the rush to hasty judgement, pointing to the many ways in which the Brexit vote signalled a complex assortment of rival impulses – often starkly at odds with a pent-up desire to embrace the global dispensation of former times.[17] At times, these rebuttals carry a distinct edge of irritability or even outright indignation, as though the national honour had been impugned. To sample just one of countless overwrought Twitter posts: 'They never, ever shut up about the empire. They're fixated. No northern leaver I know has ever even mentioned it. If people are pining for and romanticising the past, it's about industrial decline, not imperial decline. Post-colonial theory has blinded these people to reality'.[18]

This volume is intended as a contribution to that evolving debate, indeed the first concerted attempt to examine the imperial underpinnings of Britain's fractious departure from the European Union. Our shared premise is that the British Empire is indeed *history* – that there remain few political or economic vestiges that might explain these enduring entanglements, little trace of the material fragments from which the Empire might be refashioned. What, then, lies behind the perceived potency of an Empire that has long since served its purpose? How do we account for the almost ethereal presence of the embers of empire in Brexit Britain?

A fundamental problem lies in the multiplicity of histories that comprise the imperial past. As Robinson and Gallagher remarked more than half a century ago, historians are 'very much at the mercy' of their particular concept of empire, and the same applies to any attempt at assessing the enduring influence of its legacies in the present.[19] Merely posing the question invites thinking about the Empire as 'one big thing' – lumping a formidable diversity of historical experience into an insistent singularity.[20] A wide assortment of well-worn metonyms routinely stand in for the bigger picture – exploration, commerce, slavery, seafaring, settlement, colonial wars, massacres, missions, emigration – each with its own distinctive emphases and usages. This seems unavoidable for the purposes of conducting worthwhile debate, but it raises the risk of attributing long-term causality to a wildly indeterminate array of historical factors. This is equally true of the incessant polling of the British people to ascertain their 'feelings' about the Empire. Whether the response is one of pride, shame or something hovering in between, the object of popular sentiment is invariably assumed to be unproblematically unitary.

Related to this is the difficulty of evaluating the plurality of imperial afterlives without resorting to the reductive moral categories that give the debate its distinctive emotional edge. Apologists for empire frequently take aim at the 'conventional view' (as they see it) – that 'there is only one way to look at the British empire: it was A Thoroughly Bad Thing'.[21] Some point to the 'chequered semantic history' of the term 'imperialism' itself, which has become so 'heavily laden with political baggage' and 'negative connotations' as to 'make it difficult to use dispassionately or truly analytically'.[22] Yet it is claimed with equal conviction that 'colonial rule is somehow fondly remembered by a majority of Brits' – a feeling sustained at an almost subconscious level by the complex inner workings of 'historical amnesia'; or less charitably, by a 'conspiracy of silence' in the service of institutionalized racism.[23] Here, the burden of complaint is that the imperial past is deliberately 'obscured' or 'whitewashed' so that it might be represented in a more positive light.[24] Both sides of the argument routinely condemn the conceptual simplicity and moral posturing of the other, presenting their own perspective as a sorely needed 'nuancing' of the debate.[25]

Intriguingly, the anecdotal evidence of Brexit lends support to both sets of claims, attesting to the positive as well as negative collective memory of empire. The ever-readiness of Remain supporters to tar Brexit with an imperial brush speaks for itself in this regard, but there are also reasons why leading Brexiteers persist with backward-looking motifs to evoke the boundless possibilities of leaving the EU. One ardent Leave supporter attending a Save Brexit rally in Yorkshire in October 2018 achieved momentary notoriety for airing his unrepentant views in the presence of a Sky News crew: 'For God's sake let's just get on, I mean, we're British. We stood alone for years . . . Let's get back to being a British Empire again. That's what it's all about you know? It's about being a British Empire'.[26] The sense of the imperial cat escaping from the Brexit bag was palpable.

Such indications only compounded suspicions that Theresa May's advocacy of 'Global Britain' was an exercise in cynical euphemism – conjuring older, discredited enthusiasms that could no longer be articulated in polite company. The parliamentary Foreign Affairs Committee took the extraordinary step of launching an official inquiry into the term itself, strongly insinuating that the government had been less than forthcoming in explaining its meaning or purpose. The report handed down in March 2018 concluded that Global Britain, in its very vagueness, carried the risk 'of undermining UK interests by damaging our reputation overseas' – not least if the prevailing uncertainty and confusion about its historical resonances went unchecked.[27] Senior Foreign Office officials were quick to concede that there had indeed 'been shortcomings with the label', in particular the widespread conjecture that it was simply 'code for Empire 2.0'.[28]

These semantic tensions are by no means unique to the Brexit era, but extend back over a much longer time frame. Arguably, the habit of ransacking the lexicon for alternative renderings of 'empire' is as old as the Empire itself – grasping for a form of words better suited to its sprawling diversity and unburdened by pejorative connotations. More than a century and a half ago, Charles Dilke published a two-volume travelogue of his extended tour of the British world. Striving to encompass the unwieldy dimensions of his subject, he very deliberately chose not to call it the 'British Empire', convinced as he was of the need to downplay the domination of subject peoples and accentuate the achievements of the British people scattered around the world; specifically, the white anglophone constituency in the settler colonies he so eloquently lauded.

'Greater Britain' was to be Dilke's coinage, soon taken up by others equally disenchanted with the unwanted baggage of empire. When J. R. Seeley borrowed the term in 1883, he also advanced it as a substitute for an imperial syntax that somehow failed to fit the bill. 'Our Empire is not an Empire at all in the ordinary sense of the word. It does not consist of a congeries of nations held together by force, but in the main one nation, as much as if it were no Empire but an ordinary state'.[29] Then, as now, it was the moral stakes that determined the brand. Neither Dilke nor Seeley were able to define their chosen term with any degree of precision (the former never resolved the puzzle of whether the United States should be included; the latter never fully squared the contradictions of excluding India), but clearly for both, the great advantage of Greater Britain lay in the very haziness of its outward projections, blurring the limits of location and obscuring unwanted detail.

Later reformers associated with the Round Table movement promoted the use of 'Commonwealth' as part of their search for an ideal form of closer imperial association, with Lionel Curtis noting that by 1916 he had 'reached the point of seeing that that part of the world under the British Crown was not, or ought not to be, an Empire, and for months I cudgelled my brains as to some alternative form'.[30] This same, self-conscious 'cudgelling of the brains' would continue into the inter-wars years and beyond, often at the behest of Dominion leaders like Jan Smuts who bridled at the 'misleading' implications of 'empire' (a term he found thoroughly demeaning).[31] Semantic ambiguity became the order of the day, punctuated by frequent attempts to nail down the finer distinctions between empire, commonwealth, colony, and dominion (the latter memorably described by Canada's Wilfred Laurier as 'a general term which covers many words which it is not possible to define otherwise').[32]

In other words, even at the Empire's zenith alternative categories were pressed into service to reconcile tensions produced by an eclectic set of relationships that meant different things to different people. Such yearning to escape the unwanted connotations of empire was never achieved with any degree of precision, however, partly because it addressed an emotional as much as a constitutional need. Even when agreement was reached at the 1949 Imperial conference on the formula 'Commonwealth of Nations', an element of confusion remained over whether the adjective 'British' had survived the change of nomenclature. Called on to adjudicate, Labour Prime Minister Clement Attlee could only offer the most evasive of solutions: 'Opinions differ in different parts of the British Empire and Commonwealth on this matter and I think it better to allow people to use the expression they like best'.[33]

Viewed in this light, Global Britain appears as a remediation of a wider family of concepts that have jostled for recognition through the ages to convey the abiding globality that has wedged itself into a particular way of thinking about Britain. That leading Brexiteers should explicitly disclaim any equivalence with 'empire' (while subtly invoking that very equivalence) is entirely consistent with a long succession of semantic substitutions. It also suggests that the enduring purchase of empire in the context of Brexit is as much about the persistence of certain habits of mind and structures of feeling – more so than any measurable, material continuity that might be neatly adumbrated. Ironically, even the ambiguities and contradictions of the term Global Britain itself turn out to be a throwback to the troubled conscience of the imperial past.

But not all is continuity. In several crucial respects, there is more than a modicum of daylight between the former verities of Greater Britain and its latter-day reboot. What distinguished the semantic tinkering of prior generations was an interactive quality, with any number of widely dispersed claimants asserting a stake in the outcome. It was a game everyone could play within the Empire's governing writ – albeit rarely conducted on equal terms. It is significant that an early innovator like Dilke coined his concept, not in Britain but while touring the globe, influenced by the temper and attitudes of the peoples and places he visited. A century later, even the agreement to disagree on the official designation of the Commonwealth was a group effort, the sheer range of interested parties necessitating a messy compromise.

That crucial collective component seems conspicuously absent in the creative processes that gave us Global Britain. Returning from a diplomatic mission overseas in September 2018, Theresa May made a particularly revealing observation:

> What I sense from my trips recently around the world, Africa most recently, is that people are looking at us in a different light . . . because we will be that independent sovereign nation able to do our own trade deals. As a global Britain, people will look to us and the role we'll be playing in the world.[34]

According to these optics, there could be no meta-constituency of co-owners sharing a stake in the Greater British bounty. May's reasoning seemed decidedly insular, even parochial by comparison – evoking an inert world 'looking at us' from fixed positions on the global grid, all waiting for Britain to determine how far its writ should run. Oliver Daddow notes how May 'went big on the word "embrace" throughout her speeches' on Global Britain, implying a newfound freedom to engage with a new global dynamism.[35] Yet the metaphor was almost wholly one-sided, more a species of grasping for a world that had been lost. Much the same mindset attended former Defence Secretary Gavin Williamson's ambition to expand Britain's military presence abroad once the European shackles are removed. 'This is our biggest moment as a nation since the end of the Second World War', he enthused, 'when we can recast ourselves in a different way, we can actually play the role on the world stage that the world expects us to play . . . that true global player once more'.[36] It seems hard to support a simple argument for historical continuity or semantic evolution in the face of such bald evidence of arrested development.

Further, there is the question of time lag. How are we to account for the prolonged gap between the diminished purchase of Greater Britain, the 'British' Commonwealth, and indeed the Empire itself (all consigned to past tense by the mid-1960s) and this latter-day flourish more than fifty years later? How did the imperial imagination fare in the intervening years, through the tumult of Powellism, the transformations of Thatcherism, the Blairite revolution, before re-emerging at an opportune political moment in the twenty-first century? Even among Brexit's keenest adherents, it is hard to find any trace of the galvanizing potential of the imperial past until comparatively recent times.[37] To what might we attribute the delay in transmission, the temporal break in the semantic arc from Greater Britain to Global Britain?

And above all, how do we describe the process of belated recall? Is it 'memory', 'nostalgia', 'imperial legacy' or any of its ubiquitous metaphors – shadows, hangovers, remnants, phantoms, ghosts, or embers of empire? Here the lexical 'cudgelling of the brains' becomes the lot of those tasked with interpreting the provenance of the 'imperial history wars' – grasping for a name, not only of the thing itself, but the process by which it is summoned forth.[38] The successful Leave campaign in 2016 was fought on a three-word slogan: 'Take back control'. It is the purpose of this collection to examine the retrospectivity inherent in that deceptively simple phrase.

These essays first took shape as a series of public lectures at the Garrison Library, Gibraltar in September 2018, and were later refined during the dramatic denouement of the Brexit negotiations in early 2019. At no stage were they intended as a running commentary on the complex diplomatic dynamics, still less an 'expert' analysis of the likely scenarios and outcomes. The more modest aim was to bring a variety of perspectives to bear on one persistent feature of the Brexit political minefield so often taken for granted. Fundamental to the task was finding ways of unpacking 'the empire', both in terms of its many constituent elements as well as multiple registers of popular resonance, furnishing many points of departure for the essays that follow.

The collection opens with the more immediate manifestations of the Brexit-empire nexus, with David Thackeray and Richard Toye examining the uses of the past in Brexiteer projections of Britain's economic future outside the EU. Closely related to this is Mike Kenny and Nick Pearce's dissection of the remarkable lure of the historically-ordained partnership of white, anglophone nations (recently stylized as the 'Anglosphere') while Elizabeth Buettner tackles the problem of whether Britain really is unique among the former empire-states of Europe in cultivating the memory of past imperial exploits.

From here, the emphasis shifts to a consideration of the diversity of regional and sub-national perspectives, where support for Brexit is anything but uniform. Bill Schwarz looks at what he terms the 'paucity of historical perspective' in specifically English inflections of the Brexit debate, suggesting that the alleged imperial provenance of anti-EU sentiment is an argument in considerable need of refinement. The Northern Irish border loomed throughout the Brexit negotiations as the ultimate stumbling block, and here Fintan O'Toole sheds light on the remarkable turning of the tables inherent in Ireland's 'England problem'. For the people of Scotland, too, Brexit has encumbered an already fraught relationship with their southern neighbours, not least in the light of the uneven burden-sharing of the Empire's more dubious legacies, as Neal Ascherson reflects. Meanwhile,

Jennifer Ballantine Perera turns our attention to the vexed example of Gibraltar, a community that remains both British, European, imperial and post-imperial all at once.

The persistence of imperial parallels is tightly bound up in the enduring potency of race in British politics; a phenomenon by no means confined to Britain. Camilla Schofield considers the wider, transatlantic connections that cohere around shared racial tensions bequeathed from former times, sustaining manifold linkages between the ethnic populism of Brexit Britain and the advent of Trump's America. Immigration famously emerged as one of the more compelling factors influencing the Brexit vote, and Yasmin Khan looks at how this has played into the wider politics of ethnic diversity in Britain, feeding directly into the divisive 'Windrush' scandal of the spring of 2018.

The high diction of political debate is but one of many ways in which imperial memory retains its salience; more pervasive still are the meanings issuing from the adornment of everyday public space. Saul Dubow examines the 'Rhodes Must Fall' controversy that erupted in Cape Town in March 2015 and wound its way to Britain by the end of that year, chiming in with the gathering social media momentum of the Brexit referendum in unexpected ways. Slavery, too, has long furnished a ready flashpoint in Britain's culture wars, as Katie Donington elaborates in her chapter on the struggles over heritage management in Britain's museums and galleries. Olivette Otele considers these issues in relation to the streetscape of Bristol, where the advent of Brexit has seen the growing influence of 'guerrilla artists' waging an aesthetic campaign against the city's abundant physical reminders of empire and the slave trade.

Two concluding essays examine the intricate thought processes of Brexit Britain through the careers of two individuals, each in his own way emblematic of our theme. Oxford Theologian Nigel Biggar's self-proclaimed 'outing' as a spokesman for right-leaning causes has proceeded virtually in lock-step with the political sea-change wrought by the 2016 referendum, a development Richard Drayton attributes equally to the embers of empire and the 'music of the Brexit moment'.

The exploits of Harold Baillie-Grohman could hardly be more dissimilar – a British naval officer who looked to China to reinvigorate Britain's ailing shipbuilding industry in the 1930s. Robert Bickers finds food for thought in Baillie-Grohman's headlong pursuit of Eastern promises, matched only by his exaggerated confidence in British enterprise – his abject failure an object lesson in the circuit loops of empire-states of mind.

Finally, Dane Kennedy's afterword reflects on the ever-combustible properties of Britain's imperial past, of which the ructions over Brexit are merely the most recent manifestation.

Our sincere thanks are due to all of our contributors for the ideas, energy and efficiency they have brought to assembling this collection, and to Jennifer

Ballantine Perera and her team at the Garrison Library, Gibraltar for providing such an appropriate – indeed obvious – setting to gather our thoughts and pool our resources. We acknowledge, too, the generous financial support of the Velux Foundation, as well as the invaluable moral support of the 'Embers of Empire' team at the University of Copenhagen: Ezekiel Mercau, Kalathmika Natarajan, Christian Damm Pedersen, Tóra Djurhuus and Harriet Mercer. Rhodri Mogford, Dan Hutchins and Laura Reeves at Bloomsbury have been supportive of the venture from the outset, and we thank them too, for their encouragement and advice throughout.

Notes

1 British Pathé, 'Malaya Seeks Home Rule, 1956', https://www.youtube.com/watch?v=zjsuTWYoYyY
2 Theresa May, Lancaster House speech, 17 January 2017, https://www.gov.uk/government/speeches/the-governments-negotiating-objectives-for-exiting-the-eu-pm-speech
3 Ibid.
4 Fintan O'Toole, *Heroic Failure: Brexit and the Politics of Pain* (London: Head of Zeus, 2018): 79–80.
5 Boris Johnson, 'Brexit frees us to be a truly Global Britain', *Telegraph*, 18 July 2018.
6 Boris Johnson, 'There is only one way to get the change we want: Leave the EU', *The Telegraph*, 16 March 2016.
7 'Boris Johnson's conference speech', *The Spectator*, 2 October 2016, https://blogs.spectator.co.uk/2016/10/full-text-boris-johnsons-conference-speech/
8 Boris Johnson, 'The rest of the world believes in Britain. It's time that we did too', *The Telegraph*, 15 July 2018.
9 Jacob Rees-Mogg, 'My Vision for a global-facing, outward-looking post-Brexit Britain', *Brexit Central*, 21 June 2018, https://brexitcentral.com/vision-global-facing-outward-looking-post-brexit-britain/. See also Astrid Rasch, '"Keep the balance": The Politics of Remembering Empire in Post-Colonial Britain', *Journal of Commonwealth and Postcolonial Studies* 7, no. 1 (2019).
10 Pankaj Mishra, 'Brexiteers are pining for empire', *BloombergView*, 29 April 2016; Ben Judah, 'England's Last Gasp of Empire', *New York Times*, 12 July 2016, Yanis Varoufakis, 'Brexit is an empire-era trick. Only the radical case for Europe makes sense', *The Guardian*, 28 May 2016; Tony Barber, 'Nostalgia and the Promise of Brexit', *Financial Times*, 19 July 2018.
11 Nicholas Boyle, 'The problem with the English: England doesn't want to be just another member of a team', *The New European*, 17 January 2017. A simple google search of 'brexit empire' suffices to furnish an indicative sample of this line of thought.
12 Mark Salter, 'Was Brexit an Emotional Decision?', *QRIUS*, 6 November 2016. Salter was commenting on Joris Luyendijk's diagnosis of 'collective clinical narcissism'

stemming from inflated English convictions 'about their country's place in the world' in 'Britain: Narcissist Nation', *Prospect*, November, 2016.

13 https://twitter.com/heatherwheeler/status/767756321219379201?lang=da

14 Neal Ascherson, 'From Great Britain to Little England', *New York Times*, 16 June 2016.

15 Bill Schwarz, *The White Man's World*. Memories of Empire Vol. I, (Oxford University Press, 2011); Elizabeth Buettner, *Europe after Empire: Decolonization, Society, and Culture* (Cambridge University Press, 2016); Dietmar Rothermund, ed. *Memories of Post-Imperial Nations: The Aftermath of Decolonization, 1945–2013* (New Delhi: Cambridge University Press, 2015); Jordanna Bailkin, *The Afterlife of Empire* (Berkeley: University of California Press, 2012).

16 O'Toole, *Heroic Failure*; Michael Kenny and Nick Pearce, *Shadows of Empire: The Anglosphere in British Politics* (Cambridge: Polity Press, 2018); Anthony Barnett, *The Lure of Greatness. England's Brexit and America's Trump* (London: Unbound, 2017); Philip Murphy, *The Empire's New Clothes: The Myth of the Commonwealth* (London: Hurst, 2018).

17 Robert Saunders, 'The Myth of Brexit as Imperial Nostalgia', *Prospect*, 7 January 2019; Janan Ganesh, 'Forget Empire – Britain wants less of the world, not more', *Financial Times*, 10 April 2017; David Edgerton, 'The idea of deep continuity in British history is absurd. We've always been in flux', *The Guardian*, 18 November 2018.

18 Twitter post by 'R.A.G.', https://twitter.com/stonky12, posted 24 March 2019.

19 John Gallagher and Ronald Robinson, 'The Imperialism of Free Trade', *The Economic History Review* 6, no. 1 (1953): 1.

20 Richard Price, 'One Big Thing: Britain, Its Empire, and Their Imperial Culture', *Journal of British Studies* 45, no. 3 (July 2006): 602–27.

21 Jeremy Paxman, '"Our Empire Was an Amazing Thing"', 16 February 2012, https://www.telegraph.co.uk/culture/tvandradio/9085936/Jeremy-Paxman-Our-empire-was-an-amazing-thing.html; see also Niall Ferguson, *Empire: How Britain Made the Modern World* (London: Allen Lane, 2003): xx.

22 Bernard Porter, *The Absent-Minded Imperialists: Empire, Society, and Culture in Britain* (Oxford: Oxford University Press, 2004): 8.

23 Kehinde Andrews, 'Building Brexit on the Myth of Empire Ignores Our Brutal History', *The Guardian*, 7 March 2017, http://www.theguardian.com/commentisfree/2017/mar/07/building-brexit-on-myth-of-empire-ignores-history-at-our-peril. On 'conspiracy of silence' see Rothermund, 5. Kris Manjapra, 'When Will Britain Face up to Its Crimes against Humanity?', *The Guardian*, 29 March 2018, https://www.theguardian.com/news/2018/mar/29/slavery-abolition-compensation-when-will-britain-face-up-to-its-crimes-against-humanity

24 Alice Procter, 'Museums Are Hiding Their Imperial Pasts – Which Is Why My Tours Are Needed', *The Guardian*, 23 April 2018, https://www.theguardian.com/commentisfree/2018/apr/23/museums-imperialist-pasts-uncomfortable-art-tours-slavery-colonialism

25 Thus, Oxford Theologian Nigel Biggar could decry 'the erection of a straw-man' in the arguments of his anti-imperial opponents, while the latter condemned Biggar for setting up 'a caricature in place of an antagonist: an allegedly prevailing orthodoxy that "imperialism is wicked". . . . This is nonsense. No historian . . . argues *simply* that

imperialism was "wicked"'. Nigel Biggar, 'Here's My Reply to Those Who Condemn My Project on Ethics and Empire', *The Times*, 23 December 2017, https://www.thetimes.co.uk/article/heres-my-reply-to-those-who-condemn-my-project-on-ethics-and-empire-cw5f2z80x; James McDougall et al., 'Ethics and Empire: An Open Letter from Oxford Scholars', *The Conversation*, http://theconversation.com/ethics-and-empire-an-open-letter-from-oxford-scholars-89333. See Richard Drayton's chapter in this volume.

26 https://twitter.com/SkyNews/status/1053662098574716929
27 https://publications.parliament.uk/pa/cm201719/cmselect/cmfaff/780/780.pdf
28 FCO Permanent Under-Secretary Sir Simon McDonald, quoted in the *Daily Mirror*, 4 June 2018.
29 Charles Dilke, *Greater Britain*, (London, 1868); J. R. Seeley, *Expansion of England*, (London, 1883, 1891 ed.): 11.
30 Curtis to J. S. Ewart. 7 May 1941, quoted in UKNA, CAB21/1815, 'Official Title of the Commonwealth', 23 October 1948 (essay by Canadian Department of External Affairs on the use of the term 'British Commonwealth').
31 W. K. Hancock and Jean Van Der Poel (eds), *Selections from the Smuts Papers, Vol. III, June 1910–November 1918* (Cambridge University Press, 1966): 510.
32 Quoted in W. David McIntyre, 'The Strange Death of Dominion Status', *Journal of Imperial and Commonwealth History* 27, no. 2 (May 1999): 194.
33 2 May 1949, extract in Nicholas Mansergh, *Documents and Speeches on British Commonwealth Affairs, 1931–52, Vol. 2* (Oxford University Press, 1953): 1210.
34 *Daily Express*, 19 September 2018.
35 Oliver Daddow, 'Global Britain™: The discursive construction of Britain's post-Brexit world role', *Global Affairs*, 2 April 2019: 11, https://doi.org/10.1080/23340460.2019.1599297
36 Interview, *Sunday Telegraph,* 30 December 2018.
37 Boris Johnson and Daniel Hannan provide an instructive bellwether, whose extensive writings on the subject reach back to the early 1990s but reveal little recourse to the empire-family resemblance that only crept into their prescriptions for Britain's post-European destiny decades later.
38 Dane Kennedy, *The Imperial History Wars: Debating the British Empire* (London: Bloomsbury Academic, 2018).

Chapter 2
Debating Empire 2.0
David Thackeray and Richard Toye

'Britain will seek to boost trade links with African Commonwealth nations this week in a move described by Whitehall officials as "empire 2.0"' reported *The Times* in March 2017, a few weeks before Theresa May started the formal countdown to Brexit by invoking Article 50 of the Lisbon Treaty. The story claimed that the British planned to promise all developing nations that their post-Brexit trading relationships with the UK would be at least as good as in the past: 'Ministers want to go further with African nations, however, and start talks to allow Britain to work more closely with an African free trade zone.'[1] Such aspirations were in line with the vision previously described by David Davis, shortly before his appointment to the newly created role of Secretary of State for Exiting the European Union in July 2016. According to Davis, post-Brexit Britain could hope for a buoyant economic future: 'Trade deals with the US and China alone will give us a trade area almost twice the size of the EU, and of course we will also be seeking deals with Hong Kong, Canada, Australia, India, Japan, the UAE, Indonesia – and many others'.[2] Unsurprisingly, these types of claims have been subjected to strong criticisms from Remainers. Many have claimed, in particular, that Brexiteers have unrealistic expectations about the role that the Commonwealth can play in Britain's future as a trading nation. 'The empire, even at its height, never came close to absorbing the majority of our exports or providing the bulk of our imports, and neither will the Commonwealth, no matter how good a trade deal we win', wrote the public historian and broadcaster David Olusoga. 'Empire 2.0 is a fanciful vision of the future based on a distorted misremembering of the past.'[3]

The notion of a link between Euroscepticism and the yearning for lost greatness is also a significant feature of the historical literature on Britain and Europe. Following the decline of the Empire, argued Benjamin Grob-Fitzgibbon prior to the 2016 referendum, the British people developed a hostility to Europe that went hand in hand with post-imperial nostalgia.[4] There is much merit in the argument. Undoubtedly, there is significant body of journalistic, political, and popular opinion that regards the British Empire as having been a positive force for good. Equally, pride in Britishness, and the sense that Britain is an illustrious nation which has no need of the EU, have been important features of the Brexit debate. If we offer a degree of challenge to the 'misremembered past' narrative, it is not because we reject the notion that pining for former grandeur is an important feature of Brexit ideology. Rather, we suggest that it could only become effective in conjunction with other key tropes, such as 'taking back control', EU 'dictatorship', and the rhetoric of Magna Carta and 'English (or British) freedom'.

Moreover, we argue that Brexiteers, however wistful they may in fact feel for the past of formal Empire, actually seek to play it down or to avoid discussing it. They do this even as they evoke what they regard as the unproblematic parts of Britain's Great Power past. The question, then, is not whether post-imperial nostalgia is important for Brexit, but rather the precise form that it has taken and how it has been operationalized. Fintan O'Toole's concept of 'zombie imperialism' is helpful here.[5] If Brexiteers do not overtly aspire to recreate Empire, they unconsciously reproduce imperial mindsets, in which the search for British *prestige* and the humiliation/subordination of the foreigner are intimately intertwined.

There are a number of reasons for expressing caution about the standard 'imperial nostalgia' narrative. To begin with, EU states other than Britain have struggled with their imperial pasts, without developing an anti-European pathology. Moreover – and this is indeed made clear by scholars such as Grob-Fitzgibbon – many post-war British politicians were simultaneously proudly imperialistic and enthusiastically European. (Duncan Sandys, Conservative founder of the European Movement in the 1940s and Colonial Secretary in the 1960s, is a case in point.) Furthermore, Robert Saunders has drawn attention to the important role of left-wingers on the 'No' side in the 1975 EEC referendum.[6] Tony Benn, a key player, had previously been active in the Movement for Colonial Freedom. The 'Empire 2.0' label was applied by disaffected officials, not the Brexiteers themselves. It was a derisive term, not a celebratory one; and this, in fact, signifies a crucial element of the rhetorical landscape of Brexit.

For Brexiteers have been well aware that they are likely to be accused of imperial atavism. The defensive tone of Boris Johnson, cited in the introduction to this volume, is highly relevant here. Johnson claimed to want to recapture Victorian dynamism, but 'not to build a new empire, heaven forfend'.[7] There was an acknowledgement here that explicit aspirations towards empire building are to some degree problematic (or at any rate politically unwise in the current climate). But what was equally striking was the way in which the Victorian economy and the Great Power status that went with it was presented by Johnson as easily separable from the Empire with which they were so intimately connected. If only the British people would believe in themselves enough, they could once again grasp their country's late-nineteenth-century status, leaving any exploitative connotations safely to one side. It is actually the casual disregard of Empire, then, rather than its conscious or systematic evocation, that forms the key to the 'post-imperial' in much Brexit rhetoric. At the time of the referendum, it was this that helped the Leave campaign(s) to deploy a language of abstract British 'greatness' which could appeal to younger audiences as well as older, more nostalgic ones.

Thus Brexiteers have consistently presented themselves as globalists keen to build on Britain's nineteenth-century legacy as a champion of free trade but have glossed over the ways in which free trade was itself an imperial project. It is important to note the limited role that calls to redevelop trade with the Commonwealth played among the Leave campaign's arguments during the 2016 referendum. Some prominent Brexiteers, such as Davis, instead presented themselves as globalists keen to build on Britain's nineteenth-century legacy as a champion of free trade. Leaving the EU, they claimed, would make it easier for the UK to establish trade treaties with key economic partners. Calls for trade deals with New Zealand and Australia featured prominently in the Leave campaign, indeed remarkably so given that these countries account for around 2 per cent of UK exports. And yet, these calls for trade deals with Commonwealth countries were usually interspersed among claims about the need to strike trade treaties with fast-growing economies such as China and Brazil.[8]

It is worth emphasizing that arguments about trade were only one aspect of the story told by the Leave side, which involved a multiplicity of claims on topics ranging from fishing quotas to migration to excess regulation. The crowd-funded film *Brexit: The Movie*, released in advance of the referendum, offers a fascinating combination of some, but not all, of these themes. (The absence of any discussion of immigration is notable.) Over black-and-white film of various forms of industrial activity, the director/presenter, Martin Durkin, asks and answers his own questions:

> Why are the British the cussed ones in Europe? Why are we so attached to our independence and freedom? Why do we take so badly to regulation? Where does it all come from? The British freed themselves from suffocating feudal regulation, centuries before the Europeans. While serfdom still existed in large parts of Europe, the free British were carrying out the great commercial and industrial revolutions that gave birth to the modern world. In the nineteenth century, unregulated Britain was the pioneer of global free trade, workshop of the world, dominating the world economy like a Leviathan.

Throughout the documentary, though, the only hint of explicit imperial nostalgia comes from Davis, who crops up as a talking head. Rather than summon a Victorian vision of empire, he refers to swashbuckling Elizabethan heroes: 'Our history is a trading, buccaneering history – you know, back to Drake and beyond, and that's what we're good at.' Intriguingly, the film also includes a lengthy paean to Switzerland – a wealthy country, certainly, but nobody's idea of a world power. Part of Durkin's success as a persuader here lay in his ability to conjure up an attractive range of potential options, rather than a single cast-iron alternative to EU membership.[9]

In order to appreciate Brexiteers' rhetorical strategies more fully, it is helpful to consider how the outcome of the 2016 referendum fits into a wider pattern of historical change.[10] At various points since the 1880s, hopes placed in the economic future of regional blocs have reshaped Britain's identity as a trading nation. Those who have historically sought to advocate a change in Britain's economic direction have often done so by employing novel interpretations of the past to justify their cause. Efforts to promote a 'Brexitization' of history in recent years therefore build on a long legacy.

In the late nineteenth and early twentieth centuries, many argued that it was essential to invest resources into 'British world' cooperation between the UK and its settler colonies. Australia, Canada, New Zealand and South Africa were commonly seen as vast, under-populated countries which needed British investment and migrants to reach their full economic potential. Although these countries accounted for a small fraction of UK trade (around 13 per cent of British imports and 16 per cent of British exports c. 1900), they received a disproportionately large share of attention in public debate, given they were seen as key markets for the future. Growing tariff barriers in Europe, and the advance of industrial competitors such as France and Germany, meant that Britain's place in traditional continental markets was looking increasingly unsure. Moreover, the Dominions had the advantage of being seen as 'culturally British', so UK exporters felt a sense of security and familiarity in trading with countries that was not shared by frontier markets such as China.

While *Brexit: The Movie* offered a vision of a confident, buccaneering, free-trade Britain, from the late Victorian period onwards many felt the solution to the Empire's economic problems lay in promoting imperial cooperation through tariff preferences. Advocates of tariffs claimed that the UK's economic progress over recent decades had been disappointing, while the United States and continental Europe had flourished as a result of the policies of free-trade Britain. Their opponents countered such claims by invoking the spectre of the 'Hungry Forties'. Free-traders claimed that many Britons had suffered from acute poverty until the protectionist Corn Laws were revoked in 1846.

Although the experiences of the 1920s and 1930s challenged earlier assumptions that the Dominions could support vast populations of settlers, British world networks became an important feature of civic life in these years. Economic links between Britain and the Dominions were strengthened by the development of bodies such as the Federation of British Industries, which worked extensively with UK manufacturers' representatives' groups within the Empire.

Moreover, governmental bodies such as the Imperial Economic Committee and Empire Marketing Board sought to promote Empire trade by collecting data, promoting scientific research and encouraging consumers to buy national and Empire goods in preference to foreign goods. These existing strands of cooperation help explain why UK and Dominion politicians promoted a system of intra-imperial tariff preferences in conditions of an acute global economic crisis at the Ottawa Conference of 1932, when few opportunities appeared to be available in foreign markets.

This system slowly unravelled after 1945 as it became increasingly difficult to see the Commonwealth as a coherent and attractive economic bloc with a bright future. A key problem here was that the foundations of Commonwealth economic collaboration before the Second World War were based on the activities of British world networks, effectively marginalizing or excluding Asian and African politicians and businesspeople. While efforts were made after 1945 to reshape fora such as the Commonwealth Prime Ministers Meetings and Commonwealth Chambers of Commerce to reflect the character of the multiracial Commonwealth, they had limited success. UN-linked bodies generally provided more appealing fora to collaborate with international partners on trade matters. In cities such as Singapore, Hong Kong and Delhi, Asian businesspeople had long been accustomed to working within their own ethnically-based chambers of commerce (in many cases they had little choice – being excluded from British chambers) and the practice continued long into the era of decolonization. In any case, if the British public felt any loyalty to Commonwealth trade it was assumed to be with the old rather than the new Commonwealth. When cheap imports of manufactured goods from Hong Kong and India became a common sight in the 1950s and 1960s, they were an unwelcome challenge to domestic producers.

While the Empire-Commonwealth accounted for as much British trade as Western Europe in the early 1960s, the latter was by now seen by many as the more promising trade partner of the future, and this explains why there was a significant recalibration of UK trade in the decade prior to EEC membership in 1973. 'Declinist' studies recast the years after 1932 as an era of economic stagnation in which Britain had initially benefitted from 'sheltered markets' but was now falling behind more dynamic European competitors.[11] The value of imperial preferences had already been significantly eroded by the General Agreement on Tariffs and Trade (GATT) and economic growth rates in much of the old Commonwealth lagged behind countries like West Germany and Italy despite significant immigration. Moreover, it became increasingly difficult to present the Dominions as 'British' nations who shared a common culture with the UK. The international outcry which greeted atrocities committed by South Africa's apartheid government, and the actions of Rhodesia's rebel government, undermined established ideas of 'Britannic' cooperation based on racial ties. At the same time, as Britain turned towards Europe, Australia, Canada and New

Zealand were paying increasing attention to the attractive trade opportunities opening up in the Asia-Pacific region.

The 2016 EU referendum hinged to a substantial degree on competing visions of how the UK should engage with foreign markets. It was not, however, a simple choice between free trade and protectionism nor between globalization and anti-globalization. Whereas Remain campaigners urged voters not to cast aside the opportunities presented by access to the European single market, those on the Leave side held out the lure of a more globally-oriented trading future (building on Britain's historical role as a 'free trade nation').

The result of the 2016 campaign provides a stark contrast with the European referendum of 1975. When Britons went to the polls then to decide whether to remain a member of the EEC, access to the European Common Market was presented by the victorious Yes campaign as key to Britain's future economic prosperity, and indeed as a means to combat the nation's supposed economic 'decline'. It would also compensate for Commonwealth markets, whose importance to British trade had declined sharply during the 1950s and 1960s.[12]

The triumph of the Leave campaign in 2016 resulted, in part, from their ability to overhaul this earlier perception that European Community membership was vital to Britain's economic future, and to revitalize earlier narratives which presented the UK's global trade role as key to its economic prosperity. Leave depicted the Euro-enthusiasts as having been blinded by their obsession with the EU to the detriment of other, better trading opportunities around the world.[13] The EU remains vital to Britain's international trade accounting for 44 per cent of exports and 53 per cent of imports in 2015. Nonetheless, the role of non-EU countries as destinations for UK exports rose significantly in the years leading up to the referendum, rising from 46 per cent in 2006 to 56 per cent in 2015. Leave supporters could therefore argue that the recent direction of trade meant it was better to focus on global trade opportunities that could be best pursued by leaving the EU.[14] There are parallels here with claims made by supporters of Joseph Chamberlain in the 1900s, who argued that preferential tariffs were needed to fully realize the economic potential of the Dominions as Britain's key market of the future.

The Leave campaign challenged the key rationale for EEC membership presented in the 1960s and early 1970s, that Common Market membership would enable Britain to take part in a dynamic and vibrant trading bloc that had a significantly greater future than Commonwealth trade. The EU, Leave supporters claimed, was now a region of low growth, hampered by expensive bureaucracy and divisions between member states, and increasingly peripheral to Britain's trading future. One Leave leaflet claimed that 'UK exports to the rest of the world are growing three times as fast as the UK's exports to the EU', despite Britain being unable to enter into its own trade agreements with these countries, which would presumably expand this non-EU trade further.[15] A key priority then, leading Brexiteers claimed, was for the UK to be able to establish trade treaties with key economic partners, which would be far easier to achieve working outside a large trade bloc.

In the period since the Brexit vote, debates about future trade deals have developed a new prominence, with some arguing that the 'Anglosphere' can play a central role in the UK's future trade strategy due to a common language, and the common cultural and legal frameworks forged from the experience of empire.[16] However, there is an uncertainty about what the 'Anglosphere' is and whether it is a viable trading bloc. Advocates of the 'Anglosphere' idea do not agree on what it consists of – there are at least three commonly-employed definitions. For some it is an alliance of English-speaking peoples, in which the United States can play a prominent role. Others see the multinational Commonwealth as 'the soft power network of the future', to borrow Lord Howell's phrase. These advocates of greater Commonwealth cooperation point to a doubling of these nations' combined GDP over the last twenty years, and see developing countries such as India and South Africa as playing an important role in its future prosperity.[17] Finally, other advocates of the 'Anglosphere' have focused on narrower forms of CANZUK cooperation, between the core 'old' Commonwealth countries of Britain, Australia, Canada and New Zealand.[18]

This uncertainty about what the 'Anglosphere' is and whether it is a viable trading bloc, or a delusional and impractical form of imperial throwback, reflects the complex legacy of historical attempts to develop Empire-Commonwealth cooperation in trade matters between the 1880s and Britain's entry into the European Economic Community in 1973. This helps explain why many have criticized plans for CANZUK cooperation and why this cause has largely remained a preoccupation of the right. Those who favour Commonwealth collaboration today often draw on earlier efforts to adapt the existing mechanisms of British world collaboration to the realities of the multiracial Commonwealth which emerged after 1945. However, historically it proved difficult to substitute this new model of Commonwealth cooperation for earlier connections based on British world links. Indeed, a 1972 Foreign Office report cast doubt on the value of recent attempts to expand multilateral cooperation within the Commonwealth, and claimed that Britain needed to focus on promoting good bilateral relations with Australia, Canada and New Zealand: 'The British people have, in the past, paid a high, and perhaps an excessive price for their support for a multilateral Commonwealth and it will be important to avoid doing so in the future. Subject to this however, it would seem in our interests to keep the multilateral concept of the Commonwealth in reasonable repair'.[19] In any case, with Britain due to join the EEC the following year, the chief focus for all these countries was on promoting alternative forms of regional trade cooperation.

Regardless of what trading environment emerges after Brexit, what seems most striking about debates about the future of trade in Britain since June 2016 is how little voices from the new Commonwealth have featured.[20] What is essentially a debate about the global economy has played out largely as a story of national politics, with occasional interventions from 'interfering' Europeans, CANZUK, America and other leading foreign powers. Since the referendum some on the right have repeatedly called on the UK to reconnect with its nineteenth-century legacy as an international champion of free trade. For instance, Liam Fox has eulogized about how in the nineteenth century through invention and industry 'a small island perched on the edge of Europe became the world's largest and most powerful trading nation'.[21] But Britain is no longer the world's leading creditor – nor can it exploit the resources of an empire – both conditions which were essential to its dominance of the world economy up to 1914 (often to the detriment of colonized populations). India is poised to overtake Britain as the Commonwealth's leading economic power and the UK is set to leave the world's largest free trade zone.

We have argued here that although imperial nostalgia does play a part in the vision of many Brexiteers, one must be careful not to assume that the 'post-imperial hangover' alone was responsible for the UK being an 'awkward partner in Europe', or that the legacy of Empire predetermined the failure of Britain's relationship with the EU. In fact, the rhetorical skill of Brexiters during the referendum lay in their ability to conjure up an imagined future drawing on an equally brilliant imagined past in which formal Empire was largely absent but British power and prestige was enormous. As we have suggested, they have put forward many rival or overlapping visions of the future, while never really offering coherent, practical proposals.

Of course, Britain's historical trading relations with the Empire were complex, and efforts to promote cooperation with the old and new Commonwealths often sat uneasily together. Therefore, it is perhaps not surprising that advocates of Brexit have struggled to develop a coherent or commonly agreed notion of Britain's optimal trading future, and the Commonwealth's place within it, since 2016. While some have seen 'Anglosphere' cooperation as key to this future, there are at least three different notions of what the Anglosphere consists of in common use. Each of these definitions in turn builds on a different historical legacy formed by Britain's varied efforts to develop trade with the Empire-Commonwealth and the wider English-speaking world.

Yet while this uncertainty appears as a fundamental weakness at the point that Brexit actually needs to be negotiated, it was a rhetorical strength at the point that leaving the EU was presented as a simple yes/no proposition. What, to Remainers, looked like a range of incoherent and mutually inconsistent propositions, appeared to Leavers as a series of untold possibilities. The possibilities, to them, were endless. And it was their conviction that these could be willed into being through the exercise of national self-belief and imagination, rather than a desire to resurrect formal Empire as such, that made them true heirs of Victorian imperialism.

Notes

1. Sam Coates, 'Ministers aim to build "empire 2.0" with African Commonwealth', *The Times*, 6 March 2017, https://www.thetimes.co.uk/article/ministers-aim-to-build-empire-2-0-with-african-commonwealth-after-brexit-v9bs6f6z9

2. David Davis, 'Trade deals. Tax cuts. And taking time before triggering Article 50. A Brexit economic strategy for Britain', 14 July 2016, https://www.conservativehome.com/platform/2016/07/david-davis-trade-deals-tax-cuts-and-taking-time-before-triggering-article-50-a-brexit-economic-strategy-for-britain.html

3. David Olusoga, 'Empire 2.0 is dangerous nostalgia for something that never existed', *The Observer*, 19 March 2017, https://www.theguardian.com/commentisfree/2017/mar/19/empire-20-is-dangerous-nostalgia-for-something-that-never-existed

4. Benjamin Grob-Fitzgibbon, *Continental Drift: Britain and Europe from the End of Empire to the Rise of Euroscepticism* (Cambridge: Cambridge University Press, 2016).

5. Fintan O'Toole, 'The paranoid fantasy behind Brexit', *The Guardian*, 16 November 2018, https://www.theguardian.com/politics/2018/nov/16/brexit-paranoid-fantasy-fintan-otoole

6. Robert Saunders, *Yes to Europe! The 1975 Referendum and Seventies Britain* (Cambridge: Cambridge University Press, 2018); Robert Saunders, 'The myth of Brexit as imperial nostalgia', *Prospect*, 7 January 2019, https://www.prospectmagazine.co.uk/world/the-myth-of-brexit-as-imperial-nostalgia?fbclid=IwAR0cz5WQeoA4F918wioXpNP5GXK0AkRJwYg2SMJohYkwC_p3WJBsF8wDOxQ

7. Boris Johnson, 'It's time Britons believed in Britain, like the rest of the world', 16 July 2018, https://gulfnews.com/opinion/thinkers/it-s-time-britons-believed-in-britain-like-the-rest-of-the-world-1.2252374

8. Vote Leave, 'The European Union and Your Family' and '5 positive reasons to vote leave and take back control: Europe yes, EU no' (2016), https://digital.library.lse.ac.uk/objects/lse:sav235yoh

9. 'Brexit the Movie', 12 May 2016, https://www.youtube.com/watch?v=UTMxfAkxfQ0&list=PLrgytSOvo3OAnHKInQb7HmWoXyBzg1UDC

10. For a more detailed elaboration of the argument which follows see David Thackeray, *Forging a British World of Trade: Culture, Ethnicity, and Market in the Empire-Commonwealth, 1880–1975* (Oxford: Oxford University Press, 2019).

11. See, for example, Michael Shanks, *The Stagnant Society: A Warning* (London: Penguin, 1961); Anthony Sampson, *Anatomy of Britain*, (London: Hodder and Stoughton, 1962).

12. HM Government, 'Britain's new deal in Europe' (1975), https://digital.library.lse.ac.uk/objects/lse:fug282yox

13. UKIP, 'The out post. EU Referendum Special Edition, May 2016', https://digital.library.lse.ac.uk/objects/lse:hiq468qal; Vote Leave, 'The European Union and your family: the facts' (2016), https://digital.library.lse.ac.uk/objects/lse:fip763sox

14. Leave.EU, 'Dear [voter], the most important vote in your life!' (2016, http://digital.library.lse.ac.uk/objects/lse:tol227lag

15 Leave.EU, 'It's time to . . . Leave.EU' (2016), https://digital.library.lse.ac.uk/objects/lse:nem485roh

16 Michael Kenny and Nick Pearce, 'The rise of the Anglosphere: how the right dreamed up a new conservative world order', *New Statesman*, 10 February 2015, https://www.newstatesman.com/politics/2015/2/rise-amglosphere-how-right-dreamed-new-world-conservative-world-order, and also their chapter in this volume; BBC Archive on 4, 'Return of the Anglosphere', 16 Dec. 2017, http://www.bbc.co.uk/programmes/b09j6qz8

17 House of Commons, Foreign Affairs Committee, *The Role and Future of the Commonwealth* (London, 2012), HC 114, pp. 8, 36–9, https://publications.parliament.uk/pa/cm201213/cmselect/cmfaff/114/114.pdf

18 Andrew Roberts, 'CANZUK: after Brexit, Canada, Australia, New Zealand and Britain can unite as a pillar of Western civilization', *The Telegraph*, 13 September 2016, http://www.telegraph.co.uk/news/2016/09/13/canzuk-after-brexit-canada-australia-new-zealand-and-britain-can

19 'Paper on the Commonwealth After UK Accession to the EEC', n.d. [1972], FCO49/398, The National Archives, London.

20 Eve Namusoke, 'A divided family: race, the Commonwealth and Brexit', *The Round Table* 105 (2016): 463–76.

21 'Speech delivered by International Trade Secretary Liam Fox at the Manchester Town Hall on 29 September 2016', https://www.gov.uk/government/speeches/liam-foxs-free-trade-speech

Chapter 3
Brexit and the Anglosphere
Michael Kenny and Nick Pearce[1]

The claim that there is some kind of connection between Britain's imperial past and the UK's vote to leave the European Union remains one of the most notable and contentious features of the debate that has broken out since the momentous national decision of June 2016. As we have seen in the introduction to this volume, some critics detected undertones of Empire in the idea of a 'Global Britain' which was evoked by leading Brexiteers, and the Prime Minister herself, in the aftermath of the vote. For others, evidence that most Leave supporters lived in the villages, shires and towns of non-metropolitan England was sufficient proof that this represented the reassertion of post-imperial angst. And so, when the press reported that officials in the Department for International Trade had likened Brexit to 'Empire 2.0', critics enthusiastically adopted the motif to criticize the referendum result and the motives of Leave protagonists.[2]

This characterization has tended to obscure, not illuminate, a complex historical question. In our own work, we have pinpointed instead the enduring impact of the malleable and diverse 'Anglosphere' discourse in British politics.[3] The Anglosphere is a recently coined term used to denote a historical political tradition which has its roots in the celebration of racialized notions of 'kith and kin' and the political and cultural commonalities of the English-speaking world associated with the idea of 'Greater Britain' in the late nineteenth century.[4] For most of its proponents, the cultivation of political, economic and military links between the white settler colonies of the British Empire and the United Kingdom was a critical response to the rise of rival great powers. But it was also interwoven with a number of ideals – like the rule of law, free trade and parliamentary sovereignty – that nurtured romanticism about the history and virtues of the 'English race' or 'Anglo-Saxons' scattered across the world.

This dream of an alliance of the English-speaking peoples foundered upon the rocks of the geopolitical realities of the twentieth century. As the United States began to assume a hegemonic position within the world economy after the First World War, and the Dominions achieved greater independence within the British Empire, and as the Depression of the 1930s and the challenge of wartime necessitated a significant extension of the state and its role in the economy, dreams of a free trade order under English leadership began to dissipate. Moreover, in the early decades of the twentieth century a rather different political project in the name of the anglophone parts of Empire emerged instead – that associated with the conjunction of imperial preference and a concern for domestic social reform. This new politics, which was most powerfully embodied in the figure of Joseph Chamberlain, gained considerable traction in the Conservative Party and underpinned a new emphasis on pragmatic modernization, and a more active role for the state.

But while it lost its dominant position in British politics, the *laissez-faire* worldview of the Victorian era was never expunged from the outlook of the political establishment, and remained a crucial part of the mental framework of Britain's rulers up until the 1940s. So too did a commitment to the Commonwealth, the newly formed association of colonies and Dominions with which Britain traded heavily in the years leading up to, and immediately after, the Second World War. Commonwealth idealism played an important part in the geopolitical thinking of both of the main British political parties, and provided a carrier for enduring, often unarticulated, assumptions about the natural intimacy of the English-speaking countries. This way of thinking achieved new salience during the course of the referendum held in 1975 about whether Britain should retain its membership of the European Economic Community.

This line of descent resurfaced powerfully on the fringes of the Conservative Party after its major defeat in the election of 1997, and was actively promoted among a developing network of think-tanks, politicians and media figures from Britain, Canada and Australia. Increasingly this milieu proved attractive to Thatcherite politicians, a number of whom were markedly sceptical about the kinds of regulation and protection which were associated with the European model after 1987. The percolation of ideas within this milieu forms a vital, though somewhat overlooked, prelude to the public resurgence of Anglosphere idealism within the political cultures of all of these countries in the first decade of the new century. This ideal supplied important ideological and rhetorical resources for Prime Ministers Tony Abbott in Australia and Stephen Harper in Canada – politicians who were themselves sources of inspiration for British Conservative thinkers, such as Tim Montgomerie, then editor of the influential website *ConHome*. After 2010, it provided an increasingly attractive option for a cohort of leading British Conservative politicians, most notably Boris Johnson. The Anglosphere was given its most extended political articulation in the UK by the Conservative MEP Daniel Hannan, author of the widely read book *How We Invented Freedom and Why It Matters*.[5]

The popularity in some Conservative circles of this kind of thinking undoubtedly enabled the dissemination of an increasingly full-throated Euroscepticism at the top of the party. And this discourse has continued to inform one of the main currents of Brexiteer opinion, which has vigorously promoted the idea that the UK is at heart a freely trading nation that needs to be unencumbered by the EU's regulatory regime and rule-based order that impinges on its ability to engage freely and flexibly with other economies. Indeed, it is only by appreciating the importance of this particular heritage and the political-economic outlook it sustains that we can properly grasp the unalloyed opposition of some Conservatives to the prospect of an ongoing customs union with the EU, a stance that generated considerable discord within the party as the government negotiated a Withdrawal Agreement with the European Commission. More generally, this Anglospheric lineage needs to be brought back into focus by those looking to the historical roots of Brexit. The pointed accusation bound up in the characterization of 'Empire 2.0' tends to distract from the specific character and contemporary appeal of the ideological projects that notions of the Anglosphere have most effectively aided in recent years.

Above all, we need to understand better the political 'work' that has been performed by advocacy of the Anglosphere and the related, but distinct, notion of the Commonwealth in recent British politics. Judging the impact of these ideas upon the outcome of the Brexit referendum, and the political crisis generated by attempts to deliver a deal with the EU, is certainly not a straightforward enterprise. It is apparent that adherents of the Anglosphere are most usually found in the worlds of politics, finance and the media – both on and offline. Various surveys since the referendum overwhelmingly indicate that for the majority of Brexit supporters, an array of domestic issues and discontents were integral to the decision to vote against the EU, and were more important than convictions about free trade and the anglophone community.[6] At the same time, lingering affection for the Commonwealth may have been one factor in sustaining Euroscepticism among older voters and ethnic minorities, but there is no strong body of evidence suggesting that the Anglosphere commands widespread popular support.

Yet this outlook did play an important role in political terms, primarily because it was able to join up with a broader mood of concern and disenfranchisement in a growing chorus about the need to restore British sovereignty. Loyalty to parliamentary sovereignty is a signature commitment of neo-liberal Anglosphere advocates, and enabled them to find their place within the larger caravan of support for Brexit. But the themes and ideas associated with this circle have not always sat easily among the concerns and priorities of other Brexiteers. Indeed, contrary to the assertions of some of its keenest critics, far from being the dominant ideological frame for Tory Brexiteers, the Anglosphere has increasingly proved to be a distinctive, sometimes disruptive, element.

Rather tellingly, the outward-facing and free-trading ethos of 'Global Britain' was consciously subordinated as a campaigning theme in the Brexit referendum itself, having initially been given some prominence. The senior strategists of 'Vote Leave', including Michael Gove's former adviser Dominic Cummings, deliberately eschewed the references to 'Going Global' that had featured in the 1975 EEC referendum, in favour of a relentless focus on sovereignty ('Take Back Control'), immigration control and the promise of increased resources for the NHS. Yet the Leave campaign's archetypes of post-Brexit policy were replete with references to the policies of other Anglosphere countries as it pointed repeatedly to the Australian points system as an alternative to free movement within the EU, and heralded the Canadian–EU free trade agreement (CETA) as a blueprint for a post-Brexit economic and trade relationship between the EU and the UK. The Anglosphere did therefore serve as a source of policy inspiration, as well as a horizon of possibility, for Britain's role in the world outside of the EU in Brexiteer circles.[7]

In the months following the 2017 general election, and Theresa May's abortive attempt to secure an increased parliamentary majority for her Brexit negotiating strategy, advocates of the Anglosphere put their energies behind proposals for a new round of 'free trade' deals between the UK, Canada, Australia, New Zealand, and the USA. Hannan set up a new 'Initiative for Free Trade' (IFT) to champion the idea that the UK should leave the customs union and promote 'global free trade'.[8] With an advisory board drawn from international Conservative networks, including vocal supporters of the Anglosphere such as former Australian PM Tony Abbott, the IFT was formally launched in the Foreign and Commonwealth Office at an event hosted by the Foreign Secretary, Boris Johnson, and attended by other leading Brexiteers Michael Gove and Liam Fox.

Working with partners among the libertarian Washington think-tanks, and sympathetic Conservative politicians in Canada, Australia and the USA, the IFT subsequently developed proposals for 'an ideal UK–US Free Trade Agreement,' which would form the basis for a pan-Anglospheric free trade agreement.[9] Similar proposals were also published by the Legatum Institute, the Institute of Economic Affairs, and the Economists for Free Trade group (a group of pro-Brexit economists led by Patrick Minford). All of these outfits enjoy close links with Brexit-supporting ministers in the UK government, the European Research Group of Conservative MPs, and free-market think-tanks in the US and elsewhere.[10] The same networks through which Eurosceptics and neo-Conservatives relaunched the idea of the Anglosphere and proselytized for its virtues in the 1990s and early 2000s, were used to plan the shape of a post-Brexit settlement.

Free trade has become a dominant motif in the discourse of many Conservative Brexiteers, alongside the regaining of national sovereignty. Deploying the ideological resonances of one of the most powerful traditions of thought in British politics, Anglosphere enthusiasts have also revived the emphasis of their liberal forebears on sound money, free trade and balanced budgets in their arguments for the unavoidable need for the UK to leave the customs union and the regulatory orbit of the EU's single market. At the heart of this outlook is the ambition to deregulate labour and product market standards, dismantle tariffs and non-tariff barriers to trade, and open up public services, such as the NHS, to foreign suppliers. In making these arguments they have, unwittingly, inverted the political combination favoured by Chamberlainite Anglosphere advocates in the late Victorian and Edwardian eras. Instead of tariff preferences for the white settler dominions coupled with 'constructive imperialist' social reform, these Brexiteers offer 'free trade' with the Anglosphere coupled with a new phase of Thatcher-style reforms.

These contributions to an increasingly fraught set of policy debates in the UK signal the enduring malleability and influence of the Anglosphere tradition in British politics – and the rich array of transoceanic, 'world-island' themes and symbols with which it is associated. In contrast to the debates over Britain's entry to the EEC in the 1960s and 1970s, the Commonwealth itself is very rarely cited as the repository of economic or historical obligations, but is now more regularly depicted as a group of like-minded countries, bound together by the shared heritage supplied by the common law, free markets and parliamentary democracy. And, as was the case with Victorian-era arguments for Imperial Federation or Greater Britain, so too do today's Anglosphere enthusiasts believe that distances can be transcended by technology. Gravity models of trade, which consistently demonstrate the importance of geographic proximity to trade flows, are thus set aside through appeals to the internet, the weightless service economy, and the faster long-distance air travel that now connects the UK to the rest of the world, including its antipodean cousins, via single long-haul flights.[11]

The free-trading Anglosphere is not usually taken to extend to the former English-speaking colonies of the Caribbean or Africa, however. Instead, as has often been the case in its recent manifestations, the Anglosphere has been given an Asian tilt with the inclusion of the former imperial outposts of Singapore and Hong Kong by advocates like Hannan. These 'two city states are now gleaming examples of what open markets can achieve'.[12] Sidestepping the role of the developmental state in the economic growth of these cities, and the importance of publicly-owned land to their economic models, advocates for their inclusion in a putative anglophone bloc stress their low tax and open market credentials. And this pivot in Anglosphere discourse provides a rejoinder to accusations that the Anglosphere dream is saturated with imperial nostalgia and a racialized yearning for the 'kith and kin' models of yesteryear.[13]

An important – though overlooked – underpinning for the free trade ideas of this grouping is a deep commitment to the value of the voluntary, mutual recognition of goods, services and professional qualifications between countries, which is depicted as the antithesis to uniform multinational standards or common rulebooks like the EU's single market. One of the 'ideal types' for this kind of thinking is the Australia–New Zealand Closer Economic Relations Trade Agreement (known as the CER Agreement), which allows Trans-Tasman free movement, removes tariffs between New Zealand and Australia, and permits the goods and services of one territory to be sold in the other. Mutual recognition is premised on the idea that signatory countries to free trade deals recognize each other's standards as equivalent for the purposes of the import of goods and the provision of services, rather than mandating regulatory harmonization. Contemporary advocates of CANZUK – who support the idea of an alliance of Canada, Australia, New Zealand and the UK that can be scaled up from free trade deals to deeper military and political integration – have argued for the extension of CER to Canada and the UK.[14]

Brexiteers of this persuasion argue that mutual recognition protects national sovereignty, since the authority to determine the content of regulations is retained by national governments, and no supranational jurisdiction such as the European Court of Justice is required for free trade – only membership of the World Trade Organization. Indeed the implied homology between free trade and national sovereignty is integral to much Anglo-Brexiteer discourse, and has shaped strong support for the various version of 'Canada +++' or 'Super Canada' free-trade deals which have been urged by figures like David Davis, former Minister for Brexit. These are seen as superior to an agreement in which the UK would stay in a shared customs territory and single regulatory space for the provision of goods with the EU, an outcome anticipated by the White Paper advanced at Chequers in July 2018, and which featured in the Withdrawal Agreement agreed with the EU in November 2018.

Mutual recognition is an important part of the conceptual web of recent Anglospheric arguments, and it is used to disqualify the different 'anti-competitive market distortions' that are seen as inhibiting trade. The extension of mutual recognition implies more than simply removing tariff barriers to cross-border trade; instead, it aims at eliminating a wide array of constraints on market exchange, including environmental standards, labour market regulations, rules on public procurement, and even public ownership. What matters in trade relations is 'the degree to which a state shares a commitment to similar notions of political-economic order, not its degree of proximity'.[15] It is therefore through this concept that the Anglosphere ideal is converted, in neo-liberal hands, into 'an alliance of countries that are disposed to accept the foundational pillars of classical liberalism'.[16]

To give mutual recognition purchase in terms of politics and public policy, it is presented in quasi-populist terms as a blanket challenge to cartelism and bureaucracy. As Hannan has put it:

Mega-businesses loathe [mutual recognition], much preferring uniform international regulations, which they see as a way to raise barriers to entry and disadvantage smaller rivals. That's one of the reasons that corporate giants tend to be pro-Brussels. Mutual recognition works for the consumer rather than the producer, for the entrepreneur rather than the bureaucrat, for the start-up rather than the multinational. It increases competition, cuts prices and widens choice.[17]

The free-trade liberalism arising from Anglosphere advocacy is only one part of the constellation of views which have grown up around the idea of Brexit. While the argument for leaving the EU's customs union is a totemic one for the European Research Group faction within the parliamentary Conservative Party, Brexit is supported by most for reasons of national sovereignty rather than free trade. Tensions have indeed flared between those for whom the priority is to repatriate powers from the EU, and those who wish to use divorce from the EU's customs union to strike new trade agreements. This is most apparent in relation to the issue of agriculture standards, where a UK–US free trade deal would require entry onto the UK market of US agri-products such as the (now infamous) chlorinated chicken. Similar arguments also arise over environmental standards or the opening up of the NHS to US healthcare suppliers, as was the case with the aborted TTIP negotiations.

The free-market Anglosphere is also in tension with other visions of Brexit. Its economic liberalism, and outward-looking character, sit awkwardly with some of the communitarian and anti-establishment sentiments that underpinned support for Brexit. More generally, the Anglosphere idea has little directly to offer those concerned about deep inequalities associated with class, education or place, themes that have become central to a new raft of 'modernizing' Conservative MPs such as Nick Boles and George Freeman. Moreover, many of the putative benefits of Brexit which figure in the optimistic reckonings of Economists for Brexit or the Institute of Economic Affairs, rely on heroic assumptions about the deregulation of entry to UK markets, which – if implemented – would come to endanger the Tory party's relationship with key demographic groups, such as farmers or older voters reliant on the NHS.

Moreover, the election of Donald Trump – a protectionist US President who has embarked on a tariff war with China – has rendered the dream of an anglophone free trade zone deeply problematic. Trump's support for Brexit, and open hostility to the EU, are both founded upon nationalist sentiment, and are unlikely to issue forth into US support for a new Anglosphere or an Anglo-Pacific free trade bloc. Trump has also thrown key pillars of Anglospheric military and security cooperation, exemplified in the 'Five Eyes' intelligence partnership, into question. His support for Russia, readiness to question US commitment to NATO, and volatility in handling US relations in Asia-Pacific, have proved disorientating and deeply problematic in different ways for the UK, Canada, Australia and New Zealand. Trump's presidency has dramatically threatened the stability of the US-led global security and defence alliance of which these nations have considered themselves a key part since 1945.

Aside from its lingering influence upon current expectations about what Brexit should deliver, the Anglosphere idea has continued to exercise an influence by contributing to a growing fragmentation of the territorial outlook of the Conservative Party. This process has been underway since the introduction of devolution in the late 1990s, and the lengthy period which ensued during which the parliamentary party was overwhelmingly based in England and performed very poorly outside it (until the general election of 2015).[18]

Over time, Conservatism in Scotland has re-oriented its outlook in response to the rise to power of the SNP, becoming more liberal and more emphatically Unionist. Under the leadership of Ruth Davidson, the party has supplanted Labour as the main Unionist opposition party to the SNP at Holyrood, whilst developing a broad centre-right appeal. Compelled to engage with the realities of devolution, the party in Scotland, and some leading Tory figures in Wales, speak a language of shared sovereignty which is increasingly at odds with the territorial thinking of some of their English Brexiteer colleagues. As MSP Adam Tomkins has put it, 'the Union not only accommodates but requires difference ... it is not a unitary state with a single seat of power in which the entire land is ruled in a uniform way.' Rebuking English Conservatives for their intransigence on the Northern Ireland 'backstop' in the Withdrawal Agreement negotiated by Theresa May, he argues that they need to understand that 'the accommodation of reasonable difference strengthens the union'.[19]

In the same period, the growing appeal of the Anglosphere as a political ideal, and the sustenance it has given to the notion of parliamentary sovereignty as an endangered idea that needs to be rescued from external and internal menace, have worked to promote a more unitarist sensibility towards the UK's territorial constitution than was apparent among previous generations of Tory parliamentarians. And in this sense the foundational ideal of an alliance of the English-speaking peoples has returned home, coming to project a very Anglo-centric conception of the UK, as well as an exceptionalist account of why Britain can no longer remain in Europe. Not surprisingly, Conservatives inclined to think about the UK in these terms have tended to be markedly resistant to the claim that the preservation of peace in Northern Ireland requires the development of a distinctive set of political and economic arrangements in order to prevent a hard border from re-emerging. Some Conservatives have indeed been markedly sceptical about the complex model of shared sovereignty bound up in the Good Friday Agreement. And here too the Anglosphere has made an indirect contribution, bolstering a sense of disbelief towards a constitutional arrangement which has in complicated ways transcended the dictates of national sovereignty and secured the consent of the bulk of the Northern Irish population.

How then did the Anglosphere tradition return to the front rank of British political discourse, after a lengthy period of abeyance? In part the answer is to be found in the transformation of the global economy from the late 1970s onwards, which gathered pace after the fall of the Berlin Wall and was turbo-charged by the simultaneous growth of the Chinese economy and the ICT revolution in the US economy in the 1990s and 2000s. This transformation opened up new ideological vistas for Conservative Eurosceptics and made more plausible their challenge to the constraints of economic geography implied by the UK's integration in the European single market. The shift of economic growth in the world economy to Asia, coupled with advances in information and communication technologies, created the space for the reassertion of the promise of liberal free trade and the international communion of the English-speaking countries that were once part of the Empire.

The other key reason for the renewal of this tradition was the turn of many Thatcherite figures, including Margaret Thatcher herself, against the project of European integration. So long as the Conservative Party was convinced that the UK's future prospects were best served in an economic union with other European powers, Anglosphere-style dreaming was impossible. But from 1987 onwards, this influential and disparate circle of influence began to look elsewhere for inspiration. Out of power for much of the long boom of the post-Cold War era, a small group of Thatcherite Eurosceptics used their time to forge links with like-minded politicians, think-tanks and media figures in the Anglo-world, preparing a prospectus for the future of the UK outside the EU that was given its opportunity by the economic turbulence and stagnant household incomes of the financial crisis and its aftermath. Rising public hostility to EU immigration and distrust in mainstream politics then supplied a new opportunity for Euroscepticism to find a wider popular resonance. There followed a succession of contingent, unpredictable events and processes – including the opportunity supplied by a popular campaign around Brexit, and the unusual circumstances that propelled right-wing figures from the parliamentary party into office in 2016 – to enable figures like David Davis and Liam Fox, Secretary of State for International Trade since 2016, to propound their beliefs from places of influence.

The Anglosphere dream has therefore continued to play a role in the post-referendum situation. Where previously it was deployed for its critical power, sustaining the argument that a break from membership of the EU was both desirable and historically viable, since 2016 it has become a source of thinking about the nature and terms of the UK's exit. And in this very different context, it has become a very distinctive element within a larger repertoire of opinion, providing an ideologically grounded, and sometimes disputatious, contribution to deepening arguments within the Conservative Party.

In key respects, this outlook continues to feed off a deeply ingrained instinct in the UK's political class about the enduring significance and potentially exemplary influence of the British state. It has also provided an appealing garb for an ideological vision – of a smaller state and freer set of markets – which has in many ways faced serious challenge since the financial crisis of 2007–08. But whilst this extended moment of political crisis has allowed the Anglosphere project to gain a hearing and profile that it has not enjoyed for many decades, the prospects for its continued impact look far less promising.

Notes

1 The authors are indebted to Tim Bale and Duncan Bell for their comments on an earlier draft of this chapter.
2 D. Olusoga, 'Empire 2.0 is Dangerous Nostalgia for Something that Never Existed', *The Guardian*, 19 March 2017; accessed at: https://www.theguardian.com/commentisfree/2017/mar/19/empire-20-is-dangerous-nostalgia-for-something-that-never-existed
3 M. Kenny and N. Pearce, *Shadows of Empire: the Anglosphere in British Politics* (Cambridge: Polity Press, 2018).
4 D. Bell, *The Idea of Greater Britain: Empire and the Future of World Order, 1860–1900* (Princeton University Press, 2011).
5 D. Hannan, *How We Invented Freedom and Why it Matters* (London: Head of Zeus, 2013).
6 H. Clarke, M. Goodwin and P. Whiteley, *Brexit: Why Britain Voted to Leave the European Union* (Cambridge: Cambridge University Press, 2017).
7 Kenny and Pearce, *Shadows of Empire*, ch. 7.
8 The IFT was originally launched as an 'institute', but that term is protected by law and the apparent threat of a fine from Companies House forced a change of name to 'initiative'.
9 D. Ikenson, S. Lester and D. Hannan, *The Ideal U.S.–U.K. Free Trade Agreement: A Free Trader's Perspective* (Washington: Cato Institute, 2018).
10 See for example S. A. Singham and R. Tylecote, 2018, *Plan A+: Creating a Prosperous post-Brexit UK*, IEA Discussion Paper, available at https://iea.org.uk/iea-report-plan-a-creating-prosperous-post-brexit-uk
11 D. Hannan, 'EU is the past. Anglosphere is the future; a trade agreement with the chief English-speaking democracies would be best for Britain', *Sunday Telegraph*, 4 November 2018, accessed at https://www.telegraph.co.uk/politics/2018/11/04/commonwealth-booming-time-embrace-free-trade-anglosphere/
12 D. Hannan, 'For an example of the power of open markets, look no further than Hong Kong', *Sunday Telegraph*, November 11 2018, accessed at https://www.telegraph.co.uk/news/2018/11/11/example-power-open-markets-look-no-hong-kong/
13 D. Bell and S. Vucetic, 'Brexit, CANZUK and the legacy of Empire', *The British Journal of Politics and International Relations* (2019, forthcoming).

14 Ibid.

15 G. Siles-Brugge, 'Bound by Gravity or Living in a "Post-Geography Trading World"? Expert Knowledge and Affective Spatial Imaginaries in the Construction of the UK's Post-Brexit Trade Policy', *New Political Economy* (2018), DOI: 10.1080/13563467.2018.1484722,10.

16 S. A. Singham and A. M. Kiniry, *Trade tools for the 21st century* (London: Legatum Institute, 2016), cited in Siles-Brugge, 'Bound by Gravity or Living in a "Post-Geography Trading World"?'

17 D. Hannan, 'EU is the past.'

18 R. Scully, *The End of British Party Politics* (London: Biteback, 2017).

19 A. Tomkins, *Brexit: Where Raab and McVey go wrong over threat to Union – Tory MSP*, *The Scotsman*, 15 November 2018, accessed at https://www.scotsman.com/news/opinion/brexit-where-raab-and-mcvey-go-wrong-over-threat-to-union-tory-msp-1-4830439

Chapter 4

How Unique is Britain's Empire Complex?

Elizabeth Buettner

'There are two kinds of European nations . . . There are small nations and there are countries that have not yet realised they are small nations.' Thus argued Kristian Jensen, Denmark's finance minister, at a 'Road to Brexit' event held at the Danish parliament just under a year after Britain's 23 June 2016 referendum had resulted in a narrow victory for those who wanted to withdraw from the European Union. 'It is a paradox that the country that once had an empire on which the sun never sets, that ruled the waves, that in its heart is truly global, is now drawing back from the world's most successful free trade area', he continued, adding that '[t]here is still this notion in some countries that because they have been the rulers of the 20th century they will continue to be that in the 21st century'. Jensen's strong opposition to Brexit was compounded by utter disbelief: leaving the EU, in his view, would bring nothing but 'disaster for the UK' – a small nation in misguided denial whose era as a global power was most decidedly over.[1]

Statements such as these push us to think more deeply about the ways Britain compares and contrasts with its neighbours on the European stage. How much does the fact that Britain once had an empire that, for Jensen and countless others, is still remembered as sunset-free in its unprecedented reach make it distinct from other EU countries? After all, Britain undeniably shares common traits with its closest neighbours in the EU in being both 'European' and 'small', however much vocal Brexiteers might vehemently contest these descriptors. While many leading figures in the Leave campaign were as keen to highlight Britain's history of global preeminence as Jensen was, they ardently disagreed with his suggestion that imperial glories of yesteryear had nothing to offer a post-Brexit Britain. Once freed from EU shackles, Leave champions insisted, Britain could set about reviving its links with other parts of the world by building new trading and international relations beyond the European continent, particularly with the post-imperial Commonwealth – an alluring yet chimeric 'Empire 2.0' that many critics readily consigned to the realm of dangerous fantasy.[2]

Jensen was certainly not the first politician to single Britain out and attribute its exceptionality in considerable part to its imperial orientations. Charles de Gaulle famously used the same verdict when he was President of France to justify scuppering Britain's first two applications for membership within what was then the European Economic Community (EEC) in 1963 and again in 1967. For de Gaulle, Britain's insistent insularity along with its ties to countries that had once been imperial but had morphed into the Commonwealth were central to it not being 'European' enough to warrant entry. While conveniently saying little about other French agendas and reservations let alone France's own imperial engagements, de Gaulle's stated rationale nevertheless echoed claims that had repeatedly emanated from both the right and the left of Britain's own political establishment since 1945. After all, Winston Churchill's pronouncements in the late 1940s and early 1950s that Britain was geopolitically part of 'three circles' – the British Empire and Commonwealth, an 'English-speaking world' that included the United States along with Canada and other dominions, and a 'united Europe' – had stopped decidedly short of envisioning that Britain would ever merge within a continental federation.[3]

Churchill's outlook that laid emphasis on the first two 'circles' and consigned 'Europe' to a distant third place would prove as durable as it was bipartisan. Labour's 1950 *European Unity* manifesto portrayed Britain as 'the nerve centre of a world-wide Commonwealth which extends into every continent. In every respect except distance we in Britain are closer to our kinsmen in Australia and New Zealand on the far side of the world, than we are to Europe.'[4] Twelve years later, its leader Hugh Gaitskell persisted in arguing against EEC membership by equating it with 'the end of a thousand years of history' as it would curtail Britain's own independence as a state and bring an end to the Commonwealth itself along with it. 'How can one really seriously suppose that if the mother country, the centre of the Commonwealth, is a province of Europe . . . it could continue to exist as the mother country of a series of independent nations?', Gaitskell asked. As his successor Harold Wilson had also insisted in 1961, 'we are not entitled to sell our friends and kinsmen down the river for a problematical and marginal advantage of selling washing machines in Düsseldorf'.[5]

That Wilson's own government would launch Britain's second failed EEC application just six years later illustrates the extent to which the Commonwealth had declined as a British priority during the 1960s. Earlier attitudes nevertheless left a deep mark. They explain three persistent features of British geopolitical thinking: the limited enthusiasm for the European project that was destined to linger long after the third application finally bore fruit in 1973; the ongoing importance of Britain's 'special relationship' with the United States within its 'second circle'; and the uncanny ability of Britain's imperial and Commonwealth heritage to become periodically revived, as it did so spectacularly in the run-up to and aftermath of the 2016 Brexit referendum. 'Europe', in the words of Anne Deighton, remained 'an unhappy alternative to great powerdom', with the lost empire remaining an important ingredient in Eurosceptic cookbooks.[6]

Inseparable though Britain's imperial past, decolonization history and its approach to European integration may be, however, the same can be said of many other Western European countries that have joined the EU since its founding with the Treaty of Rome in 1957. Of the EEC's original 'Six', only Luxemburg lacked a history of overseas empire altogether and only West Germany, having lost its African and Pacific colonies after the First World War, had a recent history whereby its imperial ambitions under the Third Reich were continental as distinct from intercontinental or global in scope. Italy had possessed territories in northern Africa since the late nineteenth century that became so central to fascist constructions of the nation that Mussolini famously described the Mediterranean Sea as a prospective 'Italian lake'. Despite Italian colonialism's rapid wartime collapse between 1941 and 1943, the post-war republic still retained a supervisory role over Somalia as a United Nations trust territory until 1960.[7] By then, decolonizations in other European empires had gathered irrevocable momentum, yet were far from complete as the EEC took shape and ultimately expanded to include new members.

For the remaining three EEC founder states, colonialism was still very much a going concern in and after 1957, regardless of the important territories that had been sacrificed since 1945. The Netherlands' struggle to hold on to its beloved 'belt of emeralds', the Dutch East Indies, in the face of a nationalist insurgency may have ended in its embittered withdrawal from an independent Indonesia in 1949, but the Dutch still clung on to West New Guinea until the early 1960s and maintained control over Suriname until 1975, not to mention over the six Caribbean islands that are still part of the Kingdom of the Netherlands. No remaining overseas territory even remotely approached the nation's attachment to the East Indies, however, and it was no coincidence that their traumatic forfeiture opened the door for the Netherlands to shift gears and become a driving force propelling European integration forward in the 1950s.[8] Belgium also became one of the most enthusiastic of the 'Six' at a time when it still held the Congo and Rwanda-Burundi; indeed, Congo's independence in 1960 came much sooner than anyone had anticipated even three years before.[9] Like their French counterparts, Belgian policy-makers in the mid-1950s had wanted plans for a European common market to encompass both Belgian and French Africa as part of durable '*Eurafrique*', with national colonial projects meant to evolve into what Peo Hansen and Stefan Jonsson have described as 'a joint European colonization of Africa'. As such, 'the origins of the EU cannot be separated from the perceived necessity to preserve and prolong the colonial system', particularly in the case of France.[10]

For France, maintaining empire and championing European integration was not an 'either/or' proposition like it so often seemed in British eyes, but rather were complementary ways of maintaining national stature – what de Gaulle repeatedly called *grandeur* – by operating within and beyond Europe alike. France may have already sacrificed Indochina in 1954 after years of war, but when the EEC was born in 1957 much of its empire – the largest global empire after Britain's – still remained very much intact. Although most of French Africa was granted its independence in 1960, France's most important non-European territory of Algeria was still engaged in a notoriously brutal and protracted independence struggle that would last until France finally pulled out in 1962. It is deeply ironic that de Gaulle's delegitimization of Britain's Europeanness partly on account of its Commonwealth attachments when vetoing its 1963 application came less than a year after Algeria stopped being considered French against the wishes of the vast majority of its population. Up until 1962, France had vehemently insisted that Algeria was not a colony but was instead made up of three *départements* that were integral to the nation itself, thus making it effectively part of the EEC as well for nearly the first five years of the Community's existence.

The fact that France still has 'overseas departments and territories' in the Caribbean and Indian Ocean along with New Caledonia up until today not only calls France's own 'Europeanness' into question but problematizes the very notion of the 'Europeanness' of the European Union itself, whether in its early years or in the present.[11] Other member states also still retain fragments of their former empires in the Caribbean, the South Atlantic and the Pacific, rendering the EU's geographical map far from an exclusively European one.[12] What is more, the number of members that had histories of maritime empires or continued to hold smaller overseas territories of imperial vintage rose even further in tandem with the EEC's enlargement. It was not only the accession of Britain (which retains fourteen small overseas territories today) but also Spain's in 1986 that extended the EU's global reach. Although Spain had lost most of its colonies in Latin America, the Caribbean and the Pacific in the nineteenth century, when it entered the EEC its North African enclaves in Ceuta and Melilla came with it. Tellingly, Ceuta and Melilla counted as 'European' – and still serve as vital, high-tech security outposts that the EU uses to keep out African migrants who seek to enter 'Fortress Europe' – while neighbouring Morocco's own bid for membership was flatly rejected.

'Colonialism', as Gurminder Bhambra summarizes, is both 'intrinsic to the contemporary scene of European integration and yet the colonial is typically rendered unseen in most representations of Europe.'[13] Its heritage and ongoing legacy infuses not only 'bigger' European nations like Britain and France – which were nonetheless dwarfed both in size and might by the American and Soviet superpowers and thereby rendered decidedly 'smaller' in the Cold War, decolonizing world. It also characterizes countries that were far smaller within Europe but rendered far larger thanks to their empires. This described not only Belgium, transformed as it was in the minds of imperial ideologues into '*la plus grande Belgique*' – Greater Belgium – through ruling huge swathes of central Africa, but also Portugal, where authorities had proudly insisted that 'Portugal is not a small country' ever since the 1930s thanks to its territories in and beyond Africa.[14] As the poorest, least developed country in Western Europe, Portugal (like Spain under Franco) long remained ruled by a dictatorship that had emerged in the interwar era. Portugal's entry into the EEC alongside Spain in 1986 could only come about after more than a decade of colonial wars in Africa led to the fall of the *Estado Novo* regime during the Carnation Revolution of 1974 and the consolidation of democracy afterwards. Like other countries before it, Portugal's EEC accession offered 'a substitute for the lost colonies', with its retreat from Africa paving the way for an increasingly continental international orientation.[15]

In the Netherlands, imperial enthusiasts had repeatedly warned that without the East Indies their nation would lose its Great Power status and 'sink to the rank of Denmark' on the international stage – a prophecy no longer uttered after Indonesia's independence coincided with Dutch membership of NATO and the birth of the EEC.[16] Denmark had long served as a cautionary tale as a state that had drastically shrunk in terms of territory and power since the seventeenth century, most familiarly thanks to a series of wartime defeats to Sweden in the mid-1600s, to Britain during the Napoleonic wars and ultimately to Germany in 1864. When Kristian Jensen distinguished European nations that recognized their diminutive status from those loath to do so in the context of Brexit, it was clear that neither he nor any of his fellow government ministers in Copenhagen would have imagined their own country to be anything other than one that was 'small' as well as 'European'. But what he neglected to mention when invoking Britain's imperial past was Denmark's own expansive history outside as well as within northern Europe starting with the Vikings. Although often ignored in histories of European colonialism and in wider understandings of what this entailed, Denmark nevertheless once claimed small territories in India, Ghana and the West Indies before selling the first two to the British in the 1840s and the last to the United States in 1917, thereby ending its rule over regions of the Global South conventionally associated with modern European empires.[17]

If territories across the North Atlantic and Arctic region are also taken into account, however, then Danish colonialism in Iceland only ended during the Second World War, while the Faroe Islands have since been incorporated into the Danish kingdom. Significantly, moreover, when Denmark gained entry to the EEC alongside Britain and Ireland in 1973 it brought with it its Greenland territory, thus further augmenting the EU's portfolio of the non-European outposts it has encompassed since its earliest beginnings. In Greenland's case, European accession by default served to fuel demands for Home Rule that bore fruit in the late 1970s and ultimately made it possible for it to leave the EEC in 1985. Greenland's incorporation within the EEC might well have proved an ephemeral one, yet it provides another example of the European Union's entanglement with the transoceanic history of its constituent states; moreover, Greenland also qualifies as a persistent case of incomplete decolonization, given that long after becoming self-governing in 2009 it still lacks full sovereign status outside the Danish rubric.[18] Last but not least, in becoming the first case when a referendum about EEC membership resulted in voters opting to leave, it removes yet another plank in British exceptionalist arguments when it comes to European and EU history.

Decolonization, in sum, like the longer trajectory of colonialism preceding it, were intensely European *and* European integration experiences, affecting not just ex-colonies and individual European states but playing a crucial part in the history of the European Union's emergence and evolution. As such, Britain's imperial history and heritage are part of what make it unexceptionally European, not a European exception. Like so many of its European/EU neighbours, Britain is irrevocably marked by its unfinished imperial business – the lingering presence of empires within post-colonial metropoles that remains discernible in their cultural, ideological and material heritage and in their multicultural populations descended both from former colonizers and colonized peoples now long present in Europe. British experiences of remembering, forgetting, repressing, recovering and reframing its many and varied imperial legacies have clear equivalents elsewhere.[19] Regardless of their inevitable national specificities, affirmative and often nostalgic renditions of the imperial past competing for cultural air time with more critical reappraisals or demands that amends be made for historical wrongs recur, comprising a transnational European phenomenon that shows no signs of abating.[20]

Given these similarities, then, what does make Britain different from other ex-colonizing EU countries, none of which look anywhere near to contemplating their own version of a Brexit? Several interconnected factors stand out, the first being Second World War experiences that remain central within national historical memories across most of the EU today. Neither defeated nor occupied, Britain's post-war experience did not involve a comparable need to reckon with the Nazi past, either as Germans or as citizens of the many countries engulfed by the Third Reich. France, Belgium and the Netherlands, among others, all embarked upon extended painful processes of grappling with the humiliating capitulations of 1940, with divided national experiences of complicity, collaboration and resistance under Nazi domination, and with gradual roads to recovery from the devastation wrought by a war that engulfed nations and their overseas empires alike.[21]

Looking back in later decades, it was not only Allied liberation and America's combination of Marshall aid and its military umbrella against the Soviet threat but also European integration that became widely associated with recovery, democracy, the preservation of peace and ultimately with prosperity in Western bloc countries. This was also true of southern European countries that entered the EEC in the 1980s that had remained under authoritarian governments into the 1970s. Portugal, for example, lacked a comparable Second World War experience on account of its neutrality, but achieving EEC membership symbolized the successful transition from dictatorship to democracy. Infrastructural modernization and the rising standards of living that came with infusions of European funding gradually pulled many Portuguese out of underdevelopment and poverty.

Retreating from empire after long, costly and unpopular wars in Portuguese Africa was clearly a price worth paying for reaping what were widely appreciated as the benefits of European accession, no matter how central it had long been to Portuguese national identity. 'The empire is dead, long live the EU', as one dissident would later triumphantly phrase it, undoubtedly voicing the sentiments of countless other Portuguese in a country where anti-European proclivities long remained the preserve of a very small minority.[22] It is difficult to imagine anything remotely similar emanating from British commentators around the time of Britain's accession, let alone under Brexit.

Unlike other Western European EU states that underwent seismic historical ruptures involving domestic political reinventions and, at times, dramatic decolonizations overseas, Britain could proudly look back at the Second World War as its 'finest hour' when it ultimately emerged depleted but triumphant. None other than Jean Monnet, one of the EU's most eminent 'founding fathers', had concluded that 'the price of victory – the illusion that you could maintain what you had, without change' lay behind Britain's refusal to join the European project at the outset.[23] That Britain (together with its empire) was the number two player on the Allies' winning side does much to explain how its habitual prioritization of the Anglo-American 'special relationship' interfered with European orientations in a far more fundamental way than it did in other Western bloc countries that had Atlanticist priorities of their own. Dutch foreign policy has long accorded high value to the Netherlands' American alliance and membership in NATO, while Italy had its specific 'three circles' of international engagement that included Italian–American relations and being part of NATO, Europeanism, and Mediterraneanism.[24] And alongside its keen engagement with Europe in the aftermath of its own decolonization, Portugal too continued to value its Atlanticism that embraced Portuguese-speaking countries it had formerly ruled, whether long ago in the case of Brazil or much more recently in the case of Angola, Mozambique or other lusophone areas.[25] None, however, detracted from pro-European instincts as they did in Britain.

For France in particular, the turn to Europe not only overlapped with its imperial endgames and shifting priorities after decolonization but with de Gaulle's strong reservations about '*les Anglo-Saxons*' and Atlanticism by extension. Anglo-French tensions that dated back to the war years took new form after their joint invasion of Suez in 1956 was terminated upon Britain's retreat under American pressure. Suez counts not only as a key turning point that accelerated British decolonization but also became the death knell of residual illusions that Britain could go it alone on the global stage without American acquiescence. Equally, the spectre of Suez hovered over de Gaulle's vetoes of Britain's EEC applications and also reinforced France's own Europeanism alongside ongoing ties with francophone African states. European integration simultaneously offered the best guarantee of a lasting Franco-German alliance, an alternative stage upon which France could assert itself internationally and maintain as much *grandeur* as possible as its empire first shrank and then collapsed, and protection against American hegemony in Western Europe. Taking the lead in Europe was meant to safeguard France and Western Europe by extension from '*la colonisation américaine*' as 'America tries to control Europe as she looks to control Latin America and Southeast Asia', as de Gaulle saw it. Keeping Britain out of the EEC meant France refusing 'to allow ourselves to be absorbed by the Anglo-American giant', he continued, as well as rejecting a status akin to that of a 'protectorate' whereby 'France would be to the United States that which Morocco was to France'.[26]

European cooperation has thus offered member states an important means of pulling more weight both within the continent and beyond it during and after the decolonization era that often (albeit not invariably, as France's history shows) has coexisted with American and Atlantic allegiances. Britain, by contrast, has steadfastly given precedence to its 'special relationship' with the United States despite its vastly subordinate role within it and has done so at the expense of British–EU relations. For Britain, membership in the EEC/EU never entailed the same range of positive associations that it has enjoyed in other countries at different moments, with popular enthusiasm for the European project never having been anything more than muted at best. If belonging to the European Community was widely welcomed as a political and economic achievement and a chance to reinvent themselves in the aftermath of totalitarianism and often war in other member states, for Britain it never lost connotations of 'losing control', whether on a global stage or over its own sovereignty at home. Europe for Britain connoted national decline and a downward trajectory from being the heart of the world's largest empire to one of an unimpressive herd dominated by continentals.[27]

In the era of Brexit, it is no secret that Euroscepticism (and indeed outright hostility towards the EU) has become an increasingly powerful force across Europe to the extent that many question whether the EU can ultimately survive. It is immediately visible in Scandinavian countries that have always expressed their reservations as well as in Eastern European countries that acceded far more recently in the 2004 and 2007 enlargements, regardless of the extent to which they have benefitted from EU membership. Populist nationalism has undoubtedly done much to fuel these discontents, and Euroscepticism has now proliferated even in parts of the EU where the majority had traditionally been largely immune to it. In what had reliably been largely pro-EU southern European countries like Portugal and especially Italy, the toxic environment that has resulted from the financial and debt crises since 2007 and 2008 became further compounded by the refugee crisis that has brought EU countries into fraught contact with the political cataclysms occurring in (post-colonial) North Africa, the Middle East and elsewhere.[28] Hostility towards unwanted migration (whether actual or simply feared) from other parts of the EU, particularly from Eastern and south-eastern Europe, has also stoked anti-European sentiments in countries like the Netherlands, Germany, and most certainly in Britain, where it was a central feature of the debates that raged in the run-up to the 23 June 2016 referendum and which continue in its wake.[29]

Imperial legacies, as this chapter has stressed, are far from an exclusively British phenomenon, being irrevocably woven into the fabric of many of the EU's 'small nations' whose global histories greatly exceed their current confines. Where Britain is unique in post-colonial Europe is in the way common perceptions of its imperial past have fed political fantasies of global alternatives to continental associations to the extent that they have become construed as incompatible with European loyalties. Multiple international 'circles' of interest beyond the EU (including those that survive from defunct empires) certainly feature elsewhere. Britain, however, offers a distinct example in which the still-smouldering embers of empire have fuelled such extreme hostility towards Europe that future historians of Britain after it left its empire will also in all likelihood need to grapple with Britain after it left the EU.

Notes

1 Daniel Boffey, 'Brexit broadside: British officials bristle at Danish scorn', *The Guardian*, 14 June 2017.

2 Philip Murphy, *The Empire's New Clothes: The Myth of the Commonwealth* (London: Hurst, 2018); Dane Kennedy, *The Imperial History Wars: Debating the British Empire* (London: Bloomsbury, 2018), 6, 73, 150–52.

3 'United Europe': Cabinet note by Mr Churchill, 29 Nov. 1951, NA, CAB 129/48, C (51)32, reprinted in *The Conservative Government and the End of Empire 1951–1957, Part I* (*British Documents on the End of Empire*) (Series A, Vol. 3), ed. David Goldsworthy (London, 1994), Part I, 3–4; '"The Three Circles" (Foreign Policy)', 20 April 1949, Economic Conference of the European Movement, in *Winston S. Churchill: His Complete Speeches 1897–1963*, Vol. VII, 1943–1949, ed. Robert Rhodes James (London, 1974), 7810–11.

4 Labour Party, *European Unity: A Statement by the National Executive Committee of the British Labour Party* (London, 1950), 3, accessed via http://www.cvce.eu

5 'Speech by Hugh Gaitskell (3 October 1962)', 7, reproduced from *Britain and the Common Market, Texts of Speeches Made at the 1962 Labour Party Conference by the Rt. Hon. Hugh Gaitskell MP and the Rt. Hon. George Brown MP together with the policy statement accepted by Conference* (London, 1962); 'Speech by Harold Wilson on Britain's Membership to the EEC', reproduced from *Labour and the Common Market: Report of a special conference of the Labour Party, Central Hall, Westminster, 17 July 1971* (London: Labour Party, 1971), 42–49, both accessed via https://www.cvce.eu

6 Anne Deighton, 'The Past in the Present: British Imperial Memories and the European Question', in *Memory and Power in Post-War Europe: Studies in the Presence of the Past*, ed. Jan-Werner Müller (Cambridge: Cambridge University Press, 2002), 109.

7 Nicola Labanca, 'Exceptional Italy? The Many Ends of the Italian Colonial Empire', in *The Oxford Handbook of the Ends of Empire*, ed. Martin Thomas and Andrew Thompson (Oxford: Oxford University Press, 2018), 123–43.

8 Robin de Bruin, 'Indonesian Decolonisation and the Dutch Attitude Towards the Establishment of the EEC's Association Policy, 1945–1963', *Journal of European Integration History* 23, no. 2 (2017), 211–26.

9 Skander Nasra and Mathieu Segers, 'Between Charlemagne and Atlantis: Belgium and the Netherlands during the First Stages of European Integration (1950–1966)', *Journal of European Integration History* 18, no. 2 (2012): 195.

10 Peo Hansen and Stefan Jonsson, 'Bringing Africa as a "Dowry to Europe": European Integration and the Eurafrican Project, 1920–1960', *Interventions: International Journal of Postcolonial Studies* 13, no. 3 (2011): 443, 461. See also Louis Sicking, 'A Colonial Echo: France and the Colonial Dimension of the European Economic Community', *French Colonial History* 5 (2003): 207–28; Peo Hansen and Stefan Jonsson, *Eurafrica: The Untold History of European Integration and Colonialism* (London: Bloomsbury, 2014).

11 Peo Hansen, 'In the Name of Europe', *Race & Class* 45, no. 3 (2004): 52.

12 Peo Hansen, 'European Integration, European Identity and the Colonial Connection', *European Journal of Social Theory* 5, no. 4 (2002): 488–89.

13 Gurminder K. Bhambra, 'Postcolonial Europe, or Understanding Europe in Times of the Postcolonial', in *The Sage Handbook of European Studies*, ed. Chris Rumford (London: Sage, 2009), 81.

14 Elizabeth Buettner, *Europe after Empire: Decolonization, Society, and Culture* (Cambridge: Cambridge University Press, 2016), 16, 190.

15 António Costa Pinto and Nuno Severiano Teixeira, 'From Africa to Europe: Portugal and European Integration', in *Southern Europe and the Making of the European Union, 1945–1980s*, ed. António Costa Pinto and Nuno Severiano Teixeira (Boulder, CO: Social Science Monographs, 2002), 38.

16 Marc Frey, 'Dutch Elites and Decolonization', in *Elites and Decolonization in the Twentieth Century*, ed. Jost Dülffer and Marc Frey (Basingstoke, 2011), 57–8.

17 Lars Jensen, 'Postcolonial Denmark: Beyond the Rot of Colonialism?', *Postcolonial Studies* 18, no. 4 (2015): 440–52; Rebecca Adler-Nissen and Ulrik P. Gad, 'Introduction: Postimperial Sovereignty Games in the Nordic Region', *Cooperation*

and Conflict 49, no. 1 (2015): 3–32. Thanks also to Stuart Ward for sharing his thoughts with me about Danish colonialism in comparative European contexts.

18 Ulrik P. Gad, 'Greenland: A Post-Danish Sovereign Nation State in the Making', *Cooperation and Conflict* 49, no. 1 (2014): 98–118.

19 These count among the topics currently being examined within the consortium project on 'European Colonial Heritage Modalities in Entangled Cities (ECHOES)' funded by the European Union's Horizon 2020 research and innovation programme under grant agreement No 770248 (http://projectechoes.eu).

20 These issues have been explored in much greater depth elsewhere. Within a large body of scholarship, discussions in Buettner, *Europe after Empire*, Parts II and III, and *Memories of Post-imperial Nations: The Aftermath of Decolonization, 1945–2013*, ed. Dietmar Rothermund (Cambridge: Cambridge University Press, 2015) serve as useful starting points.

21 Pieter Lagrou, *The Legacy of Nazi Occupation: Patriotic Memory and National Recovery in Western Europe, 1945–1965* (Cambridge: Cambridge University Press, 2000); Tony Judt, *Postwar: A History of Europe Since 1945* (London: Pimlico, 2007); Buettner, *Europe after Empire*, Part I.

22 António de Figueiredo, 'The Empire Is Dead, Long Live the EU', in *The Last Empire: Thirty Years of Portuguese Decolonization*, ed. Stewart Lloyd-Jones and António Costa Pinto (Bristol: Intellect, 2003), 127–43.

23 Quoted in James Ellison, 'Is Britain more European than it thinks?', *History Today* 62, no. 2 (2012); see also *Britain, the Commonwealth, and Europe: The Commonwealth and Britain's Applications to Join the European Communities*, ed. Alex May (Basingstoke: Palgrave, 2001).

24 Nasra and Segers, 'Between Charlemagne and Atlantis'; Mathieu Segers, *Reis naar het continent: Nederland en de Europese integratie, 1950 tot heden* (Amsterdam: Bert Bakker, 2013); Maurizio Carbone, 'Beyond the Three Circles: Italy and the Rest of the World', *Journal of Modern Italian Studies* 13, no. 1 (2008): 1–5.

25 Pinto and Teixeira, 'From Africa to Europe', 4, 14, 27; Luís António Santos, 'Portugal and the CPLP: Heightened Expectations, Unfounded Disillusions', in *Last Empire*, ed. Lloyd-Jones and Pinto.

26 Alain Peyrefitte, *C'était de Gaulle* (Paris: Editions de Fallois, 1994), 355, 367, 374.

27 Krishan Kumar, 'Britain, England and Europe: Cultures in Counterflow', *European Journal of Social Theory* 6, no. 1 (2003): 5–23.

28 Although these topics cannot receive further attention here, useful recent discussions include *Europe's Crises*, ed. Manuel Castells et al. (Cambridge: Polity, 2018); *The Routledge Handbook of Euroscepticism*, ed. Benjamin Leruth, Nicholas Startin and Simon Usherwood (London and New York: Routledge, 2018).

29 Similar questions are also dealt with in Yasmin Khan's contribution to this volume, 'Refugees, Migrants, Windrush and Brexit'.

Chapter 5
Forgetfulness: England's Discontinuous Histories

Bill Schwarz

With the close of the initial, formal Brexit negotiations between the United Kingdom and the European Union much remains unresolved and a precipice looms. No one knows what this will bring. Yet whatever the outcome – no deal; a face-saving, gimcrack accord which over the coming years relegates the substance to an administrative ninth circle; or the eventual shelving of the very endeavour to 'leave' – the deeper issues raised by the 2016 referendum won't go away. It's not just a question of the culpable myopia of David Cameron's tactical gamble of holding back the tide of Tory disarray by alighting upon his plebiscitary legerdemain. Nor can it be attributed to the evident lack of wisdom displayed by his successor Theresa May, although her disregard for the lives and opinions of the mass of the population – notwithstanding her occasional poisoned invocations of 'the will of the people' – undoubtedly places her in the frame. Even if a second referendum were to resolve that the Brexit adventure should be revoked in its entirety there can be no 'return'. Return to what? The genie has been released. The stakes are too high. The technicalities about trade – the customs union (now in place for sixty years), EFTA (the European Free Trade Area), the single market, Norway, Canada, Norway-plus – were never really the issue: when I cast my vote I knew little of these variants and in this I was not alone. The world has turned and repairing the old political settlement has ceased to be an option.

For this reason the current collapse is not a matter of party narrowly conceived but properly a crisis of the state, in which the executive and the legislature are at odds with each other. There are signs that the legislature might be beginning to assert its authority, at long last, creating a passage out of the impasse. But even so, this is a crisis which has undone the political class as a whole. This is so in the widest sense, drawing in not just MPs and public functionaries but the broader spectrum of those who orchestrate authority and who strive to manage public opinion, whether or not they are directly affiliated to the institutions of the state. Fundamentally it's a crisis of political representation, in which the established configuration of the Westminster parties – and indeed large sectors of the established configuration of the EU – systematically fail to nourish, or even to comprehend, popular life. While politicians are regularly derided, political divisions imperil many domains of our everyday social worlds. The sclerosis of Britain's constitutional arrangement is visible as rarely before. It touches us all. It's less a democratic deficit than a democratic mudslide, the political analogue of fracking in which the structures of public life are vulnerable to what appear to be – for those who choose not to see – entirely random subterranean implosions. For the citizenry located outside Westminster, observing the purgatorial paralysis of the British state takes its toll on every one of us. Politics isn't only out there. When it's reduced to a macabre farce we are all diminished.

Yet simultaneously this is also a crisis in historical memory. Since the 2016 referendum the more that's been spoken the more intractable the political impasse becomes. In turn when this occurs the further history evaporates as a significant referent in public life. And that, simply, is my argument: that in England – the geopolitical motor of Brexit – the crisis of the state is accompanied by a pervasive historical forgetfulness.[1] Whether cause or effect, it's difficult to discern. But its operations are material.

What though, in this historical conjuncture, does historical forgetfulness mean? What's its import? What is the relation between the crisis of the state and the crisis – if that's what it is – of memory? Where is it to be located? Can a state be an agent in the organization of its own forgetfulness?

My concern here is with the grubby, mundane aspects of political practice. This isn't, in the case of Brexit, the terrain of 'deep' memory, or 'deep' forgetfulness. By invoking the idea of forgetfulness I do so in order to uncover what I regard as the phenomenon of *not caring to remember*.[2] This is not a mode of forgetting which has its origins in a resistance to the subjective endeavour to recall painful pasts, blocking all attempts mentally to retrieve the past. Forgetfulness, as I use it here, represents a different order of remembering/forgetting, in which human will and ethics lie closer to the surface of things. It's a way of thought akin to James Baldwin's judgements on the racial indifference of white America in the period of civil rights and Black Power which he named, and condemned, as 'innocence'. This was not for Baldwin the emancipatory innocence of William Blake. On the contrary, he conceived it as a criminally abject means of being in the world. Innocence, in his sense, was morally charged. *Your* innocence, *your* (racialized) refusal to acknowledge what was occurring at the end of your street, or around the corner, meant that (racialized) *others* were dying. Not caring to remember is of a part with post-truth and the dissolution of politics by the tweet.

It signifies neither amnesia nor trauma, the staple of certain lines of approach in contemporary historiography. Yet it does highlight a pathological form of forgetting in which both the intellectual demands of thinking and the ethical care that thought requires are relegated from the practices of politics.

In one sector of the British press (notably in *The Guardian* columns of Marina Hyde and John Crace) the capacities of Mrs May's cabinet are regularly pilloried as the acme of stupidity. There have been many occasions when I nod my head in agreement, no longer disbelieving secretaries of state who exult in their own ignorance (as once I did), or when I concur with the evisceration of those who parade their latest tomfoolery as a sharp-witted vindication of the deepest desires of the people. Even so, I'd sooner shift perspective and think in terms of the alternative but perhaps more damning sensibility: one constituted by the wilful disregard for taking responsibility for one's political actions and – as a further function – by a lackadaisical casualness in regard to the gravity of the historical past.

It's an occupational hazard for historians to complain about the absence of historical consciousness in the affairs of state and it seldom gets us anywhere. Unconcern with the political past happens all the time. But the coming of Brexit, and the bad faith it has generated, signal an escalation in the trivialization of the past; degrees of temporal dissociation have turned into a qualitative transformation of significance. It feels that politics is operating by new, undeclared principles which are difficult to identify and which no one owns.

The mental reflex of not caring to remember is dramatically evident in the dispositions of those (erstwhile Burkeian) Tories who have come to pose as the (neo-Jacobin) vanguard of Brexit: those who, when it comes to the labour of making a new politics, find the diligence required of them, as begetters of the new order, too arduous to contemplate – or, to resort to the vernacular of putatively ancient Bullingdon custom, when they discover that they just can't be arsed.

Ideologues of Brexit have been perversely adept in conjugating *faux* histories: eccentric, wayward, and meaningless. Telling is the appeal arising from the urbane stratum of the Brexit camp (in the figures of Boris Johnson and Jacob Rees-Mogg) to the calamities of 'vassalage', as if Eton has now turned into an institution for the creation of a modern species of serf, subject to the indignities of a re-imposed Norman Yoke master-minded from Brussels.[3] Such myth-making works as a screen-memory, camouflaging the past and placing it further beyond the reach of the present. In its highly-strung incantations, driven by the more assured populist inflections of Nigel Farage, histories of this complexion can be lauded as irrefutable proof that Europe is robbing England of what it holds most dear: its providential past.

However, the disappearance of the historical past has become a more general feature of public debate. There's a consensus that we are facing a situation which is historically unprecedented but few are inclined to give much thought to what this comprises. In the liberal media it's become a reflex to blame the nation's political ills on those responsible for forcing the pace of Brexit. Yet the extent of the paucity of historical perspective is striking, and I understand this *generalized* abandonment of history to be the fallout from the crisis of the state. 'Forgetfulness' is part of this larger situation. On occasion the recomposition of politics in 1846 is gestured; infrequent reminders of the referendum of 1975 can sometimes be heard; more insistent have been memories of the ousting of Mrs Thatcher in 1990, and of her deepening Eurosceptic sensibilities. But that's about it, the sum of histories which are acknowledged. The slipshod 'forgetting' of Ireland by Westminster – although it marks a dramatic rehearsal of the colonial past – has proved catastrophic.

With this in mind it may be valuable also to pause and reflect on the current role of the civil service as the traditional custodian of the state's collective memory, and to consider the effect of the new stratum of government-appointed advisers, whose job it is to tell authority what it wishes to hear.

To suggest that forgetfulness is a significant aspect of England's contemporary political life is hardly radical or novel. It calls for no grandiose, abstract, or moralistic injunctions to 'remember'. What it does require, more practically, is for historians to hold fast to our faith in the value of our calling.

There are scores of plausible ways of explaining historically Brexit Britain. I'll discuss only a single general trajectory, but one which recently has gained a certain currency: the reading of Brexit through the lens of end of empire.

When the extent of the Leave vote first began to take hold of the minds of those who, only a short while before, had found such an idea unthinkable, there occurred the spontaneous reflex claiming it to be the final act in the end of empire. More particularly, nostalgia for empire – for long latent but now given form by the referendum (so the argument ran) – explained the Brexit outcome.[4] I'm doubtful about this bid to elevate nostalgia as the dominant causal factor for an entire psephological rupture. In itself the proposition may not be wrong but it accounts for everything and nothing. For sure, even when invisible to the naked eye the vanished Empire continues to be, irrepressibly, a material reality. A repertoire of melancholic associations does indeed infiltrate contemporary political sensibilities.[5] English fundamentalism confronts us, even as it steadfastly disavows its very existence. (Think of Mrs May conducting her public persona.) It's impossible to understand the mentalities of contemporary England – the reflexes, the sensibilities, the subterfuge, the disavowals – without heeding its vanished imperial core, bequeathing governing instincts which carry into the present a peculiarly post-colonial imperiousness.[6] Yet it's not clear how or if these mentalities translate into nostalgia, or how or if there is an immediate correspondence between reveries of this type and what happens when citizens enter the voting booth. Attention to further levels of mediation is necessary.

Alternatively, it may be more fruitful to start somewhere else.

An appropriate precedent can be found in the Irish crisis of 1912–14, when the Westminster system could engineer no solution to the religious schism in Ireland. The Liberals were faced with the collapse of the ethical mission for Home Rule, bequeathed to them by Gladstone. This created in its turn its political antidote, the populist forces of Unionism in the North of Ireland. By 1912 Unionism and Home Rule divided Britain as deeply as the question of Europe divides the nation today. The degree to which any of the leading politicians, on either side, believed what they so vehemently proclaimed is open to doubt. There was much posturing and grandstanding. Andrew Bonar Law, the Conservative/Unionist leader, made tentative moves to align the populist Orange order with his party in Westminster. He flirted with treason and – if only rhetorically – allied himself with the radical populist right. The Westminster system entered two years of enervating political paralysis; no political leadership emerged with any conception of how the impasse might be resolved. Only the coming of world war unblocked the impasse.

The populist moment of 1912–14 was both an imperialist and a metropolitan movement, in the double manner which we have become accustomed to think of the history of modern Ireland. But in Britain those who adhered to the Unionist cause – particularly the great proconsuls who had returned from distant points of the Empire – were as troubled by the predicament of *England* as they were by Ireland, alarmed by the question of what England would be if its colonies broke away. They expressed the fear that such an England would, in fact, be no England at all. In this mental world empire functioned as the antidote to the collapse of the centre: of England itself.

Driving this populist revolt from below was the conviction that corruption was located at the summit of the state and that ethnic enemies were now operating *inside* the ruling bloc.

This produced a startling historical paradox. The populist forces of Unionism mobilized in the name of the integrity of the Union of Ireland and Britain and as militants for the greater empire. Yet at the same time they identified their encroaching enemy as the imperial British state. This contradictory dynamic – in which loyalty became treachery, and opposites met – represented a common syndrome in the ('white') territories of the overseas British world. Here the Empire simultaneously generated centripetal identifications – the pressures to affiliate to Britain's state – as well as the centrifugal pull away from the centre, manifest in the increasing authority of emerging colonial nationalisms, ultimately leading to the creation of independent nation-states.

English Unionism, organized in the massed recruits to the League of British Covenanters, marked a new type of political formation. This was exemplified in the attachments of one its foremost ideologues, Rudyard Kipling. Kipling was certain that the Liberals' acquiescence to Home Rule demonstrated the loss of political will of the governing class and that, as a consequence, the Protestants of the north were now – by default – the saviours of England. Like Enoch Powell after him, he imagined Irish Unionism to be the vehicle which would redeem England. In May 1914 Kipling was much cheered by the gathering agitation which Ulster had witnessed in 1913, believing it represented 'the first move in the revolt of the English' and the 'beginning of the counter-revolution against the radicals in the Liberal Party'.

Kipling derided members of the government as 'outlaws' and as 'conspirators'. 'The Home Rule Bill broke the pledged faith of generations,' he claimed, bringing into the realm 'officially recognized sedition . . . conspiracy and rebellion'. He went on:

> A province and a people of Great Britain are to be sold to their and our enemies. We are forbidden to have any voice in this sale of our own flesh and blood; we have no tribunal under Heaven to appeal to except the corrupt parties to that sale and their paid followers . . .
>
> Ulster, and as much of Ireland as dares express itself, wishes to remain within the Union and under the flag of the Union. The Cabinet . . . intends to drive them out. The electors of Great Britain have never sanctioned this . . . Civil War is inevitable unless our rulers can be brought to realize that, even now, they must submit these grave matters to the judgement of a free people. If they do not, all the history of our island shows that there is but one end – destruction from within and without.

In these words we confront the critical moment when the nation/'people' is mobilized against the state. On the one side Kipling positions the 'faith of generations', the 'people of Great Britain', 'a free people': in sum, 'our own flesh and blood'. On the other are the 'outlaws' and 'conspirators', 'enemies', 'corrupt parties', and 'paid followers': in sum, 'our rulers'. In this perspective Britain's statesmen are identified as ethnic traitors, betrayers of race and nation. Ethnicity – 'our own flesh and blood' – bequeaths a higher law than that sanctioned by the institutions of the state. It was absolute, transcendent even, in its remit. If the politicians failed to recognize the power of this ethnic compact then destruction would follow, 'from within and without'.[7]

England's redemption was, Kipling proposed, to be achieved by means of the overseas province-colony; and radicalism at home was to be uprooted by calling upon the 'counter-revolution' fomented by the Protestants of Northern Ireland, whose ethnic loyalties were unsullied by the corruptions of the metropole. The virtuous 'Great British' people functioned as the antidote to the machinations of the British state. The crisis in the imperial state was conceived *as* principally an ethnic crisis. Kipling believed his putative compatriots were, in truth, insufficiently national, or insufficiently racial. In turn this led him, as it must lead any who employs such thinking, to fervid imaginings of treachery. And where else does treachery happen than at home?[8]

The properties of the new ethnic populism were a product of the age of imperial democracy. The populist upsurge was not an aberration in British politics but a function of the larger political system of 'universal' democracy which was slowly assembled in the metropole between 1886 and 1928. It was the offspring of the Westminster system, articulating a political voice which could never easily be contained within the established institutions of parliamentary democracy. The inner structure of this populist upsurge was both post-colonial in inspiration – in England they were given form by presentiments of the nation 'after empire' – *and* conceived as a principal vehicle to uproot radicalism at home.

I don't wish to over-emphasize the Unionist mobilizations in Britain between 1912 and 1914. The significance of this moment was perhaps less in what it represented at the time than what in retrospect we can see it prefiguring. The mobilizations carried onto the political field a counter-force to the universal state: an ethnic populism, vociferous in proclaiming its democratic credentials, defined by its deep commitments to race and nation – to a highly charged articulation of *the people* – in order to contain and destroy the depredations of radicalism and the liberal state.

I hesitate to suggest that in the intervening years ethnic populism has constituted anything akin to a discernible 'tradition' in Britain's political life. This is not so, or not if one assumes it to have been a constant presence. But through the twentieth century, and into our own historical present, it has worked as a *discontinuous* presence; it stands as an unexhausted reservoir of popular sentiment, mobile in its inner configurations, and ready to burst into the light of day when ruling settlements begin to creak and crack. It takes many forms, from one conjuncture to the next. Obliquely, this discontinuous current within the British polity marked one element in the inchoate phenomenon we know as Thatcherism. It was manifest more vividly in the Powellite rupture of 1968–72, whose end was marked late in 1974 by Enoch Powell crossing the Irish Sea and – in his last stand – reaffirming from his County Down bunker that the purity of his vision remained intact. And the embers flash into the light of day again in the anti-EU populism of our own period, taking form from perhaps 2012 (or thereabouts), when UKIP began to organize effectively a political base outside Westminster, and continuing as significant presence in the years which follow.

This is not to imply that, from Sir Edward Carson at the start of the twentieth century to Nigel Farage today, these populist incursions onto the political stage have been *the same*. This makes no sense. But if we alter the angle of vision and think conceptually in terms of the contingent, mobile relations *between* state and nation(s), then this recurrent pattern of different variants of ethnic populism, in the plural, may be helpful.

We can grasp, for example, the submerged lines of connection between the (white) Great British people whom Kipling imagined and their descendants today, the 'ordinary' (white) folk of a contracting, defensive England, each believing their historic mission was to save the 'nation' from its rulers.

There are, though, two inhibitions in conceiving the historical past in these terms. Directly or indirectly each underwrites informed opinion both in the national media and in the formal historiography.

First is the question of populism, in general, which seems to have the capacity to induce Westminster ideologues into a state of bemused, apprehensive discombobulation. Commonly it's regarded as something alien to how 'we' do things, a kind of virus, which shouldn't rightfully settle in the cool and temperate minds of the English. There occurred a symptomatic moment just after the Trump election when the BBC's *Any Questions* felt itself obliged to turn its attention to the troubling phenomenon.[9] One of the invited panellists was Kwasi Kwarteng, a Conservative MP and historian of decolonization, an impeccably modern Tory whose views always sound gratifyingly wholesome. He struggled to understand why populist eruptions had become so evident in the classic Atlantic democracies. Yet he also was at pains to be open-minded, concluding that populism essentially was a 'corrective' coming into play when established politicians wobbled. It worked as a reminder to the power-brokers that it was time to pull their socks up. His observation stands as an elegant distillation of an old sociological functionalism, imagining that a little fine tuning here and there and all would be well. It follows that Westminster was where proper politics happened, and politics from below could only ever be an excrescence on the body politic. In this reading, populisms could never possess a rightful role in the British polity.

Second is the emphasis I give to the political right outside (or largely outside) the bounds of the Conservative Party, acknowledging that the racialized populist right has historically formed part of the life of the political nation. This jars with the liberal and progressive instincts which, to a greater or lesser degree, have formed the profession over the past two or three generations. There exists a kind of intellectual closure in recognizing that such a phenomenon could exist in England.[10] It arises, I guess, from a residual attachment to late Whiggish sentiments which favour continuity and progress, still beholden to the rightness of the hegemony of Westminster. Populism is awkward enough. But authoritarian populism?[11] Surely not. This can't be how England has worked in the past. And certainly not how it works now.

I'm not claiming that the recent history of England should be conceptualized exclusively in terms of ethnic populism. But nor should the periodic punctuations of ethnic populism be ignored, or placed outside the mainstream of England's politics. To open the story with the Irish crisis before the First World War won't tell us all we need to know. But it may provoke new questions.

It's also a perspective which places centrally the end of empire in the domestic, political narrative. As the ties of imperial belonging weakened and as, in the 1960s, the writing was on the wall, white resistance in the redoubts of the British world overseas – in the Central African Federation; in Rhodesia – reverberated with new potency in the metropolis, giving form to the lived travails of native Britons in Britain both as white and as oppressed, or more graphically, as a defeated people. The stories emanating from settler central Africa proved fertile, engendering a populism which sought to claim back the nation from the politicians. As the people, in their guise as 'ordinary' English men and women, were mobilized *against* the British state, the lineaments of a historic ethnic populism can be discerned inside the metropole itself. The old centrifugal forces of empire – the drive to pull away from the centre – began to operate *in England*, as a vociferous section of the nation voiced their disconnection from the state. In an uncanny affirmation of the old presentiments of the Edwardian proconsuls, the apprehension that without an empire the centre couldn't hold – that *England* couldn't hold – was, in an unexpected turn, vindicated.[12]

This is to shift the argument away from a preoccupation with amorphous, elusive sensibilities (nostalgia) to an analysis founded on the relations between the state and 'the people', in its many discursive entities. It's premised on a belief that the changing configurations of what politics *is*, in any single historical conjuncture, is decisive. There's one final point.

David Cameron's announcement in January 2016 that he would call a referendum was turned inside-out the following month by the electrifying announcement that his two senior colleagues, Boris Johnson and Michael Gove, were jumping ship and allying themselves to the populist ultras. This threatened a direct link between the populists outside the state and the established governing class. This – before Mrs May made her pact with the Democratic Unionist Party: a classic instance of the repressed returning – echoed the febrile times of Bonar Law and the Unionist crisis, when a harder, racialized populist politics came close to infiltrating the operations of the state.

The possibility of a Gove/Johnson/UKIP alliance signalled a frightening development. It was not to be. But the significance of the *proximity* of such an eventuality is, isn't it, unnerving? Trump's presence in the White House rearranges our expectations of what, in the old democracies, is politically possible. We should be serious in thinking what historically this means. There's good cause, as I see things, for returning to Hannah Arendt's reflections on the making of what she decided to call the totalitarian state. The capitulation of the state to populist forces of the right doesn't represent simply another instalment of political life. It's of a different order: not merely a different sort of politics, but the unhinging of what we have been accustomed to appreciate as the political world.

Notes

1. In centring England I follow Anthony Barnett, *The Lure of Greatness: England's Brexit and America's Trump* (London: Unbound, 2017).
2. With thanks to Peter Hulme: see 'The Locked Heart: The Creole Family Romance of *Wide Sargasso Sea*' in Francis Barker, Peter Hulme and Margaret Iverson (eds), *Colonial Discourse/Postcolonial Theory* (Manchester: Manchester UP, 1994); and his 'The Place of Wide Sargasso Sea', *Wasafiri* 20 (2008).
3. Fintan O'Toole, *Heroic Failure: Brexit and the Politics of Pain* (London: Head of Zeus, 2018), a magisterially profane interpretation from Ireland, which turns the historic tables. 'Vassalage' supplies one of its many comic turns.
4. Significant anticipations include Linda Colley, 'Brexiteers are Nostalgics in Search of a Lost Empire', *Financial Times*, 22 April 2016; and Pankaj Mishra, 'Brexiteers Are Pining for Empire,' *Bloomberg*, 29 April 2016, https://www.bloomberg.com/view/articles/2016-04-29/brexit-supporters-are-pining-for-the-days-of-empire
5. Paul Gilroy, *After Empire: Melancholia or Convivial Culture?: Multiculture or Postcolonial Melancholia* (London: Routledge, 2004).
6. Brexit supplies endless examples of the syndrome. The first meeting of the British negotiators late in April 2017 with their future adversary, Michel Barnier, is symptomatic. Those representing the UK exhibited a blithe ignorance of their own circumstances. All was going to be speedily resolved; Britain, in the argot of the moment, was to have its cake and eat it: Denis MacShane, *Brexit, No Exit: Why (In the End) Britain Won't Leave Europe* (London: IB Tauris, 2017): xviii–xix; and Robert Saunders, 'Britain Must Rid Itself of the Delusion That It Is Big, Bold and In Charge', *The Guardian*, 9 January 2019.
7. Cited in David Gilmour, *The Long Recessional. The Imperial Life of Rudyard Kipling* (New York: Farrar, Straus, & Giroux, 2002), 246.
8. I draw here from my *Memories of Empire. Vol. I. The White Man's World* (Oxford: Oxford UP, 2011), 102–6.
9. BBC Radio 4, *Any Questions*, 12 November 2016.
10. For a recent broadside against such unconscious assumptions amongst British, or English, historians, David Edgerton, *The Rise and Fall of the British Nation: A Twentieth-Century History* (London: Allen Lane, 2017).
11. See Stuart Hall, 'Popular Democracy vs. Authoritarian Populism', in *Marxism and Democracy*, ed. Alan Hunt (London: Lawrence & Wishart, 1980).
12. In part a historical interpretation along these lines owes much to the arguments originally deployed by Tom Nairn in *The Break-Up of Britain: Crisis and Neo-Nationalism* (London: Verso, 1981; first published 1977). In Nairn's account, end of empire lies at the heart of the renewed emergence of the local nationalisms which jeopardize the integrity of Britain's old empire-state. His perception of what he identified as the 'slow-motion landslide' of the British state is more persuasive now than it was forty years ago – even though his 'slow-motion' has been a deal slower than Nairn, and many like him, ever expected.

Chapter 6
Ireland and the English Question

Fintan O'Toole

'I remember', Winston Churchill told the House of Commons in February 1922, 'on the eve of the Great War we were gathered together at a Cabinet meeting in Downing Street, and for a long time, an hour or an hour and a half . . . we discussed the boundaries of Fermanagh and Tyrone. Both of the great political parties were at each other's throats. The air was full of talk of civil war. Every effort was made to settle the matter and bring them together. The differences had been narrowed down, not merely to the counties of Fermanagh and Tyrone, but to parishes and groups of parishes inside the areas of Fermanagh and Tyrone, and yet, even when the differences had been so narrowed down, the problem appeared to be as insuperable as ever, and neither side would agree to reach any conclusion.'[1]

It is a poignant, even tragic image: Europe is about to implode and the members of the imperial cabinet in London are peering through a metaphorical microscope at the ragged boundaries of parishes in Fermanagh and Tyrone. They are hoping to descry a clear pattern of sectarian division in those counties that would allow for the drawing of a rational and stable border between the Ireland that was to be granted Home Rule and the Protestant areas of the north-east that might be allowed to opt out. It is funny to think of the British grandees sitting around the table in Downing Street saying the strange Gaelic names to themselves in tones of pure bewilderment: Belcoo, Magheraveely, Rosslea, Aghalane, Derrygonnelly. Or at least it would be funny if we did not know what was about to happen in the bigger world.

But: the first time is tragedy; the second time is farce. As the Brexit negotiations came to crunch time at the end of 2018, the British cabinet was embroiled in a European war that was not so much a cataclysm, more a nervous breakdown.

And beneath the noise and bluster, a low but persistent voice kept whispering: Belcoo, Magheraveely, Rosslea, Aghalane, Derrygonnelly. The mock-heroic epic of Brexit was itself mocked by the contested contours of minute border parishes as the problem of what to do with the Irish frontier continually dashed the hopes of a Great Escape from the European Union. Pathos had become bathos. But the same fundamental truth applied: the problem of the Irish Border was 'as insuperable as ever'. It seemed that one could metaphorically trace all the ins and outs of its 500-kilometre meander across hills and fields, bogs and highways, bridges and streams and still not 'reach any conclusion' that would allow for the good clean, red white and blue Brexit of the Leavers' dreams. And this was, for the Brexiters, exasperating. As Andrew Lilico, economic adviser to the Leave campaign, tweeted:

> Almost everyone's tried to avoid saying, up to now, that the Irish border is not a top priority. No one wants to be responsible for any future unrest or lawlessness. But it is the blunt truth. What happens at the Irish border is far less important than that we truly leave the EU . . . I don't believe there need to be stop-&-check controls at the Irish border, but I am not prepared to see any compromises on anything fundamental to avoid them. Avoiding them (especially insofar as they are implemented by the EU not the UK) simply isn't that important.[2]

This vexation had a history. In that same speech, Churchill went on to create the classic formulation of English exasperation at the insolubility of the Irish Question. Looking back on that futile cabinet meeting from the far side of the great divide of the First World War, he said that

> The whole map of Europe has been changed. The position of countries has been violently altered. The modes of thought of men, the whole outlook on affairs, the grouping of parties, all have encountered violent and tremendous changes in the deluge of the world, but as the deluge subsides and the waters fall short we see the dreary steeples of Fermanagh and Tyrone emerging once again. The integrity of their quarrel is one of the few institutions that has been unaltered in the cataclysm which has swept the world. That says a lot for the persistency with which Irish men on the one side or the other are able to pursue their controversies. It says a great deal for the power which Ireland has, both Nationalist and Orange, to lay their hands upon the vital strings of British life and politics, and to hold, dominate, and convulse, year after year, generation after generation, the politics of this powerful country.

Hidden in this dazzling rhetoric, there is a plain and apparently banal word – 'their' repeated thrice: *their* quarrel, *their* controversies, *their* hands laid upon our life and politics. The Irish, whether Green or Orange, whether traitorous rebel or loyal subject, are Them. This is so much of a given, so apparently evident an assumption, that it is easy to miss how startling it is. All of Ireland was, at that point, not just still in the Empire (and even independent Ireland would remain in the Commonwealth for another quarter of a century) but still a supposedly integral part of the mother country, the United Kingdom of Great Britain and Ireland. Britain had just fought a nasty little war in Ireland to try to keep it so. Yet it did not seem odd to Churchill or apparently to any of his listeners, that all kinds of Irish were emphatically not 'us'. And thus the Irish Question is precisely that: not a British, still less an English question. Here is the profound ambivalence that would return to haunt the whole Brexit process. On the one hand, Ireland (now reduced to Northern Ireland) is a sacred part of a Union whose integrity must not be undermined at any cost. On the other, it is a foreign affair: the Irish, yet again, in their awkward insistence on guarantees that the residents of parishes of Fermanagh and Tyrone would not again be separated by a hard border from their neighbours to the south, are up to old tricks of laying their alien hands on the vital strings of British life and politics.

There is no serious doubt that, for the vast majority of those who voted for Brexit in England, Northern Ireland is Them. The evidence for this is threefold. First, in the 2016 referendum campaign, the Leave side consistently refused to address the problems of Northern Ireland, the Belfast Agreement of 1998 or the border. The best that could be got out of any of them was a double fantasy. The border would not be a problem because the Republic of Ireland (never really recognized as an independent country) would just have to follow the UK out of the European Union and return to the fold of what could again be called (political correctness be damned) the British Isles. And/or the European Union would have to give post-Brexit Britain a fabulous trade deal – the easiest ever negotiated – which would ensure 'frictionless' trade anyway, so again the border did not have to be considered. Asked specifically about the Irish problem in the last big televised debate before the Brexit vote, Boris Johnson replied: 'I remember vividly when the EU was given the task of trying to sort out the tragedy in the Balkans . . .' For those who had suspected that, for most of the Brexiteers, Ireland might as well be Montenegro, here was literal confirmation. Johnson spoke for two minutes. The words 'Ireland' and 'border' did not pass his lips.

Second, we know from the survey evidence that English people who voted Leave in 2016 or supported the Tories in the 2017 general election do not want to have responsibility for Northern Ireland and do not care about the peace process based on the 1998 Belfast Agreement that brought a 30-year conflict to an end. The most telling measure of commitment to a political union is whether or not you are content for taxes from the richest part to be used to subsidize services in the poorest. In the 2018 Future of England study, just 25 per cent of

Leave voters, and 29 per cent of people who say they voted Conservative in 2017, agree with the proposition: 'Revenue raised from taxpayers in England should also be distributed to Northern Ireland to help Northern Irish public services.' (Ironically, most English people still willing to subsidize Northern Ireland are Remainers.)[3] And, rather startlingly, when asked whether 'the unravelling of the peace process in Northern Ireland' is a 'price worth paying' for Brexit that allows them to 'take back control', fully 83 per cent of Leave voters and 73 per cent of Conservative voters agree that it is. This is not, surely, mere mindless cruelty – it expresses a deep belief that Northern Ireland is not 'us', that what happens 'over there' is not 'our' responsibility.

In the Channel 4 Survation study of November 2018, the largest since the Brexit referendum, voters were asked how concerned they would be 'If Brexit leads to Northern Ireland leaving the United Kingdom and joining the Republic of Ireland'. Just a third of Leave voters said they would be very concerned or quite concerned. Fully 61 per cent said they would be not very concerned or not at all concerned. Of the four grades of concern offered by the pollsters, by far the most popular among Leave voters, with 36 per cent, was 'not at all concerned'.

Third, after Theresa May triggered Article 50 in March 2017, her government produced, on the crucial border question, no concrete proposals and much magical thinking. The Prime Minister signed up twice, in the draft withdrawal deal agreed with the EU in December 2017 and in again in a reiteration in March 2018, to the so-called backstop to ensure that Northern Ireland would remain fully aligned with the Republic of Ireland to avoid a hard border. But after the signing of the original deal, her then Brexit secretary David Davis almost immediately dismissed it in public: 'This was a statement of intent more than anything else. It was much more a statement of intent than it was a legally enforceable thing'.[4] This lack of seriousness was predicated on a fanciful belief in the emergence of some as yet uninvented technology for invisible border control – Boris Johnson seriously proposed that the Irish border could be controlled like the congestion charge in London. The House of Commons select committee on Northern Ireland, after extensive hearings, concluded in March 2018, with just a year to go before Brexit:

> We have had no visibility of any technical solutions, anywhere in the world, beyond the aspirational, that would remove the need for physical infrastructure at the border. We recommend the Government bring forward detailed proposals, without further delay, that set out how it will maintain an open and invisible border. These proposals should provide detail about how customs compliance will be enforced if there is regulatory and tariff divergence between the UK and Ireland.[5]

But the British government made no attempt to bring forward any such detailed proposals.

These three factors – the refusal to debate the impact of Brexit on Northern Ireland before the referendum; the strong evidence that Leave voters in England do not really think of Northern Ireland as part of the Union; and the failure to produce concrete proposals – might at least add up to a comprehensive statement of indifference. They amount on any rational analysis to an even starker statement than Churchill's in 1922 that the Irish Question is really an Irish problem, something for Them to sort out while Britain gets on with the much more important business of Brexit. It may well be, then, that Brexit brings to a head a process of distancing that has been at work for at least a century – and that is arguably built in to the entire Anglo-Irish relationship over many centuries. But even this clarity cannot emerge through the Brexit fog.

This is Ireland's English problem. On the one side, Brexit is strongly related to the rise of English nationalism and disenchantment with the Union. On the other, no one in the British political mainstream wants to acknowledge this reality. One of the great ironies of post-2016 British politics is that May's disastrous decision to call an unnecessary general election in 2017 ended up giving a far louder and more insistent voice to a marginal expression of vestigial Britishness – that of Northern Ireland's Democratic Unionist Party – than to the English nationalism that had been a primary factor in causing the earthquake. If anything, the official rhetoric of 'defending the Union' was thus amped up to an ever-louder volume in the ensuing political panic: May in 2017, for example, pledged that 'I will always fight to strengthen and sustain this precious, precious Union', one precious clearly not being enough.[6]

Thus, one of the main responses of the Tory government to the deep lacuna in political authority created by the Brexit vote, was to reach for precisely what the people who voted for Brexit had been rejecting: an insistently unitary Britishness. To take a simple and symbolic example, the Brexiteers and their cheerleaders in the press made much of the idea of restoring the blue-covered 'British passport' as an icon of independent identity. But asked in 2011 what nationality they would have on their passport if they could choose, fully 40 per cent of English respondents chose English, not British.[7] There is good reason to think that these are the people who voted most enthusiastically for Brexit. Here we see one of the paradoxes and contradictions of Brexit itself. It is driven by a force – English nationalism – that it still refuses to articulate. It draws on English disengagement from the Union, but wraps itself in a brashly reasserted Unionism.

This contradiction and the problem it creates for Ireland is about more than immediate political contingency. It is about history and the need to escape it most memorably evoked by James Joyce. Early in *Ulysses*, Joyce's alter ego Stephen Dedalus goes to collect the wages he is due for some part-time teaching in a Dublin school. The opinionated headmaster Deasy talks to him of history:

He came forward a pace and stood by the table. His underjaw fell sideways open uncertainly. Is this old wisdom? He waits to hear from me.
– History, Stephen said, is a nightmare from which I am trying to awake.
From the playfield the boys raised a shout. A whirring whistle: goal. What if that nightmare gave you a back kick?[8]

The great difficulty of Brexit and Ireland is not just that the border itself, with its 208 official crossing-points and infinite number of unofficial ones is a legacy of a tangled history. It goes to something even deeper: two incompatible ways of escaping history. We all, in some way, desire to escape history, to imagine a future untrammelled by the accumulated uncertainties we have inherited from the past. But Stephen's expression of this desire raises two questions, one implicit, the other explicit. First, what do you awake from the nightmare *into*? Secondly, what if the nightmare kicks back? Do you awake to reality or do you merely escape into a kind of dreamtime? And if the escape hatch is the latter one, what are the consequences?

The deeper problem is, in the light of these two questions, not just that Ireland, and the Irish border in particular, is the great spoke in the Brexit wheel. It is that there is another kind of border, a line separating one way of thinking about the trajectory of history from another, very different one. In Ireland, we have been trying to awake from the epic into the ordinary, from the gloriously simple into the fluidly complex, from the once-and-for-all moment of national destiny into the openness and contingency of actual existence, with all its uncertainties and contradictions. In the England of Brexit, on the other hand, this process is working in reverse. The imagined movement is from the ordinary into the epic, from the complex to the gloriously simple, from the openness and contingency of real life in a society of multiple identities into a once-and-for all moment of destiny: 23 June 2016 as Independence Day, a sacred day of destiny from which a new history begins – a day that cannot therefore be revisited or returned from.

This is a thing that emerging nationalisms do. Since recent history is always full of compromises, complexities and contradictions, they seek out a version of the past that is not history but myth. Irish nationalism did this for well over a century: for English nationalism's June 2016, there is Irish nationalism's Easter 1916. But Irish nationalism was forced by suffering to return from the land of myth to those compromises, complexities and contradictions. The question for England is: how much suffering do you want to endure before you make the same journey from pursuing epic dreams to making peace with complex realities?

The promise of Brexit is, to borrow from T. S. Eliot, that 'history is now and England'. This is a promise of time and place: 23 June 2016 is a radiant moment in time and through it, England becomes again a radiant place. But these promises, like all of those underlying Brexit, turn out to be false. The moment of the referendum does not have a clear meaning – it is almost immediately lost in contention and confusion. But neither does 'England'. It emerges as a divided thing, bitterly split, not just between Leavers and Remainers but between the England of the big multicultural cities on the one side and the England of the villages and towns on the other. Perhaps this is always so with national revolutions – they are premised on the sacred unity of 'the people' but have a habit (as in Ireland) of morphing into civil wars.

And so, Brexit must inevitably exit its own historical condition, into mythological time. The escape hatch from actual history – the history of Anglo-Irish relations, of the Troubles and of the last 45 years of British membership of the EU, is to imagine England as an oppressed nation now engaged in an anti-colonial act of national liberation. In the Empire's prime, the British had the cult of heroic failure which was, in many ways, the ultimate colonial appropriation. Britain took to itself not just the resources of the conquered people, but their suffering and endurance.[9] In its Brexit iteration, it has to take this much further: to imagine the greatest colonial power in modern history as itself a colony. This is in its own way quite audacious – England dreaming itself into the status it so triumphantly imposed on others. It is a dramatic bypass operation. In reality, Britain went from being an imperial power to being a reasonably ordinary but fundamentally privileged Western European country. But in the apparition conjured by Brexit, it went straight from being the colonizer to being the colonized. The history of the last 45 years of EU membership is reshaped as a nightmare that is not so much to be awoken from as to be transformed into a masochistic fantasy of an intolerable oppression that is now being thrown off.

This is fundamentally imperial. In the imperial imagination, there are only two states: dominant and submissive, colonizer and colonized. This dualism lingers. If England is not an imperial power, it must be the only other thing it can be: a colony – just like Ireland used to be. The idea of a defeated and essentially conquered Britain having to rise again in a national rebirth leads naturally to a bizarre fantasy of Britain *as* Ireland. One leading Brexiteer, Tory MEP Daniel Hannan, directly compared Theresa May's Chequers proposals of June 2018 to the approach of the pro-Treaty side in the early years of Irish independence:

> When the Irish Free State left the UK, in 1921, there were all sorts of conditions about Treaty ports and oaths of supremacy and residual fiscal payments. And what very quickly became apparent was not just that those things were unenforceable once the split had been realized; it was that everyone in Britain kind of lost interest in enforcing them. And although there were some difficulties along the way in the 1920s, it turned out to have been better to have grabbed what looked like an imperfect independence and then built on it rather than risking the entire process.[10]

In this vertiginous analogy, in the 1920s and 1930s Britain is the EU and Ireland is, um, Britain. Now, in the post-referendum scenario, the EU is Britain and Britain is Ireland. When the room stops spinning and vision is restored, what can be focused on is the breath-taking nature of the shift in self-image. The British are now the people against whom they themselves once unleashed Oliver Cromwell and the Black and Tans, the gallant indigenous occupants of a conquered and colonized territory rising up, albeit as Nigel Farage boasted, without firing a shot, against their imperial overlords.

For those of us who are Irish, it is tempting to take this as a compliment, but it has one minor flaw. Britain was not colonized by the European Union. By no stretch of the imagination – and the elasticity of the Brexit imagination is astonishing – can the relationship between Brussels and London be credibly construed as being similar to that in colonial times between London and Dublin, let alone that between London and Delhi or Nairobi. This is a hyperbolic inflation of the minor irritations of EU membership into epic suffering. The EU is here playing a pre-scripted role. England needs to think of itself self-pityingly as a colony – therefore it must have a colonizer.

In all of this, we see the evasion of two obvious aspects of recent British history:

- forty-five years of the UK being deeply – and profitably – intertwined with the EU;
- the actual living history of that part of the UK known as Northern Ireland and in particular the Troubles of 1968–98.

But these are, of course, the very briars on which Brexit's coat is snagged. For here we come to the other way of escaping the nightmare of history – the one that has been unfolding in Ireland over the last twenty-five years. History on our island really did seem recurringly nightmarish – we seemed to be struck, not just with incompatible notions of national identity and belonging but with the sour dregs of the Reformation and Counter-Reformation. And yet consider a simple fact: in 2011 when it was, for the first time in a century, possible for a British head of state – Queen Elizabeth II – to visit Britain's closest neighbour, the Republic of Ireland, there were no more than 200 people on the streets of Dublin to protest. The nightmare really did seem to be over: Anglo-Irish relations were the best they had ever been, which is to say they were utterly normal. They were normal because they had ceased to be epic and become ordinary.

The Irish had radically revised their nationalism. Three big things changed. The power of the Catholic Church collapsed in the 1990s, partly because of its dreadful response to revelations of its facilitation of child sexual abuse by clergy. The Irish economy, home to the European headquarters of many of the major multinational IT and pharmaceutical corporations, became the poster child for globalization. And the search for peace in Northern Ireland forced a dramatic rethinking of ideas about identity, sovereignty and nationality. These very questions had tormented Ireland for centuries and were at the heart of the vicious, low-level but apparently interminable conflict that reignited in Northern Ireland in 1968 and wound down thirty years later.

If that conflict was to be resolved, there was no choice but to be radical. Things that nation-states do not like – ambiguity, contingency, multiplicity – would have to be lived with and perhaps even embraced. Irish people, for the most part, have come to terms with this necessity. The English, as the Brexit referendum suggested, have not. This is why the Irish border has such profound implications for Brexit – it is a physical token of a mental frontier that divides, not just territories, but ideas of what a national identity means in the twenty-first century.

In retrospect, there is some irony in the fact that the Conservative Party in Britain, now the driving force behind Brexit, was crucial to the conceptual revolution that led to the Belfast Agreement (colloquially called the Good Friday Agreement) of 1998. Traditionally, the Conservative and Unionist Party (to give it its full title) held to the line succinctly summed up by Margaret Thatcher in 1981: 'Northern Ireland is part of the United Kingdom – as much as my constituency is.'[11] But by 1990, the Conservatives were articulating a position in which Northern Ireland was very different to Thatcher's English constituency of Finchley. It was (and is) inconceivable that any British government would state that Finchley was free to go its own way and join, for example, France. In 1990, however, the then Secretary of State for Northern Ireland, Peter Brooke, announced, in a carefully crafted phrase, that 'The British government has no selfish strategic or economic interest in Northern Ireland'.[12]

This phrase, since embedded in international law through the Belfast Agreement, is remarkable in itself: sovereign governments are not in the business of declaring themselves neutral and disinterested on the question of whether a part of their own state should ultimately cease to be so. Even more remarkable, however, is that this fundamental shift in British thinking was mirrored in a similar shift in the Irish position. Since Ireland became independent in 1922, its governments had always looked on Northern Ireland as a part of its national territory unjustly and temporarily amputated by the partition of the island. Now, Ireland too withdrew its territorial claim – in 1998 its people voted overwhelmingly to drop it from their constitution and replace it with a stated desire 'in harmony and friendship, to unite all the people who share the territory of the island of Ireland, in all the diversity of their identities and traditions'. Those plurals resonate: Irish nationalism rests itself now on notions of shared space and of multiple identities.

Within this shared space, national identity is to be understood in a radically new way. In its most startling paragraph the Belfast Agreement recognizes 'the birthright of all the people of Northern Ireland to identify themselves and be accepted as Irish or British, or both, as they may so choose'. It accepts, in other words, that national identity (and the citizenship that flows from it) is a matter of choice – and is therefore, since choices may change, open and contingent. Even more profoundly, it accepts that this choice is not binary. Those lovely little words 'or both' stand as a rebuke to all absolutist ideas of nationalism. Identities are fluid, contingent and multiple. This is how you awake from the nightmare of history – into an embrace of the complex and fluid identities that real people really have.

When these ideas were framed and overwhelmingly endorsed in referendums on both sides of the Irish border, there was an assumption that there would always be a third identity that was neither Irish nor British but that could be equally shared: membership of the European Union. In the preamble to the agreement, the British and Irish governments evoked 'the close cooperation between their countries as friendly neighbours and as partners in the European Union'. The two countries joined the EU together in 1973 and their experience of working within it as equals was crucial in overcoming centuries of animosity. Particularly after the creation in 1993 of a single EU market with free movement of goods, services, capital and labour, the Irish border had itself become much less of an irritant. The peace process allowed the British to demilitarize the border region to such an extent that, today, travellers are generally unaware of when they are crossing it. The idea of a common European citizenship has real substance and it has made it much easier for people to feel comfortable with the notion that a national identity can have many different dimensions.

What no one really thought about when all of this was being done was the emergence of another force: English nationalism. There were two nationalisms, 'Irish' and 'British', and they had been reconciled in a creative and civilized way. But the United Kingdom contained (in every sense) other national identities: Scottish, Welsh and English.[13] Scotland and Wales were asserting a sense of difference in devolved parliaments and, in the Scottish case, in growing demands for independence. What could not be predicted, though, was that the decisive nationalist revolution would occur, not in Scotland or Wales, but in England. Brexit is a peaceful revolution but it is unmistakably a nationalist revolt, albeit one that is contradictory, incoherent and not fully articulated. It is England's insurrection against the very ideas that animated the Belfast Agreement: the belief that contemporary nationality must be fluid, open and many-layered. It is so unsure of itself that it escapes from an imagined nightmare into a strange and woozy Dreamtime that has no place for the complex living, evolving history of Ireland.

In *Ulysses*, Mr Deasy tries to insist, as utopians do, that history is moving secretly towards a single point of fulfilment: 'All history moves towards one great goal, the manifestation of God. Stephen jerked his thumb towards the window, saying: – That is God. Hooray! Ay! Whrrwhee! – What? Mr Deasy asked. – A shout in the street, Stephen answered, shrugging his shoulders.'[14] History doesn't move towards a single goal but it's not a shout in the street either. It is not a moment of national destiny and it is not a sacred expression of the people's will. It is an endless search for ways in which people in all the diversity of their identities and traditions can share space. Perhaps, in that light, the Irish border might be thought of not as a problem to be overcome for Brexit, but as a frontier over which the English might have to pass from a mythological history into an acceptance of the complex here-and-now that is the only place and moment from which we can move forward. Perhaps, to adapt that great Anglo-Irish thinker Johnny Rotten, Ireland might be the place for which to look for a future in England's dreaming.

Notes

1 Hansard, Irish Free State (Agreement) Bill, HC Deb 16 February 1922, vol. 150 cols 1261–372.
2 Andrew Lilico, Twitter, 9:32 AM, 13 November 2018.
3 YouGov / Future of England Survey Results, Fieldwork: 30th May–4th June 2018, https://d25d2506sfb94s.cloudfront.net/cumulus_uploads/document/8gzxmxtckl/FOE_England_June2018_Results_w.pdf
4 *Irish Times*, 10 December 2017.
5 The land border between Northern Ireland and Ireland, 16 March 2018, https://publications.parliament.uk/pa/cm201719/cmselect/cmniaf/329/32908.htm#_idTextAnchor133
6 17 March 2017, https://www.reuters.com/article/us-britain-eu-scotland-may-idUSKBN16O1K7
7 IPPR, *England and Its Two Unions: The Anatomy of a Nation and its Discontents* (London: IPPR, 2013), 8.
8 James Joyce, *Ulysses* (London: The Bodley Head, 1960): 42.
9 See in particular Stephanie Barczewski, *Heroic Failure and the British* (Yale University Press, 2016).
10 *Irish Times*, 14 July 2018.
11 Hansard, House of Commons statement, 10 November 1981, HC Deb vol. 12, cols 421–28.
12 Quoted in Hansard, HC Deb, 11 November 1992 vol. 213, cols 877–94.
13 See also Bill Schwarz, 'Forgetfulness: England's Discontinuous Histories' and Neal Ascherson, 'Scotland, Brexit and the Persistence of Empire' in this volume.
14 *Ulysses*, 42.

Chapter 7
Scotland, Brexit and the Persistence of Empire

Neal Ascherson

I want to start this chapter with a silence – or rather, by inviting you to listen to a silence.

In the 2016 referendum on British membership of the EU, Scotland voted quite heavily and emphatically to remain, by 62 per cent. Not one electoral region out of 32 voted Leave. But the British government repeated what it had stated clearly before the referendum: that the United Kingdom vote as a whole was the only total which counted. 'Regional variations' had no significance. In other words, the vote of English residents, some 85 per cent of the UK population, overruled the expressed preferences of other member-nations. Prime Minister David Cameron had promised that the United Kingdom was a 'partnership of equals'. Few people in Scotland now would recognize that description.

Many commentators north of the Border put it another way. 'Scotland was being torn out of Europe against its will.' Two years before, in 2014, Scottish voters had chosen by a 10 per cent majority to remain in the UK. But as soon as the EU referendum was proposed, politicians and journalists assumed that a Leave vote forced through by English votes might so enrage previously neutral citizens in Scotland that they would move decisively to favour the breakup of Britain. Nicola Sturgeon, who became SNP leader and First Minister in 2014, shared this view. She began to prepare for a second independence referendum, expecting that outraged Scottish opinion would swing to the Yes option.

But this did not happen. The outrage did not find that sort of voice. At the time of writing, opinion polls suggest that independence has crept only a few points up on the 45 per cent figure of four years ago: still a minority. I should add that the same crop of polls do begin to indicate that a really hard Brexit or a no-deal crash-out might change that. One sounding taken in December 2018 suggested that in those circumstances 59 per cent of the sample would vote Yes to independence.[1]

The silence, the public failure to react, surprised the media and shocked the SNP. Sturgeon lost some prestige as she was obliged to backtrack and postpone indefinitely the date for the next 'indyref'.

Brexit, in short, has not – or not yet – transformed Scottish politics in the subjective sense. But there is a curious contradiction between this almost static condition of public opinion and the simultaneous loosening of Scotland's position within the United Kingdom. Brexit has sharply accelerated a process of objective sundering between Scotland and the rest of the UK which has been developing for some time. Old assumptions on which the 1998 devolution settlement, and perhaps the 1707 Union, were based don't seem to be holding. It's not just the ugly grating and grinding of the devolution machinery in the last few years, of which the ceaseless succession of Holyrood protests and Westminster snubs accompanying Brexit are only the latest manifestations. It is also a quiet process of separation in civil society, as – for example – when an all-British association divides to create a Scottish branch which after a time morphs into an autonomous Scottish institution. It's a process not brought about by the agency of conscious political choices. Instead, it feels more like the metal-fatigue degeneration of institutions unfit to survive the pressures of change. In other words, this loosening of connections would almost certainly be coming about even if the present Scottish government were not committed to independence.

So why did Scotland stay so passive over Brexit? Scotland is in many ways more closely linked to the EU than England has been, not least by the needs of its more dramatic geography. European funds helped to modernize and extend its difficult transport infrastructure, to maintain remote areas and communities and preserve the marginal agriculture of crofting and hill farming. In a major contrast to England, immigration from Europe (Poland especially) has been deliberately encouraged by Scottish governments in order to balance an ageing population and correct Scotland's lamentable deficit in small service enterprises. On the debit side, Brexit will have devastating impact on the staffing of Scottish universities and the Scottish NHS.

All explanations for the silence are tentative. Here are a few:

1. Shock. The outcome of the European referendum was profoundly humiliating for Scots. Certain peoples, like the Catalans, react to national setbacks by pouring into the streets. Scots, like many other small nations, are liable to be felled by a sense of powerlessness and to go quiet for a time – perhaps for years. Much the same mood followed the failure of the rigged 1979 referendum on devolution where, despite a slim 52 per cent majority favouring a devolved assembly, the poor turnout failed to meet the stringent requirement of assent by 40 per cent of

eligible voters.[2] It took eight or nine years before a confident demand for self-government re-emerged.

2   The substantial minority in Scotland which dislikes the EU. It became clear that about a third of those who voted Yes to independence in 2014 also voted to leave the European Union in 2016. The wish for independence is not neatly aligned with the wish to remain in Europe. Partly, this derives from a fundamentalist feeling that independence should be total: a Scotland free to choose its own place in the world. Partly, though, it comes from the British labour movement's persistent suspicion of the European Union as a right-wing capitalist club. In the early years of this century, a massive migration of working-class voters took place from the Labour Party to the SNP, and though the SNP policy by then was Alex Salmond's 'independence in Europe', these migrants brought some old Labour attitudes and prejudices with them into their new party.

3   A sharp reluctance to enter another referendum campaign – even on the part of citizens who hoped for an independent Scotland. Here's a perilous and anecdotal generalization. In large tracts of England, people who voted Remain in 2016 often admit that they actually don't know people who voted Leave – and vice versa (perhaps testimony to England's striking segregation by class and locality). In Scotland, by contrast, families, offices, boat-crews, neighbours or social clubs were commonly split, sometimes painfully, over independence. There's no eagerness to go through that again.

4   Last and most reasonable: Scottish voters want to wait and see. The utterly chaotic spectacle of the Brexit negotiations and the evident impotence of the Westminster Parliament to command the situation mean that nobody knows what the situation will be in a few months' time. Wait till the smoke clears.

Meanwhile the SNP government has argued, interestingly, that Britain's departure from Europe is bound to undermine the devolution settlement of 1998, which reconvened a Scottish Parliament and created a Welsh Assembly. At that period, Europe was still gradually transferring power from the old nation-states in two directions: upwards to Brussels and Strasbourg, in the wake of the Maastricht and Lisbon treaties, and downwards to the European regions.

Brexit abruptly severs that current. British powers transferred to Brussels are brought back to London. But so are powers transferred to the EU by Edinburgh and Cardiff, the devolved legislatures. Some will stay in London, perhaps temporarily, perhaps for good – the so-called 'Power Grab'. Scottish governments and agencies have spun a dense web of connections to the EU over twenty years of devolution, often to the irritation of Whitehall which constantly reminds Holyrood that only the UK government has the right to conduct negotiations with the Commission. This web is now to be torn away. Mrs May's insistence that after Brexit the Union will be 'strengthened' confirmed Scottish fears that the devolution settlement may now be eroded and Westminster's central authority re-imposed.

But what has the Scottish reaction to Brexit to do with imperial memories? Before trying to answer that, I would like to digress a little to examine – from a Scottish angle – some of the concepts that we are juggling with in this volume. What is the category distinction between 'British' and 'English', as we use the terms? Does it make sense to see the current slogan of 'Global Britain' as a spark rising from some still unextinguished embers of empire?

Richard Drayton has spoken eloquently about 'Global Britain' as a 'providential' idea rather than a sober design for a future.[3] In other words, it emanates from a nation which can think of itself as 'chosen', destined perhaps for some future global mightiness, but above all exceptional, in a mystic category which removes it from comparison with mere nation-states. The choices of a 'chosen' nation cannot always be understood by members of that lower tier of polities because ... they are not exceptional. Their path, even when they are combined in a European Union, is paved with serviceable aggregate and tarmac: while the *Sonderweg* highway of an exceptional nation is paved with gold.

Now try saying 'Global UK' instead of 'Global Britain'. It's a dull, clumsy sound. Something is missing – but what? It's the Ancient British magic which is missing, the chiming appeal to a dreamland where suddenly all things are possible. The nations of England, Scotland, Wales have their own myths of providential guidance. In Scotland's case, it's perhaps the Lord of the 124th psalm: John Knox, moving spirit of the sixteenth-century Scottish Reformation, declared that by accepting Reformation principles, the Scottish nation had entered a covenant with God as one of his chosen peoples. In return for their obedience, the psalm suggests, God would rescue the Scots from the plots of their bloodthirsty enemies: 'ev'n as a bird out of the fowler's snare / Escapes away, so is our soul set free'.

But England, Scotland and Wales exist as nations, mongrel and muddled but tangible. Where is Britain, except in a passport, an airline, an island, a citizenship? And yet it is Britain – not the other three – which was a Victor Power in the Second World War, which holds a permanent seat at the Security Council, on whose Empire the sun never set. Not a nation, but an increasingly incoherent multinational state.

When was Britain? Perhaps in that century and a half when there existed a culturally homogenous ruling caste from one end of the Empire to the other. The Romans had Civis Romanus, the Soviet Empire had Homo Sovieticus, and Britain had a brief national existence through Homo Britannicus, the small elite which shared the same accent, clothes, dogs, private schooling and standard of fairness from Thurso to Penzance, Vancouver to Varanasi. As he departed, Homo Britannicus quietly poured water on the embers of empire. England, Scotland or Wales would never on their own claim to be exceptional, global, or more than mere nations. Only Britain could go on doing that because Britain was fading into an imaginary, into a dream about a deathless past, a country no more substantial than a thread of smoke rising from the doused fires of imperial glory.

Directly or superficially, the 2016 referendum outcome didn't seem to prompt broad Scottish reflections on imperial hangovers. Most Scots, I think I can say, regard the Brexit vote as an English-driven calamity, a confused outburst of English national feeling which has unfortunately dragged Scotland along with it. Michael Kenny and Nick Pearce showed in a brilliant *New Statesman* essay recently that Enoch Powell was not nostalgic for lost Raj and Empire; on the contrary, he urged the English to face reality, stop dreaming that Britain was still an imperial world power, and concentrate inwards on their own national identity and ethnic culture.[4] And perhaps that's just what the English were trying to do, with their Brexit vote. Perhaps all the silly rhetoric from Leave campaign leaders about sallying forth across the oceans to reconquer the globe's markets entirely misses the point. Perhaps the vote wasn't about post-imperial delusions at all, but exactly the opposite: a wish to stop the world and get off.

On the other hand, the connection between the decline of empire and the rise of political nationalism in Scotland seems well founded. The 1707 Union was in part a bargain: your independence in return for access to our Empire. Scots settled, managed and exploited the British Empire for two and a half centuries. Their relationship to it was sometimes generous and creative: witness the way in which certain Scottish governors protected and encouraged Hindu culture in the early nineteenth century, or the readiness of Scottish pioneers in North America to marry into and identify with indigenous societies. Often, though, their imperial function resembled that of the Croats in the Austro-Hungarian Empire: the sergeants and enforcers of imperial power, valued by their masters but disliked by their subject peoples. As Britain's Empire broke up after the Second World War, obliterating so many Scottish careers and markets, the 1707 bargain began to seem one-sided to many Scots who – again like the Croats – wondered if they might not do better on their own.[5]

But it has been a slow process. Taking the Scots out of the Empire has been easier than taking the Empire out of the Scots. The proud myth of 'the Scottish soldier', boasted to be braver and more loyal than any of the monarch's English defenders, for many years channelled patriotism into 'safe' outlets, and is not yet quite dead. And the disappearance of the Empire in the twentieth century went with a general Scottish refusal to accept responsibility for its crimes.[6]

Scotland itself, of course, could never be classified as a colony – in contrast to Ireland, in whose ethnic cleansing, military repression and settler plantation the

Scots played a vigorous part from the late sixteenth century on. An academic attempt was made in the 1970s to define Scotland's relationship to London as neo-colonial dependence, but it was soon rejected as absurd.[7] On the other hand, the inclination to regard Scotland in history as invariably a victim, never a perpetrator, gained ground in the twentieth century. It was soon contradicted. For instance, scholars brought up the 1843 massacre of Warrigal Creek, when Gaelic settlers combined in a so-called 'Highland Brigade' to murder over a hundred Australian aboriginal men, women and children.[8] But the longest struggle concerned Scottish participation in slavery.

This was a subject historians preferred to avoid. It was pointed out that Glasgow's participation in the actual slave trade was tiny compared to the dominance of Bristol and Liverpool. But energetic research in the last few decades has made that complacency untenable. Glasgow's tobacco and sugar merchants and Scottish bankers vigorously financed the slave trade, while seldom owning the ships themselves. Above all, Scots were massively involved in plantation slavery, mainly in the Caribbean. The Campbells of Argyll, especially, poured into the west end of Jamaica from the eighteenth century on, buying sugar estates and the African slaves to work them. Fortunes were made: after the abolition of slavery in 1833, the Malcolms of Poltalloch received nearly £40,000 in compensation payments (about £3.25 million in today's values) for the loss of their property: over two thousand slaves. Two-thirds of the island's doctors were Scots. So, apparently, were most of the 'surgeons' hired to accompany English slave ships on the terrible Middle Passage.[9]

In England, the rise of 'black history' and the rediscovery of the full scale, horror and profit of slavery went together towards the end of the twentieth century. At the heart of this revision was pioneering work at University College London, where the 'Legacies of British Slave Ownership' database published the names of those who received compensation after 1833 and the number of their slaves.[10] This work took some of the glitter off self-congratulatory official celebrations, organized in 2007 to mark the bicentenary of Britain's abolition of the slave trade.

Scotland was much more reluctant to accept the new history, although the compensation register was packed with Scottish names. The poet Jackie Kay recalled a woman telling her that 'we don't have racism up here, that's an English thing that's down south'.[11] The new Museum of Scottish History, opened in 1998, initially made no mention either of slavery or of Scotland's many eloquent abolitionists. A study commissioned by the Scottish executive for the 2007 anniversary met so many objections and requests for watering-down that the two authors gave up and resigned. The 'comforting myth' of Scottish moral superiority died hard.

But writers and historians made a concerted and fruitful effort to break through this barrier of wilful ignorance at the time of the 2014 Commonwealth Games.

The novelist Louise Welsh helped to run an 'Empire Café' project at the games, devoted to spreading information about Scotland's part in the worst atrocities and oppressions of the British Empire. A few years before that, James Robertson had written the bestselling novel *Joseph Knight*, based on the case of a slave liberated by the Court of Session in 1788 on the grounds that the state of slavery was not recognized by the laws of Scotland.

Today, it can be said that the amnesia has been penetrated and new rules of 'correctness' accepted, at least in Scottish public life. In September 2018, the University of Glasgow announced that it was setting up a 'centre for the study of slavery' with a memorial to the enslaved.[12] This is a sort of atonement for the discovery that in the eighteenth and nineteenth centuries the university received huge donations from the profits of slave-worked estates. Robert Graham, an ex-rector who endowed a gold medal prize for the best student work on 'political liberty', was himself the owner of many Jamaican slaves.

To sum up, fantasies of regaining lost global grandeur have no influence on Scottish attitudes to Brexit. To the contrary, the speed with which Scots have forgotten about the British Empire and the prominent part they played in it is itself pathological. Rising national consciousness has much to do with this amnesia. Scotland, to generalize, prefers to regard itself as a virtuous little country which has tried to do good things in the world but has often been misled by its big neighbour: as Jackie Kay put it, sardonically: 'a hard-done-to wee nation, yet bonny and blithe'.[13]

So far, however, political nationalism has avoided the worst temptations of victimology. 'Scotland the perpetrator' is now unwillingly recognized in the nation's activities overseas (at home, it has always been accepted that the brutalities of the Highland – and Lowland – Clearances were overwhelmingly committed by indigenous landowners and their agents against their own tenantry – 'Scot on Scot' offences).

Other neighbouring countries have found it possible to apologize for their own colonial atrocities. Germany has confronted the genocide of the Herero people. France, after long silence, took responsibility for sending French Jews and their children to the gas chambers, and has at least engaged with some of the crimes of the Algerian war. Portugal debates its long record in central Africa; Belgium argues, often bitterly, about its legacy in the Congo. Forget Brexit! Scotland, by recognizing its ugly face in the imperial mirror, has become more European.

Notes

1 "Majority Back Independent Scotland Over Staying In UK After Brexit: Poll", LBC, 9 December 2018, https://www.lbc.co.uk/news/uk/independent-scotland-over-uk-after-brexit/

2 John M. Bochel et al. (eds), *The Referendum Experience: Scotland 1979* (Aberdeen: Aberdeen University Press, 1981).
3 Richard Drayton, Garrison Library Gibraltar, 21 September 2018.
4 Michael Kenny and Nick Pearce, 'Will Post-Brexit Britain Overcome or Fall Further upon Enoch Powell's Troubling Legacy?', *New Statesman*, 20 April 2018, https://www.newstatesman.com/politics/uk/2018/04/will-post-brexit-britain-overcome-or-fall-further-upon-enoch-powell-s-troubling
5 Jimmi Østergaard Nielsen and Stuart Ward, '"Cramped and Restricted at Home": Scottish Separatism at Empire's End', *Transactions of the Royal Historical Society*, vol. 25 (December 2015): 159–85.; cf. T. M. Devine, 'The Break-up of Britain? Scotland and the End of Empire', *Transactions of the Royal Historical Society*, 16 (2006): 163–80.
6 T. M. Devine, *Scotland's Empire, 1600–1815* (Penguin, 2004).
7 Michael Hechter, *Internal Colonialism: The Celtic Fringe in British National Development, 1536–1966* (London: Routledge and Kegan Paul, 1975).
8 Peter Gardner, *Gippsland Massacres: The Destruction of the Kurnai Tribes, 1800–1860* (Bairnsdale: Ngarak Press, 2001).
9 See T. M. Devine, *Recovering Scotland's Slavery Past: The Caribbean Connection* (Edinburgh University Press, 2015).
10 'Legacies of British Slave-Ownership', https://www.ucl.ac.uk/lbs/
11 Jackie Kay, 'Missing Faces', *The Guardian,* 24 March 2007.
12 Helen McArdle, 'Glasgow University Reveals £200m Slave Trade Windfall – and Plans for New Slavery Study Centre', *The Herald* (16 September 2018), https://www.heraldscotland.com/news/16882171.glasgow-university-reveals-200m-slave-trade-windfall-and-plans-for-new-slavery-study-centre/
13 Kay, 'Missing Faces'.

Chapter 8
Gibraltar: Brexit's Silent Partner

Jennifer Ballantine Perera

Of all of Britain's former imperial enclaves, Gibraltar's interest in the June 2016 Brexit referendum was bound to be keener than most – not only because of its strategic footprint in Europe, sharing as it does a border with Spain, but especially because of Spain's long-standing territorial claim stretching back for over three hundred years. Gibraltar is perhaps not dissimilar to the Irish border, in terms at least of jurisdictional procedures in a post-Brexit scenario. However, there has been one marked difference between Gibraltar and Ireland, in that whilst the latter has been exhaustively debated politically both in the UK, Ireland and throughout the EU, not much has come to light on Gibraltar – that is, until the point at which final proposals emerged from the withdrawal negotiations in December 2018.

Gibraltarians voted overwhelmingly to remain with a 95.9 per cent majority, which although substantial was clearly not sufficient to impact on the outcome in the UK as a whole. Uniquely among the UK's overseas possessions, Gibraltar is an EU territory having joined the European Economic Community alongside the United Kingdom in 1973, a status which in practice only applies to Gibraltar and one which it will lose when the UK ceases to be an EU member state. Thus, Gibraltar raises the peculiar dilemmas of an overseas territory situated in Europe, a geographical positioning that challenges received notions that locate territorial possessions at some distance from the European metropolis.

As such, Brexit offers us a good example of how Gibraltar is bound to the UK; and destined to remain so despite the fact that this is likely to prove damaging, and despite the fact that the Brexit vote was motivated by impulses that, on the whole, Gibraltarians do not share. Ultimately, Gibraltar is leaving Europe because the alternative, co-sovereignty with Spain in return for continuing in the EU, is considered to be incomparably worse.[1] These convictions are based on practical as well as emotional reasoning, furnishing insights into the political bind and the sentimental bond informing Gibraltar's relationship with the UK. The decision-making process demanded by Brexit has not only brought attention to these underlying ties, but has also brought tensions that test Gibraltar's British attachments. The aim of this chapter is to engage with question of bonds and binds as they have come to define Gibraltar's relationships with the UK and Europe, with Spain's territorial claim trailing on the coattails of the EU. In a volume addressing the embers of empire in Brexit Britain, Gibraltar is uniquely situated at the crossroads – the prevailing colonial link inherent in Gibraltar's bind with the UK directly determining its fate at the frontier of Europe.

Gibraltar and the UK act in unison because of an age-old strategic partnership – driven by emotion, loyalty to the Crown and a deep-felt certainty by Gibraltarians of their Britishness, all of which is dependent on the presence of a diffused colonial bind. The bind is now considered non-colonial, following the 2006 Constitution, but as a British Overseas Territory, Gibraltar still awaits 'delisting' on the United Nations agenda. Established in 1962, the UN's Special Committee of Decolonization currently has sixteen territories remaining on its list, with Gibraltar remaining one of the most problematic for several reasons. Spain has always maintained its claim under Article X of the Treaty of Utrecht for the restoration of the territory. What keeps this claim alive is the reversionary clause in the Treaty which entitles Spain to reclaim Gibraltar should Britain ever relinquish sovereignty – an element which has greatly constrained the options of the UN when considering the prospects for decolonization. A further claim relates to the isthmus that joins Gibraltar to the Iberian Peninsula, which is not covered by Utrecht but which is a separate dispute between Britain and Spain.[2] All these factors suggest that Gibraltar will remain for delisting, unless the UN reconsiders its terms for decolonization in cases where independence is not possible or if Spain drops its claim. Whilst Britain and Gibraltar have stated before the Special Committee that they have a constitutional relationship that justifies delisting, albeit without the granting of independence, neither Spain nor the UN accept this position.[3]

Brexit invariably brings to the fore the uneasy balance between a colonial past and present, with Gibraltar working towards an unwanted exit while pulling firmly together with 'the whole of the UK family', as recently defined by Theresa May, in working out its future relationship with Europe (which is to say, Spain). With a historic territorial claim pressing hard against any possible Brexit deal, the sense of 'togetherness' with the UK is vitally important to Gibraltar. As one of Europe's smallest economies (with Spain enjoying one of the largest) Gibraltar's exclusion has been interpreted as part of a far wider question on Gibraltar. As such, Gibraltar is in an additional bind. The first, entered into knowingly with the UK in respect to the terms which signify remaining British, now equated with exit from

Europe, and a second bind by way of a claim from Spain that seeks, in some shape or form, to suck her back in.

Brexit is clearly not ideal for Gibraltar for many reasons, but above all, because of its proximity to Spain with this added layer of geopolitics. Gibraltar is also a very small territory given its size and dependency on the UK for protection. Although it is occasionally suggested that Gibraltar should seek another option in going it alone as a means of remaining in Europe, thus keeping fluidity across the border, (which the ex-British Foreign Secretary Boris Johnson has referred to as 'Gibraltar's choke-point'), the price tag, co-sovereignty, is not acceptable to Gibraltarians. The *sine qua non* therefore for Gibraltar lies in the safeguarding of British sovereignty, a necessity in any deal that may be brokered. Notably, sovereignty is mentioned in the header of the Gibraltar Protocol in the draft Withdrawal Agreement and highlighted by Brian Reyes in the *Gibraltar Chronicle*, 15 November 2018:

> The Gibraltar Protocol contained in the draft UK/EU Withdrawal Agreement respects the UK's constitutional relationship with Gibraltar. It also makes clear that the agreement is without prejudice to the respective legal positions of the UK and Spain on sovereignty and jurisdiction.

For Gibraltar, these two sentences are vital. Whilst prompted by the Brexit negotiations, constitutional and sovereignty relationships with Britain have a long trajectory. I would go as far as to say that the positioning of these key terms at the head of the protocol document function as a preamble, such as the preambles to both the 1969 and 2006 Gibraltar Constitutions, to safeguard Gibraltar's sovereign relationship with the UK that was cemented in 1713 with the signing of the Treaty of Utrecht. So powerful are these terms that barely a few weeks after Gibraltar's 1969 Constitution was published, Spain closed the border on the grounds that the preamble gave Gibraltarians leverage over decisions relating to any transfer of sovereignty to Spain.

Brexit therefore triggers all sorts of sovereignty safeguards for Gibraltar and indeed the UK, for as much as these principles underpin Gibraltar's democratic right to remain British they also uphold the UK's sovereign right to a strategic military base in Europe, vitally important at this juncture of exit. Because of this, and as hard as the Brexit decision is, Gibraltar will always align itself with the UK. Still, this is a relationship that is being tested. References now to Brexit as a divorce settlement suggest that in all the talk of access to markets, penalty charges, mobility and potentially, territorial rights, Brexit could also become the locus for a custody battle over Gibraltar.[4]

Although constitutionally devolved to the extent that Gibraltar's 2006 Constitution was described by Jeff Hoon, then Labour's Minister for Europe, as non-colonial,[5] colonial layers remain as do neo-imperial ones, for any sovereignty transfer to Spain would be seen by Gibraltarians as falling under neo-imperial Spanish dominance rather than securing independence. While the UK has offered a level of assurance that no transfer would take place in the absence of the wishes of the people of Gibraltar, such a transfer still remains in the UK's gift. Implicit in this understanding lies the reality that the UK has some overarching power to broach that sovereign decision if need be.

A serious amount of geopolitical baggage, which acquired traction at key historical junctures, informs this space; from sieges during the eighteenth century, to a turbulent twentieth century which saw Spain close its border with Gibraltar for more than thirteen years. Brexit is now seen as one more stumbling block in this trajectory. It is interesting to note that in 1982 the UK backed Spain's entry into the European Community on the basis of re-opening the border with Gibraltar; a move that now sits awkwardly alongside Brexit.

The fact that Gibraltar is to depart the EU, while remaining part of Europe's geographical footprint is another major consideration which brings into focus questions of proximity and distance. Gibraltar has always maintained and reiterated an abiding Britishness and closeness towards Britain; in political terms, however, Gibraltar is firm in asserting its political distance from Spain. Still, we need to also address the proximity to Spain, clearly in terms of economic, kinship and cultural ties, but also in the very close relationship with the Campo de Gibraltar in the immediate Spanish hinterland, with the border functioning as a hugely porous barrier/bridge that provides a life-line. It is also the case that the Spanish hinterland enjoys little in the way of a consolidated economic infrastructure, with unemployment at around 25 per cent in the Campo area, ten points higher than in other regions in Spain.[6] Figures for La Línea, which borders Gibraltar, are estimated in a 'Socio-Economic Study of the Impact of Brexit in La Línea' at approximately 35 per cent unemployment,[7] with many of those employed working in Gibraltar. Data for December 2016 from the Gibraltar Statistics Office show that 14,441 registered frontier workers entered Gibraltar on a daily basis, 9,016 of these Spanish.[8] There is a day-to-day routine that informs the border, with an affinity between businesses, work colleagues, friendship bonds, marriages, academic relationships and a reciprocity that belies the presumption of a dispute. Residents in La Línea colloquially refer to themselves as *la cenicienta* (Cinderella), destined to be the child abandoned by parents (that is, Madrid), looking instead towards Gibraltar for their main source of work and income. Yet this is also an unbalanced economic relationship, with the Cinderella motif indicative of the service-based jobs many work in. There has now been recognition from Spain that a post-Brexit border will bring hardship to the Campo area, testament to which is an injection of 900 million euros to boost the Campo's economy.[9] This is a very human story about people who have suffered historically and will suffer greatly in the eventuality of any post-Brexit arrangement which hampers fluidity at the border.

The reality, however, also remains that at certain junctures, Gibraltar has become a lever in wider geopolitical brokerage between the UK, the UN and Spain (and latterly the EU). Consider for example the very unsettling period for Gibraltar of the 1960s which led to proposals and counter proposals being exchanged between Spain and the UK. Had they come to fruition, these proposals could very possibly have paved the way for the eventual handover of Gibraltar to Spain, with the UK securing its red line demarcation across the vital strategic base.[10] A similar pattern arose in 2002 with a joint-sovereignty deal devised between the Tony Blair Labour government and Jose Maria Aznar's Partido Popular (Popular Party) government in Spain. On both occasions, attempts to dilute British territorial sovereignty or to instigate a decolonization process floundered, not only because they were resisted by Gibraltar but also because Spain and the UK could not agree on two vital issues: Spain's reluctance to reject their historic claim over Gibraltar and the question of British sovereign control over the military base.[11] Both points remain as alive today as they did then.

Although there are key differences now in terms of constitutional advances, as mentioned above, and despite the introduction of a non-colonial constitution, the colonial tag nevertheless resists all attempts to disappear into history. Gibraltar remains scheduled for delisting at the UN's Special Committee for Decolonization, and independence can only be an option for Gibraltar with Spain's consent given the reversionary clause in the 1713 Treaty of Utrecht. Herein lie the binds that are clearly colonial in their inception but now serve to create an uneasy even ambivalent space in which the colonial and the non-colonial coexist. The ambivalence created within this undefined space is nevertheless a very creative one in which independence is not the end game. Instead we see Gibraltarians articulating their identity though politics, institutions, in their cultural expression and in their writings, which celebrate a strong sense of emancipation. Many Gibraltarian authors, such as Mark Sanchez,[12] deploy post-colonial narrative strategies in their writings, signifying a colonial past against a present which is far removed from those days of Empire. Whilst bordering remains in terms of the triangulation of Britishness, the Empire and Spain, it seems as if this very bordering is also a generator of the terms under which Gibraltarians construct and express their identity. It is also the case that this sense of bordering is a source of vulnerability in a Brexit exit strategy, because the process towards emancipation can only remain incomplete as long as Spain's territorial claim remains alive.

In effect, to the extent that the EU backs Spain's territorial claim, it enters into the colonial debate by way of endorsing a neo-imperial initiative in Europe. Equally, being silent on the non-colonial yet perversely colonial relationship between Gibraltar and the UK triggers all sorts of unresolved questions.

In an *Irish Times* article of September 2018, Fintan O'Toole rightly suggests that 'Gibraltar is, in a sense, all border', and not simply because of the land border with Spain but because of its strategic position, controlling the border as it does between Atlantic and Mediterranean oceans. In this respect, argues O'Toole, 'Gibraltar has some things to tell us about both the physical realities of Brexit and the complexities of the post-imperial Britishness that surround it'.

I would challenge the post-imperial tag, preferring instead to think of this undefined space as somehow not quite past the post, neither imperial nor entirely after empire. Nothing infuriates Gibraltarians more than UK media depictions of a coddled, cowering people, trapped uncritically in the loyalties and symbolism of centuries past. When *The Guardian*'s Simon Jenkins, for example, derides 'a tribe of gilded "Britons" who live in a perpetual other-world', he not only obscures a complex political reality (conveniently labelled 'imperial') but also misrepresents the motivations and aspirations of the community that lies at the centre of the dispute.[13] To take the example of one man in his 30s who offered the following response to a question about his identity:

> Then they ask me 'what is Gibraltar,' I say 'it's a British [country] in the southern tip of Spain.' But in no way are we Spanish. But we have a very good relationship with Spain. Then they ask 'and where is your family from?' So that is when it goes back to . . . Italian, Maltese. But that's the first . . . the third answer I give. After British and Gibraltarian. At no point do I say we are . . . Spanish.[14]

The same is applicable in the current Brexit climate. *Panorama*, Gibraltar's tabloid paper brandished the headline on 23 November 2018: 'We have stuck with Britain in the past, and we will stick with Britain in the future, says [Gibraltar] Government'. For ultimately, if nothing changes Gibraltar will leave the EU alongside the UK, for this is where all of its principal markers of identity, nationality, sovereignty, way of life and protection lie.

I wonder if we can consider these articulations as somehow akin to a reciprocal albeit Faustian pact that binds Gibraltar to the UK in a manner that resists simple explanation; a pact dependent on protection, trust on both sides, uncertainty on both sides, and geopolitics that far exceed Gibraltar's footprint in the Mediterranean. An invisible yet palpable line is drawn between colonialism as understood in history, and this other, perhaps hybrid version of colonialism as experienced today.

As O'Toole suggests, the Gibraltar Spanish border is deceptively straightforward in that it is a clearly drawn line, but it bears the load of the UK's constitutional relationship with Gibraltar and the respective legal positions of the UK and Spain on sovereignty and jurisdiction. It seems, therefore, as though the colonial and nascent post-colonial find expression in the same space; one that is informed by a colonial period that has not yet entirely passed, and a post-colonialism that has not quite and may never fully arrive.[15] It is not a question of suggesting that Gibraltar is neither colonial nor post-colonial but rather that Gibraltar occupies a space where both coexist. This is particularly pertinent to the Brexit dilemma, which heightens tension around Gibraltar's relationship with the UK as negotiations press all the colonial buttons which have been submerged beneath the counter-current of the non-colonial. In the meanwhile, Gibraltar is caught up in a dual colonial and post-colonial period signified by, on the one hand, a bind, and on the other a bond. A messy situation, to be sure.

What is certain is that Gibraltar did not need Brexit; following the UK out of Europe is the only option as co-sovereignty is considered far worse. Caught in a complex set of binds and an indelible bond with Britain, Gibraltar offers an insight into a state of affairs that veers sharply from any colonial definition presently promulgated by the UN's Special Committee. Brexit is not simply about borders but also about a people, Gibraltarians, who live on a territory subject to a claim from Spain. Gone are the days of the Treaty of Utrecht when agreements would be brokered along territorial lines irrespective of human rights and wishes. Yet, Brexit has brought these very days back into the present with Spain seeking to harness the negotiations to the long-standing goal of reclaiming Gibraltar irrespective of the rights and wishes of Gibraltarians. We need to move away from definitions for colonialism set in the past and address the need to challenge these to pave the way for a progressive framework which engages with colonialisms in the present. For Gibraltar, the bond and bind continue, and in Nietzschean fashion, Gibraltar carries the greatest burden of eternal recurrence, yet this is a cycle that defines Gibraltar, informed as it is by binds and a bond it cannot break free from. Ultimately, the real story here is a human one of Gibraltarians who continue on their journey, navigating hugely challenging times and Faustian pacts to secure their right to their homeland.

Notes

1   I am grateful to Dr Jamie Trinidad for reading a draft of this chapter and for his suggestions. Any errors are entirely mine.
2   Peter Gold, 'Gibraltar at the United Nations: Caught Between a Treaty, the Charter and the "Fundamentalism" of the Special Committee', *Diplomacy and Statecraft* 20, no. 4 (December 2009): 697–8.
3   Ibid.: 698.
4   Lluis Pellicer and Álvaro Sánchez, 'España exige revisar el acuerdo del Brexit por la "falta de claridad" sobre Gibraltar', *El Pais* (20 November 2018). This refers to Article 184 in the draft proposals. The Spanish government seeks to insert a reference to the effect that Gibraltar be considered a bilateral issue between the UK and Spain rather than, as currently stated, an EU and UK matter. See also Brian Reyes, 'Spain's PM threatens to vote against Brexit deal over Gibraltar', *Gibraltar Chronicle* (21 November 2018).

5 *Panorama*, 20 June 2006. See also House of Commons Library, Research Paper 06/48, 11 October 2006, 'Gibraltar: diplomatic and constitutional developments', 63.

6 Marison Hernández, 'Pedro Sánchez invierte 1.000 millones en el Campo de Gibraltar el primer día de la campaña andaluza', 16 November 2018, https://www.elmundo.es/espana/2018/11/16/5beed532ca4741f8418b45c3.html

7 Joe Duggan, 'Major new study shows Brexit impact on La Línea-based Gibraltar works', *Gibraltar Olive Press* (12 January 2017), http://www.gibraltarolivepress.com/2017/01/12/major-new-study-shows-brexit-impact-on-la-linea-based-gibraltar-workers/

8 'Frontier workers by nationality', Department of Employment, https://www.gibraltar.gov.gi/new/sites/default/files/HMGoG_Documents/EMP.2_19.pdf

9 'Spanish Government allocates 900 million euros to boost Campo de Gibraltar', *The Diplomat*, https://thediplomatinspain.com/en/2018/11/spanish-government-allocates-900-million-euros-to-boost-campo-de-gibraltar/

10 *Gibraltar Chronicle* (28 July 1966).

11 Andrew Grice, 'Blair and Aznar fail to break deadlock over Gibraltar', *The Independent* (21 May 2002), https://www.independent.co.uk/news/world/europe/blair-and-aznar-fail-to-break-deadlock-over-gibraltar-130134.html

12 See for example, Mark Sanchez, *Jonathan Gallardo*, CreateSpace Independent Publishing Platform, 2016.

13 Simon Jenkins, 'Gibraltar and the Falklands defy the logic of history', *The Guardian* (14 August 2013).

14 This interview excerpt is derived from a major oral history project on Gibraltar, 'Bordering on Britishness' (2013–17). I am grateful to the ESCR for their generous grant in support of this project and to my partner in this project, Andrew Canessa, University of Essex.

15 I am compelled to make reference to Néstor García Canclini, Translators, Renato Rosaldo, Christoper L. Chiappari and Sylvia L. Lopez, *Hybrid Cultures: Strategies for Entering and Leaving Modernity* (Minneapolis: University of Minnesota Press, 2005). The strategies outlined refer to a Latin America caught between tradition and modernity and the contradictions that arise by occupying the space between both.

Chapter 9
Brexit and the Other Special Relationship

Camilla Schofield

In a three-piece suit, his waistcoat patterned as the Union Jack, Raheem Kassam strode out onto the mainstage of the 2018 Conservative Political Action Conference in Oxon Hill, Maryland, USA. He was there to introduce a headline speaker at the conference: 'Mr. Brexit', Mr Nigel Farage. Kassam was, at the time, the editor-in-chief of Breitbart News London and, in 2016, had served as chief adviser to Farage when he led the United Kingdom Independence Party (UKIP). Farage was, as one reporter noted that day, Trump's 'only competition for crowd favourite' with attendees at the most significant Conservative activist conference in the US 'stream[ing] back into the main hall to hear his usual mix of boasts about his love for Trump and alcohol'.[1] Kassam introduced Farage – in a booming upper middle-class English accent – with a familiar refrain, that Farage's Brexit and President Donald Trump's electoral victory were two parts of the same story. 'I believe the fate of our nations are [sic] inextricably linked,' he began (at that moment opening up the inside of his jacket to reveal the American flag as the inner lining) 'not just through history but right now in the present'.[2] Kassam then immediately turned to condemning what he called the 'attempted nullification project' against their shared victories, led in the US by 'Antifa and George Soros and CNN.' In the UK, he added, 'they are trying to do to us – [to] our voices and our choices – the same things they are trying to do to you'. Boos flowed through the CPAC audience.

> One of those voices in the Brexit nullification process, a man you have probably heard something about, he's the London Mayor. [More boos.] So you've heard of him: Sadiq Khan. Send a bigger message to Sadiq Khan now please. [Louder boos from the audience.] Who spent his first year in office

publicly attacking President Donald Trump and [is] spending his time overseeing heaping up Britain's funeral pyre, overseeing London crime rates skyrocketing, rape up 18%, youth homicide up 70%, robbery up 33%.

At that time, London's first Muslim mayor was quickly becoming a household name among Conservative voters in the US, serving on Fox News as the near embodiment of the horrors of 'liberal multiculturalism'. To wild applause, Kassam then presented the hero of Britain's story, Nigel Farage, whom he strangely likened to a famed historical American patriot. 'There is a man,' he bellowed, 'who like Paul Revere riding through the night to warn "the British are coming, the British are coming"; there is a man who has rode for nearly thirty years in the face of the European Union and the BBC to scream, "the British are leaving, the British are leaving."' Before Farage took the stage, a short video of 'Nigel's journey' then played, presenting Brexit as a personal victory, starting with Farage running for a by-election in 1994 as the 'first ever UKIP candidate' and ending with him proclaiming 23 June Britain's 'independence day'.

This effort to align the US historical myth of independence *from* Britain with Brexit is noteworthy. It perhaps reflects a wider strategy to emphasize Britain's place within the shared settler colonial heritage of the 'English-speaking world', now embraced by a small but well-connected network of Conservative policy-makers, journalists, business leaders and politicians who see in this shared heritage the foundation of a post-Brexit trading future for Britain with Canada, Australia, New Zealand and the United States.[3] Brexit is, in this telling, Britain's opportunity to join the settler colonial tradition of claiming sovereign independence as it throws off the shackles of the (EU) empire. Kassam's allusion to Paul Revere and Farage's 'independence day' might be read then alongside Jacob Rees-Mogg claiming that there should be 'no taxation without representation' for Britain in Europe;[4] the former Conservative Australian Prime Minister Tony Abbott insisting that Britain must 'seize its destiny' with 'nothing to lose but its chains;'[5] and the right-wing free speech activist Milo Yiannopoulus and Allum Bokhari arguing in *Breitbart News* (US) that Britain has a long history of 'standing defiant against tyrannical continental empires'. 'She wants to be free, she wants to improve,' they insist. 'In short, she wants to be great again.'[6]

Michael Kenny and Nick Pearce have tracked the shifting presence of the idea of the 'Anglosphere' of English-speaking peoples within British political thought since the late nineteenth century. In their reading, the discourse of the Anglosphere and the Atlantic orientation of some British Conservatives is at best ambiguous on race. This political faith views Britain, Canada, Australia, New Zealand and the United States as tied together by a shared cultural inheritance rooted in history, religion, language and family and inherently oriented towards democratic governance, the rule of law and – significantly – economic individualism and free-market principles.[7] Duncan Bell and Srdjan Vucetic have highlighted the increasing influence of this idea within Conservative think-tanks, transnational networks and institutions since 2016. As they put it, this is a 'reheated version of a specific settler colonial vision' in which the history of 'Global Britain' is largely shorn of its vast multiracial and culturally diverse character.[8] While faith in the Anglosphere has largely moved away in these elite Conservative circles from *explicit* articulations of the Anglo-Saxon race, the emphasis on a shared 'cultural heritage' remains key. As James C. Bennett argues in The Anglosphere Challenge (2007), the advance of multiculturalism can therefore be seen as a perpetual threat to the global ties of the Anglosphere.[9] Of course, the absence of explicit articulations of race is not equivalent to its true absence. As a vast scholarship has shown, whiteness itself derives its authority from 'its seeming invisibility, its absence of particularity'; it is invested here with 'a universal register of value and meaning' as synonymous with civilization, the rule of law, commerce and freedom.[10] White men (and less so white women) remain in the historical world of the Anglosphere 'the natural agents of modernity'.[11] This is, in Douglas M. Haynes' pithy phrase, 'the whiteness of freedom'.[12]

In 2015, historians Robin D. G. Kelly and Stephen Tuck coined what they called the 'other special relationship'[13] between Great Britain and the United States, in order to describe the two countries' largely under-analysed shared experiences of white supremacy and empire as well as the resultant struggle for black liberation, equal rights and political reform that have defined their recent histories.[14] Beyond Paul Revere, modern British historians listening to Kassam would be struck by another short phrase in his introduction to Farage: that London's Mayor was 'heaping up Britain's funeral pyre'. Drawn directly from Enoch Powell's 1968 'Rivers of Blood' speech, Kassam gave an unsuspecting CPAC audience a taste of Powell's apocalyptic medicine. Enoch Powell remains largely unknown to contemporary US audiences but in 1968 he offered a view of white victimization and national crisis that would have fit perfectly well on Fox News, some fifty years later. Contemporary debates about the extent to which we should read 'the legacy of empire' in the outcome of the Brexit referendum tend to focus on the political purchase of the idea of the 'Anglosphere' and 'Global Britain', failing to consider the impact of decolonization itself. The imperial legacy is here an 1880s vision of settler colonial unity and British trade dominance that, as Gary Younge argues, undergirds the 'hubris' of the Brexit vote.[15] As this chapter will argue, however, the effort to uncover the imperial legacy in contemporary nationalism – in Britain and in the United States – must also contend with its most immediate legacies. It must contend with the racial politics of the unravelling of empire and the concomitant crisis of white supremacy in the latter half of the twentieth century. In response to the efforts to challenge white racial privilege in the 1960s and 1970s, a reactionary discourse emerged that rejected any liberal 'guilt complex' over the long history of white supremacy and viewed these challenges, both international and domestic, as existential threats to Western civilization. This discourse is, remarkably, still at work today. Powell, for one, offered a particular reading of contemporary global history, a distinctly post-colonial Manichean world view, that infamously warned in 1968 that continued migration from Britain's former colonies would bring violence, anarchy and the eventual end of the British way of life – a 'colonization in reverse'. As Kassam noted in his 2018 self-published book, *Enoch was Right:* 'Farage is arguably the greatest inheritor of the legacy left by Powell, and perhaps indeed part of the legacy himself.'

When Farage took the stage at CPAC, he told an excited audience that both the Trump and Leave voter had 'stuffed the establishment' and their 'revolution . . . is still rolling across the West'. Farage presented here one transatlantic populist movement rising in opposition to migration from the global south. He warned in his speech of the dangers of George Soros and others committed to a globalist plot who 'don't believe in national identity' and 'want us to live in a world with open borders'. A 'world with open borders' – a world without national identity – appears, in Farage's telling, as a new international politics of the left, the enemy of the West in a new Cold War. Remarkably, the new American conservativism of the Trump era has similarly embraced a world view that no longer categorizes the world in terms of its relation to capital, between the free and the unfree world, or even simply between the West and Islam. Instead, we see the strength of a global worldview that turns on a racially-coded North-South axis, rooted in the history of colonialism and decolonization. The so-called 'caravans' of Central American refugees attempting to cross borders into the US – and coming from areas once under the informal economic and political control of the United States – dramatize America's own post-colonial moment. At times borrowing from the post-colonial imaginaries of the right of 1960s and 1970s Britain and Europe, the new American conservatism has developed a global view of white victimization, wherein demographic change, the decline of a white majority, signals social and political annihilation.

'Who do the Americans think they are getting with Farage?' asked *The Guardian* journalist Nesrine Malik at CPAC. 'Do they see him as some Churchillian English gent who lives in Downton Abbey and has managed to single-handedly secure Brexit against the efforts of the entire political establishment by sheer force of personality and capital?' For an answer, it might be best to turn to the insights of historian Antoinette Burton who, looking to a very different political world in 2003, noted that there was a specific racial politics to America's Anglophilia. She explains:

> The United States has been and remains the audience perhaps ripest for performances of Britain's eternal Britishness. In the last three decades of the twentieth century, Britain emerged as a poignant, almost pathetic figure in American culture, a safe and utopian place where very little distinction between past and present could be discerned – a place untroubled, specifically, by the

kind of racial strife that has torn at the fabric of modern American society . . . Britain for export has in fact been a whitewashed Britain, a commodified balm for a certain segment of the American public seeking relief from racial tension and ugliness in the apparently racially harmonious past (and present) of the mother country.[16]

As Burton makes clear, this whitewashed image of Britain *is* imperial – ordered by class and race – but shorn of a racial politics within Britain. The 'persistent American image of Britain as a kind of Victorian and Edwardian oasis was possible because in its commercialized forms, both high and low, Britain has most often been stripped of its histories of blackness and imperial culture "at home" – even while, paradoxically, empire "over there" was (and remains) a central feature of Britain for export.'[17] Burton underscores what is at stake in America's 'Brexit' – the protection of a commodified and eternal Britishness. In this sense, the folksy figure of Farage promises a throwback, a familiar, palatable performance of whiteness and a potential antidote to Sadiq Khan.

Enoch Powell began his 'Rivers of Blood' speech by recounting a conversation with one of his constituents. As he put it, 'a middle-aged, quite ordinary working man employed in one of our nationalized industries' had told him, 'If I had the money to go, I wouldn't stay in this country . . . I have three children, all of them been through grammar school and two of them married now, with family. I shan't be satisfied till I have seen them all settled overseas. In this country in fifteen or twenty years' time the black man will have the whip hand over the white man.'[18] This 'ordinary working man' saw his family's future in settlement – no doubt in the Anglosphere – in the ordered settler worlds, perhaps, of Australia or South Africa. Powell went on:

> Here is a decent, ordinary fellow Englishman, who in broad daylight in my own town says to me, his Member of Parliament, that the country will not be worth living in for his children . . . What he is saying, thousands and hundreds of thousands are saying and thinking – not throughout Great Britain, perhaps, but in the areas that are already undergoing the total transformation to which there is no parallel in a thousand years of English history. We must be mad, literally mad, as a nation to be permitting the annual inflow of some 50,000 dependants . . . It is like watching a nation busily engaged in heaping up its own funeral pyre.

Powell's words offered an apocalyptic view of non-white migration. This was a moment when, with African nationalist movements and what Malcolm X called the global rising tide of colour against white supremacy, the era of domination by the 'white man' appeared to be coming to a close. As Bill Schwarz has examined, this view of being overwhelmed and swamped drew heavily on fears of the white minority in colonial Rhodesia.[19] In this context, decolonization and new legal challenges to white supremacy were presented not as a politics of equality but increasingly as a 'race war' between civilization and barbarism, wherein the future of white people – whether in Britain, Europe or the ex-colonies – was in a state of perpetual threat, in a state of existential crisis, holding the (racial) frontline of 'civilization'. Whole areas in Britain were, Powell said, being colonized. This was, according to Powell, the fault of the madness of Britain's 'liberal establishment' failing to defend the nation from an invasion.

British anti-immigrant populism of the 1960s and 1970s was informed by post-colonial anxieties about British decline but also by an increasingly visible call for racial justice in both Southern Africa and the United States. After a trip to the US in late 1967 as UK Shadow Defence Minister, Powell hired a man to send him local newspaper clippings of evidence of unrest and violence within the African American community in Detroit. In the context of major protests there, Powell warned in speeches across the UK that Birmingham would soon become Britain's Detroit. In 1971, Dr Roger Pearson, a former British Indian Army officer and ethnographer at the University of Southern Mississippi, helped to arrange a speaking tour for Powell of Louisiana and Mississippi. The tour was subsidized by the Citizens' Council, who led campaigns against desegregation. Powell's status as the politician who stood against the 'oppression' of white people resulted in speaking tours in Australia and South Africa in the early 1970s too.

In 1973, a French travel writer named Jean Raspail – at times referred to as the 'French Enoch Powell' – dramatized Powell's vision of an existential crisis of the West. That year he published a novel of apocalyptic proportions entitled *The Camp of the Saints*. The title itself draws from St John's Apocalypse in the Bible. It is this work of fantasy that has, in fact, had a direct impact on the contemporary American right. The story occurs in the near future when almost a million Indian peasants take to old colonial steamships to colonize Europe, and land in Southern France. The result is mass rape, devastation and the fall of European civilization. The story is a starkly racist parable, where Indian peasants become one heaving animal mass, without individual identity. Race, not class or ideology, is the organizing logic of history in the story. With the arrival of the Indian steamships, non-white people across the West proceed to destroy what Raspail calls the 'white world'. This is, in Raspail's mind, the outcome of the rise of Frantz Fanon's 'wretched of the earth', an expression of 'an antiworld bent on coming in the flesh to knock, at long last, at the gates of abundance.'[20] *The Camp of the Saints* was translated into English in 1975. In the mid-1980s, Raspail began to argue that his prediction was coming true. Even the mayor of Paris, Jacques Chirac, agreed, noting in 1984 that, 'In demographic terms, Europe is disappearing.'[21] Importantly, the novel proceeded to become a cult classic within the US Conservative movement and was published over six times by American presses over the years. American Conservative activist William F. Buckley Jr called the book a 'great novel' in the 1990s. But the man who has probably done the most to publicize this book in the US is former chief strategist to President Donald Trump, Steve Bannon. Raspail's vision remains crucial to Bannon's understanding of the state of Europe and the world: 'The whole thing in Europe is all about immigration,' he said in January 2016. 'It's a global issue today – this kind of global Camp of the Saints' – noting again that year, 'It is not migration. It's really an invasion. I call it the Camp of the Saints.'[22]

The black man's 'whip hand over the white man' would come about, in Powell's view, due to a demographic shift from migration from the ex-colonies but also due to what he viewed as a crisis of authority *within* Britain. The British government, he argued, had lost confidence in its own moral authority, it had gone 'mad', in the context of decolonization. Powell describes this in 1965 as a 'post-imperial neurosis'.[23] Lord Elton similarly argued in 1969 that the notion that Britain had a 'moral obligation to admit great numbers of Commonwealth citizens' was due to the 'strange guilt complex' that 'has been fostered in respect of our imperial record.'[24] In Powell's view, equality law and efforts to counter racism – the internal decolonization of Britain – were not animated by liberal political principles but by this 'guilt complex'. As the Conservative campaigner George Young notes in 1971, 'liberalism has become self-hate.' Britain was, he insists, facing 'a destructive element.' The 'laws men created for their self realization are being turned against us', the 'whiteness of freedom' was under threat. 'Genuflection to the extravaganzas of Afro-Asian nationalism is the liberal's method of trying to cure himself of his neurosis.'[25] Sixteen years later, the Australian Conservative theorist Kenneth Minogue argued that the key ideological achievement of Thatcherism was its rejection of the 'culture of guilt'.[26] This persistent critique of a liberal 'guilt complex', due in large part to the unravelling of empire, would find its way into the making of the new right.

This critique of racial justice as a product of a post-colonial guilt complex – and rejection of it as an extension and continuation of the liberal political traditions of 'Western civilization' – has had a significant impact on contemporary Conservative thought. Mass migration sits at the centre of the British Conservative Douglas Murray's bestselling *The Strange Death of Europe*, but so does his argument that Europe has 'lost faith in its beliefs, traditions and legitimacy'. Europe, he insists, is 'committing suicide' by continuing to accept migration from the global south.[27] The 'tyranny of guilt' – the abiding guilt for slavery, colonialism and racism – has resulted, he argues, in the 'masochism' of Western civilization, which he warns is now facing the 'sadism' of radical Islam.[28] Murray told Representative Devin Nunes, Steve Bannon and major US Conservative donors at Restoration Weekend in Palm Beach, Florida, in November 2017, that people write to him 'from Canada, from America, from Australia' to say 'this book is about us isn't it'. As a means of countering equality, the rejection of 'guilt' for the history of white supremacy is central to America's new Conservative radicalism.

David Horowitz is an important actor in far-right fundraising in the US and a long-time anti-immigrant and anti-Islam campaigner. His David Horowitz Freedom Center is a charity and is therefore tax exempt, but raises millions in donations each year to support a hard-right Conservative agenda. It is a key funder of a nationwide network of Conservative organizations including Students for Academic Freedom, Jihad Watch and the *TruthRevolt* news website as well as the yearly fundraising event Restoration Weekend. Like Murray, Horowitz uses a 'guilt complex' to understand what he also calls the 'death of Europe'. In 2016, he told high school students at the Young America's Foundation that 'Civilizations die when they cease to believe in themselves ... We are witnessing the death of Europe as we speak for that very reason. Europe has accepted millions, millions of people who absolutely despise them. There are rape epidemics across Europe and the governments protect the rapists. And persecute and prosecute heroic objectors to the rape epidemics like Katie Hopkins ... Europe has been persuaded by the left of a gigantic guilt complex. It is one of the greatest, if not the greatest, civilizations in the history of the world, European Civilization, yet they can't summon the will to defend themselves.'[29] In 2014, Horowitz provided a quarter of a million dollars in funding to the Dutch Party for Freedom, after it proposed closing all Dutch mosques and banning the 'fascist' Qur'an in the Netherlands. Murray, Horowitz and other influential British and American Conservative campaigners combine a narrative of the death of Europe with profound Islamophobia.

Horowitz's reference to Katie Hopkins is also telling. Hopkins, UK media personality turned far-right journalist, has transformed herself – like Farage and others – into a folksy British talking head for US audiences. As she put it in 2017, 'It feels good to be here in the land of the free – a phrase I would not use to describe my own country.'[30] Unlike Nigel Farage, who when he speaks in the US emphasizes the coincidence of the nationalist resurgence of Trump and Brexit and favours an optimistic picture of a transatlantic partnership, Hopkins offers a very different view of both Britain and Europe for Conservative US audiences. According to Hopkins, true Brexit, as the Leave supporter imagined it, will 'never happen'.[31] While Farage's optimistic portrayal of the future of nationalism gets some traction at Conservative fundraising events, Hopkins is on Fox News far more often – delivering a vision of Britain and the West that is perhaps now more compelling to the new American Conservative and those sympathetic to the Alt-Right.

After leaving her syndicated column at the *Mail Online* in November 2017, Hopkins became a key contributor to Canada's online Alt-Right equivalent to Breitbart News, *Rebel Media*, with a regular 'Hopkins World' feature. With this, she has effectively entered the North American Conservative media circuit – presenting herself, first, as a Leave voter, but also as someone uniquely able and willing to tell hard political truths about Britain and the world to American audiences. Hopkins first came to the British public's attention in 2007 when, as a 'global brand consultant,' she became an outspoken, famously 'bitchy' contestant on the British *Apprentice*. That was then followed by two more reality-television appearances, on *I'm a Celebrity . . . Get Me Out of Here!* and *Celebrity Big Brother*. She became, with these appearances, a well-known right-wing controversialist with columns in the *The Sun* and then the *Mail Online*. There she made numerous inflammatory public statements, praising the efficiency of Ebola for 'cleaning certain types of people' and calling refugees in the Mediterranean 'cockroaches' who should be met by gunboats rather than charity.[32] That Hopkins purposefully cultivated a hated media personality – becoming a 'pantomime villain' – can be rooted in contemporary reality-television culture.[33] In this sense, Hopkins is, in many ways, a joke in Britain.

Yet, despite this, she has managed to cultivate a persona in the US as the voice of silenced middle England, the voice of the Leave voter in the United States. If Farage is Mr Brexit, Hopkins is to many Americans Mrs Brexit. She began her talk at one major fundraising event in the US by presenting herself as an embattled figure: 'I am a straight, white, Conservative female with one husband and three children under 13. And where I come from, back in Blighty, that virtually makes me an endangered species.' She is, as she put, 'a deplorable . . . from Normalville.' But she also presents herself as a silenced voice in Britain, a victim. Hopkin's own experiences falling foul of European anti-hate speech law is presented as proof of this and proof of a world turned upside down by 'political correctness'. 'My message is simple,' she said at Restoration Weekend in 2017: 'Do not let this great country become the United Kingdom. Do not let America fall, as Europe has fallen. Look at us. Let us be a warning. Be better than us.'

In her TV appearances, Hopkins insists that Britain and Europe have fallen on multiple fronts, overwhelmed by migration from Africa and the Middle East, by so-called 'black gangs' in London, by creeping Islamization and – even – by Europe's own anti-hate speech laws. While America's settler-migrant was constructive of the 'Anglosphere', the racialized-migrant is the very opposite. As she puts it:

> We imagine somehow in this great nation [of the United States] we have people arriving and starting a new life. We like to believe that we are a nation of migrants. You hear it all the time. Yeah, but the immigrants that arrived in New York wanted to start a better life. The immigrants that arrive in the jungle camp at Calais come with every single old hatred they ever had.[34]

Here, Hopkins joins the 'We' in 'We like to believe that we are a nation of migrants.' As though the 'We' can slip between Britain, the United States and the West.

Of course, the fact that Hopkins is a white, middle-class woman is in no way incidental to the way she presents her vision of a fallen Europe to US audiences.

Hopkins draws from a long tradition of middle-class women's right-wing activism in Britain. In keeping with these traditions, she speaks often as a mother, as a moral arbiter warning of national decline. Hopkins should also be placed in the wider context of the recent advance of post-feminist, far-right female leaders across Europe and the United States. These female public figures can inhabit a near fascist agenda while speaking up for white women's supposedly distinct vulnerability; she frames her racial world view as a global defence of white women. She draws on the rape of white widowed female farmers in post-Apartheid South Africa, the rape of Swedish women by migrants and their fear to walk in 'Muslim no-go areas', the threat of rape at Calais's migrant camp, and her own battles to maintain 'free speech' – to tell the story, in part, of the rape of white girls by British Asian men – as chapters in the same story, of white female victimization. As Wendy Webster's work has done the most to highlight, the defence of white women and white domesticity has functioned both in the colonies and the metropole as a means to defend white supremacy, colonial violence and the dehumanization of people of colour.[35] Through this, Hopkins offers a global vision of the white victim to American audiences, a means of regaining moral authority and rejection of what Murray calls that 'tyranny of guilt'. As Stefan Molyneaux, a Canadian Alt-Right author and contributor to *Rebel Media*, put it, North Americans are interested in what is happening to white farmers in South Africa, because of 'the declining population of whites in the West'. This 'white genocide', he argues, gives them a 'glimpse of what happens when whites slide into the minority'.[36]

In April 2018, Katie Hopkins appeared on Fox News to explain the recent reports of a high murder rate in London. She blamed 'black gangs' and said that, as a mother, she 'wouldn't dream' of taking her family to London. The discussion between Hopkins and Tucker Carlson on violence in London revolved around Mayor Sadiq Khan. In the very opening of the segment, Carlson describes Khan – in passing – as 'a demagogue'. In Hopkins' telling, Sadiq Khan is the main perpetrator of a new liberal fascism that continues to insist that London is safe. A month later, when the leading anti-Islam activist Tommy Robinson was charged with contempt of court for publishing a live video of a court case in Leeds involving British Muslim men in Rotherham grooming young white girls between 2004 and 2011, Hopkins returned to Carlson's nightly show. The control of media coverage of the story, like police investigations against her for hate speech, represented what she called 'very dark times' in Britain. The country, she said, is 'on a knife edge' with 'the establishment' willing to 'cleanse' the country of voices it doesn't like. When Tucker Carlson interviewed Robinson on Fox News three months later, Carlson noted: 'The United Kingdom has become a mere shadow of the nation that gave us freedom of speech, freedom of press, a host of other rights that we take for granted, but probably should not. Nobody knows that better than Tommy Robinson.'[37] As Carlson shows here, the shared cultural heritage of the Anglosphere and that 'other special relationship' are now being marshalled in support of the extreme right.

Raheem Kassam, Nigel Farage, Douglas Murray and Katie Hopkins offer a view of Britain and Brexit to Trump's America. The 'eternal Britain' of Antoinette Burton's 2003 analysis still makes its way into US homes as, for instance, the Netflix original series, *The Crown*. This whitewashed Britain of the modern royal family is, perhaps, what some US conservatives think Brexit is fighting for. But it is in conflict, now, with another imagined Britain that was produced in the shadow of decolonization, first pictured by Enoch Powell and dramatized by Jean Raspail. This is a Britain overwhelmed by Sharia Law, by multiculturalism, by a post-colonial 'guilt complex' and by Raseem Kassam's image of Sadiq Khan 'heaping up Britain's funeral pyre.' Against this 'state of Londonistan', Hopkins maintains that Brexit Britain lives on. 'There is a place called the rest of the UK,' she told David Horowitz, Steve Bannon, Devin Nunes and others at Restoration Weekend: 'There is a place where hardworking Brits want to do a fair day's work for a fair day's pay. They want to look after their families. They want to love their country. They will fight for their country. They support Trump. They voted Brexit.'[38]

Notes

1 Ben Jacobs, 'Nigel Farage gets warm welcome at gathering of US right wing,' *The Guardian* (23 February 2018), www.theguardian.com/us-news/2018/feb/23/cpac-nigel-farage-sadiq-khan-us-conservatives

2 Raheem Kassam, Conservative Political Action Conference, 23 February 2019, Oxon Hills, MD, www.youtube.com/watch?v=RqQ6eSRduWc

3 Duncan Bell and Srdjan Vucetic, 'Brexit, CANZUK, and the Legacy of Empire,' *British Journal of Politics and International Relations* (forthcoming, 2019).

4 As cited in Oliver J. J. Lane, 'Jacob Rees-Mogg on Brexit: "No Taxation without Representation"' *Breitbart News* (10 December 2018), www.breitbart.com/europe/2018/12/10/jacob-rees-mogg-on-brexit-no-taxation-without-representation/

5 As cited in Oliver J. J. Lane, 'Tony Abbott: Brexit Britain has nothing to lose but its chains,' *Breitbart News* (25 October 2018), www.breitbart.com/europe/2018/10/25/tony-abbot-brexit-britain-has-nothing-to-lose-but-its-chains/

6 Allum Bokhari and Milo Yiannopoulos, 'Brexit: Why the Globalists Lost,' *Breitbart News* (24 June 2016), www.breitbart.com/social-justice/2016/06/24/the-end-of-globalism/

7 Michael Kenny and Nick Pearce, *Shadows of Empire: The Anglosphere in British Politics* (London: Polity, 2018): 128.

8 Bell and Vucetic (forthcoming).

9 Kenny and Pearce, 128.

10 Haynes, 'The Whiteness of Civilization: The Transatlantic Crisis of White Supremacy and British Television Programming in the United States in the 1970s,' in *After the*

Imperial Turn: Thinking with and through the Nation (Durham: Duke University Press, 2003), 325. See also Gurminder Bhambra, 'Trump, Brexit and "methodological whiteness"', *The British Journal*; Richard Dyer, 'The Matter of Whiteness' in *White Privilege: Essential Readings and the Other Side of Racism*, ed., Paula Rothenburg (New York: Worth, 2005); *Postcolonial Whiteness: A Critical Reader on Race and Empire*, ed. Alfred Lopez (New York: SUNY Press, 2005).

11 Haynes, 'The Whiteness of Civilization,' 326.

12 Haynes, 'The Whiteness of Civilization,' 325.

13 The 'special relationship' is a term commonly used in international relations to emphasize the close diplomatic, economic, military, and historical ties between the UK and US.

14 Robin D. G. Kelley and Stephen Tuck, *The Other Special Relationship: Race, Rights, and Riots in Britain and the United States* (New York: Palgrave Macmillan, 2015).

15 Gary Younge, 'Britain's imperial fantasies have given us Brexit,' *The Guardian* (3 February 2018), https://www.theguardian.com/commentisfree/2018/feb/03/imperial-fantasies-brexit-theresa-may; see also chapters in this volume: David Thackeray and Richard Toye, 'Debating Empire 2.0' and Mike Kenny and Nick Pearce, 'Brexit and the Anglosphere'.

16 Antoinette Burton, 'When Was Britain? Nostalgia for the Nation at the End of the "American Century"', *Journal of Modern History* 75, no. 2 (June 2003): 359–374, 360.

17 Ibid.

18 For a discussion of the use of the 'ordinary' man on the street, see Judi Atkins and Alan Finlayson, '"A 40-Year-Old Black Man Made the Point to Me": Everyday Knowledge and the Performance of Leadership in Contemporary British Politics,' *Political Studies* 61, Issue 1 (2013): 161–77 (Politics of ordinariness).

19 Bill Schwarz, *The White Man's World* (Oxford: Oxford University Press, 2011).

20 Jean Raspail, *The Camp of the Saints* (translation of *Le Camp des saints* (Paris: Laffont, 1973)): 2.

21 As cited in Matthew Connelly and Paul Kennedy, 'Must it be the rest against the West?' *The Atlantic* (December 1994).

22 As cited in Paul Blumenthal, 'This Stunningly Racist French Novel is How Steve Bannon Explains the World,' *The Huffington Post* (4 March 2017).

23 Enoch Powell, German Service, 17 June 1965. POLL 4.1.27

24 Lord Elton, 'Burdens of Past,' *The Times* (8 January 1969).

25 Younge, 12, 33.

26 Kenneth Minogue, 'The Emergence of the New Right,' in *Thatcherism*, ed. Robert Skidelsky (London: Chatto & Windus, 1988), 133.

27 Murray, *The Strange Death of Europe*, 3.

28 Ibid., 157.

29 David Horowitz, Young America's Foundation, Ann Arbor, MI, 16 March 2018.

30 Hopkins, Horowitz Freedom Center, Los Angeles, CA, 27 March 2018.

31 Hopkins, 'After Boris Johnson's Brexit comments, it's clear: "No deal may be the best deal"', *Rebel Media* (8 June 2018).

32 Hopkins, 'Wither Freedom?' panel, Conservative Political Action Conference, 23 February 2018, Oxon Hill, MD.

33 Paul Bleakley, '"Love me or hate me – I don't care": Katie Hopkins, *Celebrity Big Brother* and the Destruction of a Negative Image,' *Continuum: Journal of Media & Cultural Studies* 30, no. 4 (2016): 419–32, 419.

34 Hopkins, 'Wither Freedom?' panel.

35 Wendy Webster, *Englishness and Empire 1939–1965* (Oxford: Oxford University Press, 2005).

36 'White Farmers Slaughtered in South Africa | Lauren Southern and Stefan Molyneux', 10 February 2018, https://www.youtube.com/watch?v=0TfAq3Lrljg

37 Tucker Carlson interview with Tommy Robinson.

38 Katie Hopkins, Restoration Weekend, Palm Beach, FL, 19 November 2017.

Chapter 10
Refugees, Migrants, Windrush and Brexit

Yasmin Khan

The charge of racism is a serious one in Britain; acting on racist beliefs, by perpetrating racist hate crimes or discriminating against others on racial grounds are criminal offences. It is little wonder then that the charge of racism against Brexiteers has been hotly contested and vigorously debated in Britain since the referendum. It is clear that Leavers and racism cannot be simplistically aligned and that there are complicated lines of connection between race and the Leave campaign. Race operates as a complex signifier in British society, and other Leavers expressed allegiance to English-British culture, multiracial Britishness or even post-imperial-Commonwealth identities which could leave ample room for people of colour. Indeed, many black and Asian British people voted to leave, and there are plenty of arguments for wanting to stand outside the EU which are not related to racial discrimination or white supremacy.

Yet, there is also an evident and undeniable connection between the referendum, the result to 'leave' and 'take back control' and the feeling that Britain has become a less welcome place for people with heritage that lies outside of Britain. The feeling that those with a true hold on English or British identity – which may be coded as white – are the rightful heirs to the land, to resources, to the political power of the state has given a nativist tone to political speech. Reducing immigration has often been the number one factor uniting Leave voters when polled, and cuts across social, party and class divisions.[1] Although for many Brexiteers this is a reaction to the free movement from the European accession countries, and, they argue, detached from issues of race, it inevitably makes those of us who are migrants ourselves – or descended from them – feel nervous when these opinions become so prominent in political and media debate.

This was made evident in a number of startling developments at the time of the referendum. At its most extreme, it was manifest in the killing of the British Labour MP Jo Cox on 16 June 2016. Jo Cox had repeatedly campaigned for the British government to go further in responding to the needs of Syrian refugees, organizing a parliamentary group in support for the cause, and it is likely that this drew her to the attention of her killer. But it was also significant that the murder happened just six days before the referendum in the feverish atmosphere of the time. At the trial, the judge concluded that the assassin was motivated by 'admiration for Nazis and similar anti-democratic white supremacist creeds',[2] yet he was regularly described and excused in the British tabloid press as a mad or lone actor. Separately, in the four weeks after the referendum, over six thousand racist hate crimes were lodged with the police in Britain including physical assault, property damage and verbal abuse in many cases using language related to the referendum, such as 'Go Home'.[3] The referendum left many people with non-white heritage feeling less secure in the country, more anxious about the borders being drawn between 'us' and 'them', less at ease in their own home towns – whether in terms of a general lack of acceptance of their Britishness or public recognition of their right to residence; whether as overseas students, asylum seekers, or EU workers in the UK with the right to freedom of movement.

Refugees in particular have had a shadowy and unclear place in British consciousness in recent years. Britain has made far less effort than most European countries to accept refugees displaced by the Syrian war. In February 2018, just 10,538 refugees from Syria had been settled in Britain, a drop in the ocean compared to the efforts of other European countries, especially Germany.[4] Yet the optics of the refugee movements and the Syrian refugee crisis in 2016 seemed to underscore a repeated refrain. There was an attack on 'fortress Europe' by non-Europeans, it was argued in the tabloids, and these refugees would inevitably move onwards to Britain through the gateway that the EU seemingly provided. There was a deliberate and sustained campaign of obfuscation by right-wing tabloid newspapers in Britain which muddled and confused the issue of who was an economic *migrant* from within the EU and who was a *refugee* from without. These unspecified outsiders would make claims on the services of the state and compete with rightful natives for access to resources – health services, education, housing.

This is most glaringly seen in headlines from the time. In 2016 in the weeks leading up to the referendum, the *Daily Mail* and the *Daily Express* ran over sixty full-page headlines which explicitly provoked fears about migrants (including: 'We can't stop migrants', 'Kick out foreign crooks', 'Migrant crisis will cost 20bn' and 'Britain's wide open borders'). Invariably, the catch-all word *migrant* encompassed both refugees from the Syrian war coming into Europe and migrants (including EU workers) in the UK. In reality Britain was under no obligation to accept refugees from the Middle East – and indeed has still not taken many at all, largely resisting pressures to be more hospitable – but the impression which was created in the public mind was one of influx and deluge, the need to 'take back control'. The obfuscation and blurring of who was a migrant in modern Britain contributed to the feeling of a lack of control, a sense (reflected in numerous popular overestimates) that the numbers of incomers were running ahead of anything remotely sustainable.

On 17 November 2015, the *Daily Mail* published a cartoon by their regular contributor Mac (which can still be purchased as a print through the news organization's website) which depicts black figures with guns, Pashtun caps, exaggerated noses, burkhas and headscarves crossing the EU border, as rats scurry among their feet.[5] The sign in the cartoon reads, 'Welcome to Europe: Our free borders and the movement of people'. This cartoon, located in unspecified time and space, deliberately and maliciously muddled the purpose and role of the EU, the question of incoming refugees and migrants, and Britain's perceived exposure to lax European entry rules. It was also undeniably Islamophobic in its stereotyping, and – in a storm of social media protest – it was pointed out by many at the time that there were distinct echoes of a Nazi cartoon, published in a Viennese newspaper *Das Kleine Blatt* in 1939 which portrayed Jews as rats to be swept out of Germany.[6] Some argued that the cartoon had been misinterpreted, and that the cartoonist was making a more direct link between Isis fighters and the terror attacks that had taken place in Paris that year, but it is exactly this porousness of meaning, the form of floating signifier – general enough to mean many things to many people, yet specific enough to galvanize action – that is so dangerous when associated with refugees.[7] One particularly pernicious and unifying theme seems to be the way that resistance to Islam, and suspicion of Islam, appears to be intensifying in Britain across many levels of society, and cutting across political divisions, and even across racial divisions. The idea of some kind of cultural chasm appears to have intensified in recent years – a trend with a longer and more complex history, rooted in post 9/11 political formations, the growth of domestic European jihadists and social and economic inequalities. But it is a politically expedient and useful tool for galvanizing populist reaction.

This kind of unspecified fear of the outsider (particularly the male Muslim outsider) was most emphatically and disingenuously harnessed to the Brexit cause by one of UKIP's campaign posters for the Leave campaign. Unveiled by the UKIP leader Nigel Farage in 2015, it employed a photograph of a long line of refugees moving in a seemingly endless sea of humanity towards a border. The tag line on this poster was 'Breaking Point: the EU has failed us all. We must break free of the EU and take back control of our borders.' Almost every person in the photograph was young, male and brown-skinned – mostly the individuals were from Afghanistan and Syria. Again, the conflation of refugees and migrants was deliberate and pernicious: this photograph showed a crossing place for refugees moving between Croatia and Slovenia but the location and source of the photograph were deliberately obscured. Again, there was a public reaction, and attendant social media storm, as critics reflected how this photograph had little to do with Britain's own experience of the EU. Yet when polled, 90 per cent of Brexit supporters in 2016 believed that the UK had taken too many refugees from Syria and Iraq, suggesting that this kind of propaganda was effective at blurring public understanding of the difference between economic migration and the presence of refugees, and a gross misunderstanding of Britain's real policy towards the Middle Eastern refugees.[8]

It could be argued that these are egregious and extreme cases, which were spotted immediately as going 'beyond the pale' and exceeding the permitted boundaries of social and political propriety. Boris Johnson and other Conservative Leavers distanced themselves immediately from UKIP's poster, which was widely denounced in the press. Farage could always be portrayed as the outlier, the unacceptable face of British Brexit debates. However, these examples are also reflective of a more widespread and more acceptable argument, which surrounded the referendum and had a part to play in the Leave victory. This was the hazy spectre of Turkish membership of the EU, the question of economic migration and Britain's connection to Europe. During the 2015 general election campaign, UKIP was, like all parties, given the chance to broadcast a party political broadcast on the BBC. The party

> devoted its entire three-and-a-half-minute broadcast to the danger posed by Turkish membership of the European Union. Emphasizing the country's size and its Muslim heritage, UKIP insisted that Turkey was just five years away from membership. The message was clear. Britain had to leave the EU before Turkey joined.[9]

This became a regular line of attack, leveraged by Brexiteers in the following referendum campaign. On numerous occasions, Leavers, including more 'mainstream' conservative MPs such as Boris Johnson, Priti Patel and Penny Mordaunt, drew on the idea of Turkish accession as a fright tactic. Notions such as the Turkish rate of gun-ownership, levels of crime and the Turkish birth-rate were circulated in the media. Xenophobia was in full force, in particular in relation to the idea of Turkey as a Muslim country. The idea that Britain was actively considering giving one million Turks visa-free access to the UK was repeatedly cited. The prospect of Turkish accession was leveraged with full force by the Vote Leave campaign in the final weeks of the campaign before the referendum. The MPs Michael Gove, Boris Johnson and Gisela Stuart even wrote a letter to David Cameron asking for assurances that the government would not agree to Turkish accession: 'If the Government cannot give this guarantee, the public will draw the reasonable conclusion that the only way to avoid having common borders with Turkey is to Vote Leave and take back control on 23 June.'[10]

The term 'dog-whistle' quickly made its way into British political discourse in the first decades after the millennium. The *Oxford English Dictionary* describes this as 'a statement or expression which in addition to its ostensible meaning has a further interpretation or connotation intended to be understood only by a specific target audience'. It is perhaps worth pausing to reflect on the ubiquity of this word in the referendum campaign coverage, and also the relative novelty of its usage in British political discourse. The term was used only sporadically in the mid-1990s, emerging in Canada, America and Australasia, before being widely understood in the UK. The speed with which it has caught on tells us something about the nature of racist language and speech, and the way that political signals can work in the modern age. It suggests an audience primed and ready to read meaning from suggestions, in an age when politicians are unwilling or unable to come out with outright racist language, but still wish to nod to racism or Islamophobia in order to trigger political allegiance and belonging. It is, in short, a classic political tool of nationalists and xenophobes. It is additionally troubling that the euphemism 'dog-whistle' is used itself to critique what might otherwise be identified as (albeit suggestively) racist and xenophobic language.

A somewhat surprising and very different, contrasting and countervailing series of events – suggesting perhaps a corrective to this rise of xenophobia and exclusion – was set in motion in early 2018 with the uncovering of the so-called Windrush scandal. Extensive journalistic investigations by *The Guardian* newspaper, particularly by the journalist Amelia Gentleman, revealed the extent to which British citizens had been affected by the 'hostile environment' policy of the Home Office, initiated when Theresa May was Home Secretary.

Individuals who had migrated to Britain as Commonwealth citizens between 1947 and 1973 had been given 'indefinite leave to remain in the country', i.e. the right to reside with full citizenship rights, but many were not issued with any documentation at the time, and the Home Office had failed to keep records confirming these individuals' status. Therefore, many individuals (possibly thousands – the numbers are still unknown) suffered deportation, being stopped when leaving the country or prevented from re-entering Britain. Numerous families affected by this unjust and illegal action came forward to tell their stories of detention and deportation, or the denial of public services, especially health services, because of their inability to prove their rightful Britishness. The scope and extent of this scandal – which included elderly British citizens detained and deported overseas, and at least one man who had been refused free cancer treatment by the NHS because he could not prove his arrival date in the UK – was astonishing. Also striking was the extent of public outrage, and a sense that a line had been crossed in the treatment of these Windrush generation migrants. The Home Secretary Amber Rudd was forced to resign in April 2018, ostensibly for failing to accurately tell MPs the target number for removing illegal immigrants;

this was a political scalp in the midst of widespread disapprobation of her department's general approach.

It is very easy to forget that *net migration* to Britain did not occur until the 1980s, and that in the 1950s many white people were leaving Britain to go to the so-called white dominions, such as Australia, New Zealand and Canada, exacerbating the extreme labour shortage. Winston Churchill was so worried about the number of British people emigrating after the war that in 1947 he spoke on BBC's Home Service and begged them to stay – 'do not desert the old land'. Away from the microphone he was less diplomatic – he is reported to have called them 'rats deserting a sinking ship'.[11] There was a massive demand for labour, on building sites, in factories and in the NHS. The black and Asian people who came in the 1950s were part of a labour market, different in type but not dissimilar in general principle to today's migrants; they came because demand was high for their kind of labour and they were willing and able to do hard, dirty and low-paid work.

Today, people with origins in over sixty countries of the world could technically be considered under the new Windrush Scheme for British citizenship. The British Empire and Commonwealth after all included one fifth of the world's population and these people were all Commonwealth citizens. Hundreds of thousands came to Britain from numerous countries in the 1950s and 1960s. This was a point reinforced by the British Nationality Act of 1948, which underscored the rights to citizenship of all Commonwealth peoples.

The story of this time, both in the British press and from the government, has focused squarely on the Windrush moment as a particularly iconic moment of arrival – linked to the arrival of 492 West Indians on the MV *Empire Windrush* ship which came into Tilbury port in June 1948, and to the contribution of Caribbean individuals recruited directly by the British state. But this narrative contains and excludes a much greater story of British imperial pasts and Commonwealth citizenship, which has been rolled back from popular memory. Many Windrush generation victims of the 'hostile environment' are likely to be Indian, Pakistani, Bangladeshi and from numerous other countries too. An inquiry by the National Audit Office, published in December 2018, into measures by the Home Office to rectify the Windrush scandal, is immensely critical of serial failings and omissions. In particular, it points out the restricted investigations into the scale of the problem since the story broke, suggesting that deportations and detentions of many other nationalities also would have occurred. Indeed, the National Audit Office report criticizes a 'lack of curiosity' on the part of the Home Office about the extent to which people had been affected: 'The department is taking steps to put things right for the Caribbean community but it has shown a surprising lack of urgency to identify other groups that may have been affected.'[12] In response the Home Office points to the sheer scale of the issue. Yet – legally, morally – the Windrush generation might properly be expanded to include all Commonwealth citizens, beyond those from the Caribbean. Insistence on the Caribbean story presents an important but rather constricted and narrow version of events, about the arrival moment of one community at one point in time.

As a number of people have pointed out, including the historians Kennetta Hammond Perry and David Olusoga, the official, popular Windrush narrative has a 'feel-good' ring to it. Some of these individuals were – and are – undoubtedly patriots but there is often the ascription to them of some kind of hyper-nationalism. It obscures as much as it illuminates, hiding the real racial challenges and obstacles that these individuals faced.[13] These new arrivals to Britain in the 1950s and 60s suffered appalling discrimination in housing, work and education during their early years in Britain – and beyond – but this is seldom referred to. The Windrush generation are seen as coming to the aid of the motherland, without much further interrogation of how this came to be. As Hammond Perry writes, this tends to 'pigeonhole Windrush into an ahistorical frame that uncritically props up a progressive image of a multicultural nation' and she asks instead that we question 'what aspects of British history are extolled, and which facets remain illegible in popular renditions of the Windrush narrative?'[14] Only some aspects of the Windrush story are palatable and politically expedient in the current British political climate. Furthermore, the whole long and difficult story of Britain's past role in the Caribbean – or wider empire – is seldom mentioned, although it is in many ways the elephant in the room. The moment of arrival becomes year zero. The ties which bound colonies to metropole are ignored. The context of slavery, imperialism, and economic deprivation in the empire is written out of this version of history. The lack of institutional memory and appreciation of Britain's imperial past has shaped official responses to the rights of these 'Windrush' migrants. It is hard to think of an example of a policy failing so closely tied to a lack of historical insight and understanding: in essence it is a failure of institutional memory about the sort of place that Britain used to have in the world, the kind of nationalism that used to animate the Empire-Commonwealth. Its erasure and replacement by something else has had grievous effects on the lives of thousands of people.

What do we gain by seeing the Windrush episode in the same frame as the wider discourse on migration and refugees? It might be argued that these are two sides of the same coin. It is noticeable that right-wing papers such as the *Daily Mail* and *The Telegraph* were in the forefront of celebrating the Windrush heroes and calling for the heads of the politicians who had wronged them. How can we square this paradox? Just as the deserving poor of the nineteenth century were separated out from their less deserving cousins, we might also be wary of the designation of 'deserving migrants' and the multi-tier system which singles out (and, it is implied, should therefore reward) those who have integrated and become British, while at the same time vilifying the poor, male, and often Muslim bodies – unnamed, unknown and collectively stigmatized and represented collectively, beyond individualization. Histories of migration tell us that these are false dichotomies – as much as *citizenship* is a binary issue (you either have it or you don't) – the reality of lived and felt *nationalism* is far more tricky and amorphous, developing over time, held by some and not others, malleable and slow-burning. An unspoken, imperial paternalism hovers over this discourse, suggesting that those who were 'loyal' imperial citizens – and therefore had a subjectivity anchored closer to home – are more deserving of widespread public indignation. Yet this is a misreading of much more contested and more complex imperial, and global, relations.

During and since the Brexit campaign, white and non-white migrants and refugees have been confused and sometimes fused in the public mind. The lines of race intersect with other identities: of language, class and religion. Britain is not in any way post-racial as some have suggested, but the lines of race are complicated by generational moments of arrival, beliefs about connection to Britain and Britishness (and claims on this) and cultural assumptions of belonging, distance and difference. This leads to hierarchies and pecking orders between migrants themselves – for instance, in the discrimination against *freshies* (new arrivals to Britain) from settled South Asian communities.[15] Older migrants can be among the first to challenge the legitimacy of newcomers, especially as they are also often living in close physical proximity. The will to pull up the drawbridge to further incomers can be as pronounced among second and third generations of migrants as anyone else, as evidenced in the prominent role in anti-migration debates by Conservative MPs of South Asian background, such as Priti Patel and Sajid Javid.

Nationalism is by design a force that defines insiders and outsiders, in-groups and out-groups. It draws lines in the sand and circles around who belongs in the nation and who doesn't. This has never been a straightforward process, and the questions of who creates and defines the nation – and how this is achieved – are always fluid and contested. The place of race, ethnicity, language and generational belonging in this are not easily captured by statistics or opinion polls. Yet it seems difficult to deny that there has been an upsurge of nativist nationalism in Britain and that this has been a powerful force driving Brexit. Sometimes this has been a British nationalism, sometimes an English. Sometimes it has looked back nostalgically to a whiter past, sometimes it has been grounded in other compulsions. But all varieties of nationalism draw tighter circles, and emphasize some form of exclusion, otherness and difference between 'us' and 'them'. The only real question about nationalism is where this feeling originates: is it tapping into deeply rooted primordial beliefs, or more cynically managed and manipulated from on high? The 'others' in Britain these days may signify EU bureaucrats, black and Asian British citizens, refugees from Syria or migrant workers from Eastern Europe. The zones of exclusion and otherness are drawn differently in different contexts and by different actors. Some would exclude the EU but look nostalgically to a shared Commonwealth identity for instance, or say that it's fine to bestow Britishness on deserving Windrush migrants, retrospectively, when they have worked and lived in the country for half a century. But underlying all these assumptions and political postures is an emphasis on a truly British/English core, never fully defined or known, apart from in opposition to its other, which is often (though not always) non-white. It is the nature of nationalism that it can't be easily pinned down or explained by opinion polls – it is inherently shifting and nebulous. Historical narratives are vital for either underpinning nationalist tropes or myth-busting some of the assumptions that they are based upon. And it is only through a more complex understanding of nationalism, that the differences between people can be complicated, understood and ultimately overturned.

Notes

1 In the year or so before the EU referendum, between June 2015 and June 2016, immigration was consistently named as the most salient issue facing the country, peaking at 56 per cent in September 2015. http://migrationobservatory.ox.ac.uk/
2 Judge's sentencing remarks republished by BBC news online, 23 November 2016.
3 Jon Burnett, 'Racial violence and the Brexit state' *Race and Class* 58, no. 4 (2017): 85–97.
4 'Over 10,500 refugees resettled in the UK under flagship scheme', 22 February 2018, https://www.gov.uk/government/news/over-10000-refugees-resettled-in-the-uk-under-flagship-scheme
5 The *Daily Mail* (17 November 2015).
6 Ryan Grenoble, 'This Daily Mail anti-refugee cartoon is straight out of Nazi Germany', *Huffington Post* (17 November 2015).
7 'Rats: the history of an incendiary cartoon trope' *The Guardian* (18 November 2015).
8 *The Guardian* (25 September 2017).
9 James Ker-Lindsay, 'Turkey's EU accession as a factor in the 2016 Brexit referendum', *Turkish Studies* 19, no. 1 (2018): 1–22.
10 'Letter to the Prime Minister and Foreign Secretary: Getting the facts clear on Turkey', Voteleavetakecontrol.org, 16 June 2016.
11 Marilyn Barber and Murray Watson, *Invisible Immigrants: the English in Canada Since 1945* (University of Manitoba Press, 2015): chapter 1.
12 The National Audit Office, 'The Handling of the Windrush Situation', report published 5 December 2018.
13 Kennetta Hammond Perry, *London is the Place for Me: Black Britons, Citizenship, and the Politics of Race* (New York: Oxford University Press, 2015). See also David Olusoga, 'The Windrush Story was not a rosy one even before the ship arrived,' *The Guardian* (22 April 2018).

14 Kennetta Hammond Perry, 'Undoing the Work of the Windrush Narrative', *History Workshop Online*, 11 September 2018.

15 Katharine Charsley and Marta Bolognani, 'Being a freshie is (not) cool: stigma, capital and disgust in British Pakistani stereotypes of new subcontinental migrants' *Ethnic And Racial Studies* 40, no. 1 (2017): 43–62.

Chapter 11
Rhodes Must Fall, Brexit, and Circuits of Knowledge and Influence

Saul Dubow

If you visit the University of Cape Town (UCT) by foot, you will walk up from the Woolsack, designed as a holiday cottage by the great imperial and colonial architect Herbert Baker, and built for Rudyard Kipling's summer holidays on the instructions of Cecil John Rhodes. Further up you pass a plinth which was, until 2015, topped by the statue of Rhodes brooding northwards and downwards over the Cape Flats towards the African hinterland. From the site of the plinth you proceed up a broad avenue of stairs, still known as Jammie Steps, where generations of students have hung out, and from there up towards Jameson Hall, now Memorial Hall, soon to be renamed Sarah Baartman Hall. This was named after Leander Starr Jameson, leader of the failed plot to overthrow Kruger in 1895–96, the notorious event that occasioned Rhodes' public fall from grace and loss of prime ministerial office. Further up the mountain slopes with Devil's Peak in the background, a track leads to Rhodes Memorial. This deeply coded temple of memory was also designed by Herbert Baker. It features a bronze statue of a horseman, *Physical Energy* by George Frederic Watts, the noted Victorian symbolist sculptor. As Norman Etherington shrewdly points out, this complex, inspired by the Temple of Zeus at Pergamon, was designed to project imperial power in such a way that it emerged organically out of its majestic natural surroundings in order to root whites *in* Africa. Rhodes Memorial 'falsely asserts that the white man was no intruder but belonged to the landscape'. Rhodes himself 'liked that idea'.[1]

Attempts to decolonize UCT's physical environment from contamination by Rhodes and his pals is an incomplete revolution. Rhodes' statue in the public gardens remains, notwithstanding traces of an angle grinder on his ankle;

highways are still named after him; as is a university, and a small village. Part of the reason for this is that the statue of Rhodes was only ever a proximate trigger point in a much wider student movement that has now turned its attentions to even greater injustices. Just as Rhodes was despised, discredited – and then mostly ignored by the first decades of the twentieth century – so the broad imprint of Rhodes remains mostly intact, while the hurricane moves on. As psychologist Sally Swartz puts it, Rhodes had long been 'lived with, partly seen, partly made invisible by the magic of dissociation, as we walked, rode or drove by'.[2] The power of targeting Rhodes' statue rendered him a unifying symbol of opposition; but with the removal of the statue, the protests themselves fragmented into multiple competing demands.

It is generally agreed that the Fallist movement began in March 2015 when a UCT student, Chumani Maxwele, covered Rhodes' statue in human faeces.[3] I happened to be present at the University of the Witwatersrand giving a research seminar in October on the subject of race when the campus exploded uncertainly into protest. Uncertain because for some time it was unclear precisely what the protestors wanted. Or who they represented. This 'leaderless revolution' was in part a deliberate tactic but it put even sympathetic vice chancellors in an impossible position.[4] The Economic Freedom Fighters, led by populist politician Julius Malema and with national representation in the South African parliament, exerted some influence at Wits but was never a controlling one. At first the protest was largely peaceful, albeit tense, and leaders either refused to identify themselves or to meet with the university authorities. When the protests arrived at Stellenbosch, these focused on the continuing use of Afrikaans, once the sole medium of instruction, and on broader issues of inclusivity.

The focus of the protests in South Africa differed markedly from campus to campus. Soon they transmuted into different forms of 'Fallism' as well as a high level of violence, some of it nihilistic. The proximate cause here was the rise in university tuition fees announced in October 2015. Protests against unacceptable fees morphed into calls to impose a cap on inflationary rises and then to demands for free, decolonized, tuition. 'Fees must Fall' eventually triumphed amidst considerable campus desecration and destruction, with a government announcement that university tuition fees would indeed end – but without any provisions for additional state funding (a situation that has since clarified). This was a most cynical response by the Zuma government, all too happy to watch left-liberal universities take the heat for generational anger and frustrations about the absence of full-scale 'transformation' in post-apartheid South Africa.

At UCT, the RMF movement transmuted – or fragmented – into campaigns around pan-Africanism, intersectionality, hegemonic masculinity and gender violence. There was a great deal of idealism and innovative progressive thinking which imagined emancipation – personal as well as collective – in strikingly new, often creative, ways. Material and bodily expressions of anger like the erection of

'Shackville' at UCT as well as a series of 'naked protests' extended the repertoire of rejection. Yet there was unmistakable tension between the impulse to destroy in order to build again on uncontaminated decolonized foundations, and constant demands for concessions and subsidies from tertiary institutions whose foundations and funding models were already visibly shaky. The student uprising – for this is what it had become by 2016 – gathered strength from the Black Lives Matter movement in the United States. A powerful rhetoric of bodily and psychic black 'pain' now came to frame the protests in which the language of collective 'trauma' and 'dehumanization' became ubiquitous. This was new and notably different in tone from the defiant and often masculinist Black Consciousness movement of the 1970s, led by Steve Biko, to which it often referred.[5] So, too, was the language of coloniality and decoloniality – subjective terms rich in affect and often expressive of deep alienation.[6]

Try as one might, it is very difficult to scrutinize coloniality in the same way that historians have looked at concepts like colonialism, imperialism and decolonization, namely, as objects of investigation with more or less recognized temporal and spatial boundaries, with discernible and contestable political logics, and as discursive practices inviting rigorous textual readings. If decolonizing the curriculum means expanding reading lists so as to include hitherto ignored voices and thereby shift the terms of academic debate, this can only be a positive development; but if it amounts to a contraction of conversation and replication in the academic sphere of the sorts of self-selection and confirmation bias so evident in social media feeds, the risk is that it may become highly restrictive. Achille Mbembe, quoting Fanon, issues a powerful warning against 'decolonization-as-Africanization'.[7]

There seems to be a profoundly existential aspect to the idea of coloniality that is unimpressed by and indeed resistant to historical analysis. This is one reason why historians who debate issues of public memorials (one thinks of the recent collection titled *Dethroning Historical Reputations* put out by the Institute of Historical Research in London where 'Rhodes Must Fall' (RMF) figures prominently) have little or no relevance to many activists.[8] Mutual incommensurability of paradigms is as true of the debates around historical legacy and decoloniality, as it is in respect of Brexit where antagonists no longer hear each other and where advocates of fundamental change outbid each other in their appeals to purity.

As a historian of ideas, it is difficult to make sense of all of this. One might conceivably chart the wave of protests starting with Rhodes Must Fall at UCT to Oxford and beyond. It is also possible to track influences radiating outwards from Cape Town to Charlottesville. But the profound differences in context between Cape Town, Oxford and Charlottesville confound easy analogies. There was little opposition to Rhodes' removal at UCT, quite a bit at Oriel College, Oxford (which ultimately decided not to take its statue down), and a very real neo-Confederate presence in Charlottesville standing by the statue of Robert E. Lee.

Nor is it easy to discern victories. In the case of 'fees must fall', the Zuma government cynically acceded to demands for free education. But by making no provision for further funding of universities, it simply ducked the problem – leading many to wonder what the future of university education in South Africa might be.[9] There are legitimate fears that the tertiary education system in South Africa could buckle under the twin demands for free and decolonized tuition, coupled with the pressures to 'in-source' previously 'outsourced' services and to 'decommodify' higher education. Oxford, Cambridge, Yale and Princeton are better placed to survive: the challenge for these wealthy institutions is not existential.

Attempts to trace the intellectual influences of the Fallist and associated social movements are very tricky. I have tried to do so in the case of 'decolonizing' but so far without much success. US and Latin American activist-intellectuals such as Peruvian sociologist Aníbal Quijano, Colombian anthropologist Arturo Escobar, or Argentine theorist Walter Mignolo are much cited in South Africa, but often out of context and frequently to the exclusion of African thinkers whose ideas would seem to me to be more pertinent.[10] One of the paradoxes here is that scholars and intellectuals in South Africa who call for decolonization of the curriculum and eschew euro-centricity, are apt to defer to the authority of fashionable theorists from the north and to overlook local traditions of scholarship in doing so. This is a point made by intellectuals with early sympathies towards Fallist movement such as Achille Mbembe and Xolela Mangcu who have since complained that student radicals are not sufficiently prepared to do the hard critical reading in recovering the work of thinkers like Biko and Fanon whom they endlessly quote.[11]

As a student of global intellectual history, I have been much absorbed in tracing circuits and mutual influences in constellations of ideas such as Darwinian evolution, eugenics, and human rights. It is challenging work. But in the age of social media, it is so much more difficult to discern the signal from the noise. In the case of Darwinism, for instance, it is possible to chart influences through journals, newspapers and correspondence. We have a rough and ready methodology to deal with what I like to call 'messy' intellectual history, and some rudimentary but well-tried theoretical tools to assist. At the height of the controversy over AIDS denialism in South Africa, at the start of the twenty-first century, it became clear that South African president Thabo Mbeki and others were unable to discern medical truth from fiction, partly because of undifferentiated over-reliance on dissident sites that popped up on the web. A widely circulated denialist monograph called 'Castro Hlongwane', likely to have been penned by Mbeki in 2002, shows the aetiology of his thinking (or rationalization) precisely because it is presented in academic form with footnotes. It is therefore possible to show how he was influenced, and by whom.[12] This is more difficult to accomplish in the new world of Tweets and Facebook.

Typically, historians of global intellectual history focus on flows and blockages, alight on examples of mutual exchange, and are sensitive to the interactions between so-called imperial and indigenous knowledge systems. In principle the same techniques could be deployed to examine social movements like Fallism; in practice the project proves elusive. Separating these entangled histories is not easy. Perspective and distance will eventually come to our aid and the publication of memoirs featuring activists in the Fallist movement is beginning to bring some clarity.[13]

Intertwined connections of influence, relying heavily on the crossover from social to mainstream media, are also a feature of the radical right. These too are difficult to unpick, in part because they increasingly eschew traditional forms of political organization, preferring pop-up rallies and free-floating foci like Britain's Tommy Robinson. But there are moments when the circuits of influence *can* be clearly demonstrated.

In August 2018, Donald Trump tweeted about the 'large scale killing of farmers' in South Africa, echoing Fox News presenter Tucker Carlson's stories on this theme. The story played large in South Africa amidst the politics of compulsory redistribution of land. A brilliant exposé by Jason Wilson traces how a largely unfounded but persistent far-right rumour about imperilled white farmers moved from the margins into the realms of mainstream news. As Wilson points out, fears of white genocide in Rhodesia and South Africa have been a long-standing radical right trope. A South African website, 'Suiderlanders.org', describing itself as 'an emergency plan initiative officially founded in 2006 to prepare a Protestant Christian South African Minority for a coming violent revolution', has been preparing the ground. Suiderlander's Simon Roche travelled extensively in the United States in 2017, propagating stories about land confiscation and ethnic cleansing. British journalist and agitator Katie Hopkins contributed to the fear-mongering by means of a news documentary. The story was picked up by NewsCorp papers in Australia from March 2018 and given airtime by talk radio host Michael Savage. From here, NewsCorp outlets in the United States picked up the baton, which was then grabbed by Trump and mainlined to Twitter.[14]

Without seeking to equate white survivalist fantasists with Fallist movements on the decolonizing left, it is nevertheless worthwhile pointing out family resemblances in the ways in which radical ideas travel underground, gain political traction, and acquire measures of legitimacy in the internet age. For historians of ideas, curious about the ways in which concepts move between metropoles and peripheries, these bifurcated rings of influence offer instructive examples. As ever, they have precedents. From the 1960s, radical right intellectual networks grouped together through the pseudo-academic journal *Mankind Quarterly* linked eugenicists in America, Britain and South Africa in a shared campaign to defend white supremacy against liberal egalitarianism.[15] *Mankind Quarterly* was shunned by the vast majority of university libraries and by the 'liberal elite' it was so viscerally opposed to. But their ideas and preoccupations never quite went away. The new world of social media has provided instant means of propagating ideas, without even the self-imposed restraints of a journal like *Mankind Quarterly* that meticulously mimics the forms of academic debate: footnotes, attributions and structured discussion.

In the case of Brexit, there is evidence that agencies and networks of influence have gained strength and experience by working transnationally to effect upwellings of nativist nationalisms. The speed and intensity of social media have facilitated opinion-making in new ways. Influence-peddling corporations have proved adept at exploiting these possibilities.

Allegations that Cambridge Analytica's data mining relationship with Facebook may have had an undue effect on the Brexit vote and on Trump's election victory are very well known. Less well appreciated is the extent to which the abuse of democratic practices in Britain and America form part of a broader global pattern. Here, again, South Africa figures as a centre of calculation and manipulation, building on its established place in the British imaginary over some two hundred years. Here too, circuits of capital, ideas and personnel tell us much about the insidious nature of colonialism and post-colonialism. Consider three recent examples of corporate entanglement and ideological influence.

First, Bell Pottinger. This public relations firm founded by Mrs Thatcher's famous PR man, Tim Bell, collapsed in 2017 after it emerged that the company had taken on a lucrative contract in South Africa with the Gupta family, brokered through a corporate entity under their control known as 'Oakbay Investments'. The Guptas, small-time entrepreneurs who arrived in South Africa from India in the 1990s, soon formed a corrupt relationship with President Jacob Zuma and together became involved in a programme of 'state capture', that is to say, wholescale larceny of the fiscus and concerted takeover of key sectors of the state. It was Bell Pottinger that secretly devised the corrosive idea of 'white monopoly capital' – a deliberately mendacious faux Marxisant slogan that was ruthlessly deployed by Zuma's supporters to allow them to cover up their own malfeasance with a toxic spray of populist anti-white racism. Bell Pottinger was implicated in attacks on journalists critical of Zuma and the Guptas (the 'Zuptas') as well as assisting an organization styling itself 'Black First Land First' and giving voice to a chorus of ranting Twitter accounts and fake 'bots'.[16]

Chris Geoghegan, a former top executive at the defence company BAE Systems, was responsible for introducing the Guptas to Bell Pottinger in January 2016. He also inserted his daughter Victoria to front up the destabilizing racist campaign. She supplied Zuma's son Duduzane (currently on trial for corruption and culpable homicide) with helpful populist slogans and seems also to have been instrumental in targeting Johann Rupert, one of South Africa's wealthiest businessman, as the exemplar of white monopoly capital (this, notwithstanding the fact that Rupert's Swiss luxury goods company, Richemont, was an established Bell Pottinger client).[17] Bell Pottinger collapsed into administration in September 2017 amidst recriminations between Tim Bell and CEO James Henderson and protests in South Africa – including the hashtag #bellpottingermustfall. The company's demise was not because Bell Pottinger was unprofitable – the firm did good business working for despots around the world – but rather as a result of its losing high-profile corporate clients and bringing into disrepute an international PR industry not always known for high ethical standards. In the wake of Bell Pottinger's collapse there has also been a string of high-level resignations from accountancy firm KPMG which was responsible for auditing the Gupta accounts. Police and judicial investigations continue to unearth dirt.[18]

Second, Cambridge Analytica. In addition to its notorious harvesting of Facebook data to manipulate the Brexit and Trump elections, secretly recorded interviews with the defunct company's founder, Alexander Nix, have shown him and business associate Mark Turnbull boasting of his company's role in manipulating dozens of elections elsewhere in the world – often in ex-colonial countries in Africa and the Caribbean. The highly divisive and violent election campaigns in Kenya in 2013 and 2017 are prominent examples. Ghana, Nigeria and a host of other countries were mentioned by Mark Turnbull, previously a Bell Pottinger executive, as examples of countries where Cambridge Analytica 'ghosted in and ghosted out'. Cambridge Analytica honed its techniques in politically fragile African, Asian and Latin American countries around the world before deploying these dark arts back in Brexit Britain.[19] The cynical and arrogant manner in which Nix worked is tellingly indicated by the offensive racial language he used in emails referring to Barbadian political leaders who spurned his offer to manage their election campaigns in 2010.[20]

Finally, Vote Leave and Arron Banks, whose links to UKIP, Cambridge Analytica and Russian money are now subject to intensive journalistic and criminal inquiry. Channel 4's investigative journalism, supplemented by work done by the *Daily Maverick*, has found a significant South African connection. In this case, it seems probable that the source of Banks' funds may have Russian origins and that some of this hot money may be connected with a mysterious diamond mine owned by Banks in Lesotho and situated in an area that no geologist considers capable of producing diamonds – let alone the handful of high-quality gems which Banks has assayed. Banks' southern African connections are now well known. He has also been closely associated in his endeavours with James Pryor, a louche South African born adviser to Margaret Thatcher and F. W. De Klerk, as well as a 'U-Kipper' described by Banks in his autobiography as his 'fixer in Africa'. *Daily Maverick* journalist Marianne Thamm draws this very plausible conclusion: 'This is a new breed of economic mercenaries who destabilize democracy not with guns or military hardware but using data, the internet and good old bribery and corruption.'[21]

Rhodes Must Fall and Brexit have no direct connections but there are uncommon contexts and associations. Both bear familial resemblances and are manifestations of the populist politics of anger and disruption. In both cases empire and colonialism figure prominently. Superficial resemblances between the South African and international echoes of the Fallist campaigns have to be unpicked very carefully. Tracing the circuits of knowledge around Fallism and decoloniality is perilously difficult, but they are becoming clearer as participants reflect on this moment in books and memoirs. These concepts are not necessarily subject to the same kinds of logic that we might apply to other historical ideas, partly because questioning is apt to be couched in the language of identity politics such as positionality, gender, race and power.

Also post-modern, perhaps post-factum, and certainly post-colonial, are the networks of power and influence that link Brexit and Trump with shadowy networks in Russia – and countries like South Africa. Here again we may see evidence of how experimentation on the global periphery rebounds on the centre, having already done an awful lot of direct harm in the case of the Guptas and State Capture.

In keeping with their cavalier blustering there is now ample evidence that the Bankses and the Nixes have been highly effective in using shadowy networks, brokered through London, to wreak havoc around the world. They have progenitors. Recall Mark Thatcher's attempted coup in Equatorial Guinea which he plotted with Simon Mann from his base in the affluent Cape Town mink and manure suburb of Constantia. Jeffrey Archer and Tim Bell were implicated then. The Guptas bought Thatcher's home after his arrest in 2004.

Decolonizing Africa has played host to other derring-do escapades and interventions, including by David Stirling, founder of the Special Air Service (SAS), who created the Capricorn African Society that promoted multi-racialism in Zambia and Rhodesia. He later formed a secretive mercenary agency, Watchguard International, which became involved in security operations in Africa and the Middle East. Motivated in part by a desire to restore British power in the post-war world, Stirling moved freely in right-wing establishment circles. He was, on balance, a well-intentioned British patriot and he was undoubtedly a war hero, but his modes of operation were recognizably colonial and thoroughly Henty-esque. By contrast, Bell Pottinger's Henderson, Cambridge Analytica's Alexander Nix, and Aaron Banks' shadowy band have more the feel of Harry Flashman.

This post-colonial bunch of bad boys bears some lineal resemblance to high imperialist heroes such as Cecil Rhodes who, along with other Randlords and political outriders like Leander Starr Jameson, behaved ruthlessly as plundering robber barons in Southern Africa. In the late nineteenth century, they built up fortunes when imperial controls were weak, the power of the City of London was untrammelled by regulation, and the Union of South Africa had yet to be born as a unitary state. Before them were the Clives of India and Raffles of Singapore. By the start of the twentieth century, such permissive conditions underwent marked tightening, a result of state-formation in South Africa and the consolidation of the imperial 'pax Britannica' more generally. It so happens the Randlords chose to invest much of their wealth into good causes, such as universities, art galleries and museums, at a time when it was fashionable to turn mining into social capital. This is no longer the case. But it does mean that, a century on, we continue to live with Rhodes' vaunting ambition and complex legacy: now transmuted into calls to decolonize on the one hand, and to flying the flag of 'Global Britain' on the other.

Notes

1. N. Etherington, *Imperium of the Soul. The Political and Aesthetic Imagination of Edwardian Imperialists* (Manchester: Manchester University Press, 2017): 95.
2. S. Swartz, *Ruthless Winnicott: The Role of Ruthlessness in Psychoanalysis and Political Protest* (New York: Routledge, 2019): 101.
3. On Maxwele's motivations, see F. B. Nyamnjoh, *#Rhodes Must Fall: Nibbling at Resilient Colonialism in South Africa* (Bamenda, Cameroon: Langaa, Research & Publishing, 2016), 72–3, 82–3.
4. See e.g. Jonathan Jansen, *As By Fire: The End Of The South African University* (Cape Town: Tafelberg, 2017).
5. *#Hashtag: An Analysis of the #FeesMustFall Movement at South African universities*, ed. Malose Langa, 2017, https://csvr.org.za/pdf/An-analysis-of-the-FeesMustFall-Movement-at-South-African-universities.pdf, 40.
6. Anye Nyamnjoh, The Phenomenology of *Rhodes Must Fall*: Student activism and the experience of alienation at the University of Cape Town', *Strategic Review for Southern Africa* 39, no. 1 (2017): 256–77; Sabelo J. Ndlovu-Gatsheni, 'Decoloniality as the Future of Africa', *History Compass* 13, 10 (2015): 485–96.
7. Achille Mbembe, 'Decolonizing Knowledge and the Question of the Archive' [n.d.], https://wiser.wits.ac.za/. . ./Achille%20Mbembe%20-%20Decolonizing%20 Knowledge . . .
8. J. Pellew and L. Goldman (eds), *Dethroning Historical Reputations: Universities, Museums and the Commemoration of Benefactors* (London: Institute of Historical Research, 2018).
9. For a useful survey of the problems facing South African universities see Andy Carolin, 'The Uncertain Future of the South African University', *Journal of Southern African Studies* (online, 2018, DOI: 10.1080/03057070.2018.1506418).
10. Sabelo J. Ndlovu-Gatsheni, *Coloniality of Power in Postcolonial Africa: Myths of Decolonization* (Dakar: Codesria, 2013): viii-ix.
11. Joel Modiri, 'In the Fall: Decolonisation and the rejuvenation of the academic project in South Africa', *Daily Maverick* (16 October 2016), https://www.dailymaverick.co.za/opinionista/2016-10-16-in-the-fall-decolonisation-and-the-rejuvenation-of-the-academic-project-in-south-africa/

12 M. Gevisser, *Thabo Mbeki: The Dream Deferred* (Johannesburg: Jonathan Ball, 2007): 736, 749.

13 See e.g., the collection collectively put together by Roseanne Chantiluke, Brian Kwoba and Athinangamoso Nkopo, *Rhodes Must Fall: The Struggle to Decolonise the Racist Heart of Empire* (London: Zed Books, 2018).

14 Jason Wilson, 'White farmers: how a far-right idea was planted in Donald Trump's mind', *The Guardian* (24 August 2018), https://suidlanders.org/who-we-are/; see also Camilla Schofield's chapter, 'Brexit and the Other Special Relationship' in this volume.

15 S. Dubow, 'Racial Irredentism, Ethnogenesis, and White Supremacy in High-Apartheid South Africa', *Kronos* 41, no. 1 (2015): 236–64.

16 Bell Pottinger – FOI Material – FOI 0870-17, https://www.gov.uk/government/publications/foi-release-bell-pottinger-south-africa; Ed Caesar, 'The Reputation-Laundering Firm that Ruined its own Reputation', *The New Yorker* (25 June 2018).

17 amaBhungane and Scorpio, '#Guptaleaks: Bell Pottinger – spinner of a web for 'pioneers of economic transformation', 1 June 2017, https://www.dailymaverick.co.za/article/2017-06-01-amabhungane-and-scorpio-guptaleaks-bell-pottinger-spinner-of-a-web-for-pioneers-of-economic-transformation/#.WTeZoCOlCHs

18 Mark Sweney, 'Bell Pottinger: father of executive at centre of scandal quits Rentokil board', 18 September 2017, https://www.theguardian.com/business/2017/sep/18/bell-pottinger-scandal-rentokil-chris-geoghegan-gupta-family

19 'SCL influence in foreign elections', https://publications.parliament.uk/pa/cm201719/cmselect/cmcumeds/363/36309.htm

20 Juliette Garside and Hilary Osborne, 'Former Cambridge Analytica chief used N-word to describe Barbados PM', *The Guardian* (8 October 2018), https://www.theguardian.com/uk-news/2018/oct/08/former-cambridge-analytica-chief-alexander-nix-used-n-word-to-describe-barbados-pm

21 J. J. Patrick, 'Leave.EU's diamond in the rough', *Byline* (9 May 2017), https://www.byline.com/column/67/article/1643; Marianne Thamm, 'From South Africa with love: Arron Banks, Brexit, the Russians and the SA connection', *Daily Maverick* (24 July 2018) https://www.dailymaverick.co.za/article/2018-07-24-from-south-africa-with-love-arron-banks-brexit-the-russians-and-the-sa-connection/

Chapter 12
Relics of Empire? Colonialism and the Culture Wars

Katie Donington

'Too much Hampstead and not enough Hull' was how the former Labour MP Andy Burnham characterized the cultural identity of the Remain campaign in 2016.[1] The divisions within society which the Brexit result exposed have been attributed to differences in class, age, education, geography, ethnicity and nationalism. Cultural identity has formed a key site of contestation demarcating the so-called metropolitan liberal elites of Hampstead from the common-folk of Hull. The citizens of nowhere, with their embrace of globalization and multiculturalism, have been pitted against the earthy rootedness of the citizens of somewhere, those native tribes who have been displaced and discarded by a political class which has 'more in common with international elites than with the people down the road'.[2] The rise of a nativist populism expressed in both the vote for Brexit and across the Atlantic in the election of Donald Trump, has manifested itself culturally in what historian David Olusoga as termed a series of 'history wars'.[3] Debates over the national narrative and the meaning(s) of its signs and symbols have long been a way of delineating who can stake a claim to belong, and who will be accepted as belonging. The cultural battle lines have been drawn in relation to histories of slavery and empire, highlighting the racial fault lines which have long existed within both societies. In America this issue reached a tragic nadir in the summer of 2017 following a prolonged and vitriolic public debate over the proposed removal of the statue of Confederate leader Robert E. Lee from Emancipation Park (formerly Lee Park) in Virginia. Following a 'Unite the right' rally which took place in Charlottesville on 11–12 August, the anti-racist activist Heather Heyer was murdered by a white supremacist. In the following days, President Trump gave a speech at a rally in Phoenix in which he told the crowds that 'they are trying to take away our history and our heritage'.[4] The question of whose history and whose heritage forms the collective 'our' is central to an understanding of the exclusionary politics of who is inside and outside of the President's vision of the nation.

As the previous chapter has shown in the case of Cecil Rhodes, public debate in Britain has focused on a variety of figures with links to both slavery and empire – Rhodes himself, but also a range of others including Edward Colston, Admiral Horatio Nelson and Winston Churchill. These iconic figures represent the kind of buccaneering imperial nationalism that Brexiteers have invoked as part of their vision of a reinvigorated 'Global Britain'. There has, however, been a growing move to challenge this interpretation of history. Calls have been made by a variety of groups to remove or recontextualize the physical legacies – statues, street names, buildings – that shape a public understanding of both these men and the histories that they represent. Campaign groups like Countering Colston in Bristol and Rhodes Must Fall in Oxford, have demanded that the brutality of colonialism be re-centred in the stories we tell about the imperial past. These contestations raise uncomfortable questions for contemporary society regarding the ways in which empire benefitted different local communities, and indeed the nation as a whole, both then and now. They pose a challenge to the idea that only those directly involved with the imperial project were enriched by it. These visible markers of British imperialism are a continued source of tension in part because they serve as a tangible reminder of the continuity of privilege, persisting forms of inequality, and the limits of local and national belonging.

Attempts to shift the narrative have met with entrenched resistance from those who view the critique as a frontal assault on British national identity. When the journalist Afua Hirsch wrote an article linking Nelson's Column to the debates about the removal of white supremacist statues in America, she was met with a barrage of racial and misogynistic abuse.[5] In an article written by Stephen Glover for the *Daily Mail*, he framed her as a thankless immigrant asking 'Couldn't she summon a smidgen of gratitude for the institutions that have nurtured her?'[6] The story was picked up by almost every national newspaper. In an echo of Trump's statement at the rally in Phoenix, the *Daily Express* included a quote from an irate teacher who claimed that 'This makes me rather angry. These Left-wingers should grow up. They want to do away with our heritage.'[7] The conflation of historical critique with historical destruction is demonstrative of a worrying impulse to shut down discussion – a move to 'silence the past' in the words of Michel-Rolph Trouillot.[8]

The removal (or not) of individual statues is perhaps less important than the public dialogue that has emerged around the place of empire in the history of Britain. This is a necessary conversation and one which is long overdue. Brexit has been framed around the notion of imperial nostalgia, but arguably it is also indicative of a deep imperial amnesia. The history of empire is not a mandatory part of the national curriculum in schools, nor are there any public history institutions which deal explicitly with this history. This lacuna has allowed for the geographic distance of empire to be compounded by a distancing of the mind. This has led to a mythologization of Britain as standing alone against the world – a sturdy little ship on the global waters. Britain however, as Gurminder Bhambra reminds us, 'has not been an independent country, but part of broader political entities; most significantly empire, then the Commonwealth and, from 1973, the European Union. There has been no independent Britain, no "Island nation".'[9] In an interview during the by-election in Sleaford in 2016, journalist John Harris asked a pro-Brexit voter why she had made that decision. Her reply was that 'I think it's better to come out . . . we've stood on our own in the past, and I think we can do it again.'[10] The ability to perceive Britain's history as one of splendid isolation and ethnic homogeneity, requires the forgetting, or active suppression of the memory of empire.

Brexiteers have been characterized as harbouring a nostalgic longing for an imagined past, one in which the Empire is both recalled and suppressed at different times and in different ways. As Charlotte Lydia Riley has noted:

> The vote to leave the European Union was framed by many as going 'back' to some moment of mythical British power. The paradox of plucky little Britain, standing alone against the bureaucratic monolith of Europe, yet backed up by a vast imperial network (now repackaged as a Commonwealth of equals), pervades politics, media and culture.[11]

There are multiple frameworks for understanding the concept of nostalgia but perhaps the most pertinent is Svetlana Boym's notion of 'restorative nostalgia'.[12] She argues that 'restorative nostalgia stresses *nóstos* (home) and attempts a transhistorical reconstruction of the lost home . . . Restorative nostalgia does not think of itself as nostalgia, but rather as truth and tradition . . . restorative nostalgia returns and rebuilds one's homeland with paranoid determination'. This sense of nostalgia can be read clearly in the cultural policies of the European project's greatest detractor – the United Kingdom Independence Party (UKIP). In 2010 UKIP published a document entitled 'Restoring Britishness' which outlined their vision of British cultural identity.[13] The language of threat and loss was threaded through the document – a manifestation of the paranoia that Boym sees as a definitive hallmark of restorative nostalgia. The title immediately indicated to the reader that the nation has somehow been lost and must be restored to its former self. The issue of just when exactly it was lost and to whom it should be restored raises precisely the same questions as Trump's use of the slogan 'Make America Great Again'. The opening sentence wasted no time in driving this message home. It stated 'Britain and Britishness are in trouble. They are being attacked and undermined, both externally and internally.' British national identity was presented as imperilled and in need of saving from multiple threats including the European Union, cultural Marxism, the liberal elite, political correctness, devolution, globalization, multiculturalism and in particular Islamicization.

The relationship between history, culture and the construction of national identity was a central concern of the document. It decried the undermining of patriotism citing 'an uncharitable reading of British history' which has 'led many to conclude that Britain is a country undeserving of affection and loyalty'. The nation's history of slavery and colonialism was identified as being 'deliberately used to undermine Britishness'. Instead emphasis was placed on the need to present an uncritical national narrative, with the text arguing that the teaching of empire in schools would be 'improved' if it was done in a way which 'celebrates its achievements in terms of democracy, freedom and trade'. Unshackled from the burden of grappling with colonial violence and exploitation, the British Empire could instead be restored to a nineteenth century understanding.

Recognizing the importance of public history in shaping a popular understanding of the past, the manifesto asserted that UKIP would establish a national collection to 'celebrate British and Commonwealth achievements, heritage and legacy'. Suggested sub-sets of the collection included aviation, maritime, transport and manufacturing. In a move which recalled both the Great Exhibition of 1851 and the later Empire Exhibitions of the early twentieth century, UKIP argued for the establishment of a 'Best of British' exhibition which would 'illustrate in an educational matter of fact (not jingoistic) way the contribution inhabitants of the British Isles have made to the world'. The Royal Naval College at Greenwich would be transformed into a new Commonwealth Institute replete with 'a major exhibition of the Commonwealth and its history, including suitable historic ships'. This maritimization of the history of commerce and colonization has been identified by John Beech as a common interpretative strategy for the repackaging of slavery heritage for cultural consumption.[14] Harking back to a sense of British national identity anchored to what historian Kathleen Wilson has described as 'the empire of the seas', the proposed exhibition drew on a romanticized notion of the island race.[15] The centrality of seafaring within Brexiteers' construction of national culture and identity could be read in the deployment of the 'Brexit Flotilla' in 2016, as well as the ongoing politicization of the contestations over Britain's fishing fleets.

The interventions made by the cultural policy document were based on UKIP's unabashed desire to instil what they describe as 'uniculturalism'. It is vital, they have argued, that 'all UK citizens must learn a common history and draw from a unified heritage'. But who gets to decide what the single interpretive framework is? In a Britain in which the descendants of the formerly colonized live and learn alongside the descendants of the former colonizers, indeed when some peoples' heritage draws from both sides of the historic divide – what stories are we to tell about empire and who should have the right to tell them? Britain's imperial history is a difficult and divisive one which has involved systematic acts of exclusion and silencing. Yet it is also a narrative that binds the nation and creates claims to citizenship and belonging for a whole range of different people who have been made British through the processes of imperialism. As the Labour MP David Lammy pointed out in a speech relating to the deportation of British citizens to the Caribbean in 2018 during the 'Windrush scandal':

> My ancestors were British subjects. But they were not British subjects because they came to Britain. They were British subjects because Britain came to them, took them across the Atlantic, colonized them, sold them into slavery, profited from their labour and made them British subjects.[16]

Despite its claims to uphold the true history, heritage and traditions of Britain, UKIP's cultural manifesto is an exercise in the control and containment of the uncomfortable realities which underpinned imperialism. These acts of historical suppression chime with Boym's assertion that 'The nostalgic desires to obliterate history and turn it into private or collective mythology'. The plaintive cries of historical desecration emanating from the far-right conceal the ways in which it is engaged with a process of historical destruction through the closing down of critical debate.

The controversial relationship between Britain and Empire can be read through the nation's museums and art galleries. The birth of the public museum in the nineteenth century coincided with a period of imperial expansion. When India became a formal part of the Empire in 1857, this greatly influenced the collecting practices of the South Kensington Museum which would later to go on to become the Victoria and Albert Museum. The imperial connections of the nation's cultural heritage have created a series of legacies which Britain's public history institutions are increasingly being forced to confront. In 2018 the Museum of London in Docklands launched an exhibition *Slavery, Culture and Collecting* which explored both the cultural accumulation enabled by the profits of slavery, as well as the ways in which culture was used to construct racial hierarchies. Many of Britain's national and regional collections contain objects which tell the history of colonial exploitation and expropriation. Some of these institutions were founded by, and owe a debt to, those whose fortunes and collections were funded through the profits of slavery and empire. Hans Sloane, for example, was married to a Jamaica heiress and drew revenue from her plantations. His collection formed the basis for the British Museum.[17] Museums not only displayed the captive objects of empire, they were also an active site for the production and dissemination of racial hierarchies based on civilizational difference. Housed within glass cases and removed from the cultural context of their production, these objects became totemic of both exotic otherness and primitive inferiority. Informed by practices of ordering and categorization that were themselves bound up in the project of European imperialism, museums became places which constructed knowledge of the colonial other for the consumption of a metropolitan audience.

In the wake of multiculturalism and with the emergence of post-independence sovereign nations, questions have been asked about the ongoing colonialism of the object. Issues of repatriation and demands for different kinds of histories (and historians) have highlighted the complicity of the museum in the structures of imperialism. The Victoria and Albert Museum is currently considering returning (on long loan) the Maqdala treasures which were looted from Ethiopia in 1868 by British troops. Similarly, the British Museum has explored this idea in relation to the Benin Bronzes and their return to Nigeria. A lack of diversity both within visitor demographics and among museum staff had led to calls for museums to 'decolonize' in order to maintain relevance for their twenty-first-century audiences. As with any perceived break with tradition, moves to make the museum a more inclusive space have met with claims that these institutions are pandering to political correctness. In 2015 the far-right website Breitbart published an article by Liam Deacon 'History rewritten: Museum conducts politically correct purge of art' in relation to the Rijksmuseum's decision to change its labelling to remove racial terms like 'Negro'. The article criticized the International Council of Museums for endorsing the move and suggested that 'scores of works have already been altered here in the UK'.[18] Despite the claim that the museum was rewriting history, the project entitled 'Adjustment of Colonial Terminology' did in fact retain a reference to the original wording on its online catalogue in order to provide additional historical context for the works.[19] The attempt to make the museum a space in which colonial power – whether through language or representation – is challenged and discussed was rejected outright by Deacon who denounced the initiative as a 'purge'. This deliberate stoking of anxieties around the destruction of history and heritage is one strand of a cultural strategy which has weaponized restorative nostalgia as part of a wider political project to empower the far right in both Europe and America.

It is not just more extreme websites like Breitbart that fan the flames of cultural tension. On 23 April 2018, the *Daily Mail* published an article about a series of art history tours which have taken place in London across a range of institutions including the Victoria and Albert Museum, the National Maritime Museum, the British Museum, and the National Gallery. The 'Uncomfortable Art' tours are run by independent guide Alice Procter who places her intervention within the context of 'a country that's repeatedly failed to come to terms with its colonial past, led by politicians who seem to think the past is the future'.[20] The tours aim to 'resist triumphalist nostalgia with art history' in order to 'unravel the role colonialism played in shaping and funding these collections'. Procter's promotional images rebrand some of Britain's most iconic national figures including Elizabeth I, Admiral Nelson and James Cook as slavers, thieves, invaders and white supremacists. In reference to the controversial provenance of some of the nation's collections, those attending her tours are encouraged to wear badges emblazoned with the phrase 'Wear it like you stole it'. Her approach to negotiating the politics of empire within the museum is uncompromising in its critique of both the imperial past and the role that cultural institutions have played, and continue to play, in representing it.

The article, patriotically published on St George's Day, took umbrage at what it viewed as the defilement of Britain's national heroes, institutions, heritage and identity, opining that 'Britain's museums have traditionally offered visitors the chance to appreciate our national treasures in all their glory.'[21] Setting aside the question of whose national treasures are actually on display, the whole tenor of the piece mourned the demise of the museum as a space of uncritical national celebration.[22] The comments section read like a form of Brexit catchphrase bingo, with Procter accused variously of being a 'millennial', a 'snowflake', a 'privileged metropolitan poppet', a 'social justice warrior', an 'anti-British lefty', a 'virtue signaller', spouting 'PC nonsense' and almost certainly heading for a job at the BBC. Although not directly related to the debates over Brexit, the exposé was nonetheless viewed by some readers as being bound up in the wider cultural wars which have intensified within the context of Brexit. One comment decreed that Procter's tours were an example of 'the communist ideology of the EU in action', adding 'destroy a country's history and you destroy their national identity'. Whether one views Procter's methods as 'sensationalist', in the words of Conservative MP Kwasi Kwarteng, or a necessarily blunt corrective to a dewy-eyed imperial nostalgia, the content of her tours raises important questions about the nature of Britain's cultural debt to empire. In doing so she challenges a celebrational narrative of the Empire as the civilizing mission, highlighting instead the cultural pillaging which took place under the guise of imperial benevolence.

The issue of who gets to shape the narrative of Britain and empire is particularly resonant for the museum sector. According to Museum Detox – a network of BAME heritage professionals – the percentage of people identifying as BAME who work within the sector is currently around 7 per cent. Current census data puts the overall BAME population of England and Wales at 14 per cent. This figure varies within different institutions, for example, only 4.3 per cent of Historic England's staff identified as BAME in 2016–17.[23] The data does not break down how many of those people are in permanent curatorial, education or senior management roles. The lack of diverse voices within Britain's cultural institutions impacts on the nature of the narratives included within the museum space. In recent years there has been a shift towards engaging more critically with the history of empire, however change has been slow and uneven. More recently the practice of 'community co-curation' has emerged as a possible, if problematic, antidote to criticisms around a lack of representation.

The exhibition 'The Past Is Now' was displayed at Birmingham City Art Gallery and Museum between October 2017 and June 2018. It focused on how Birmingham's historic collections could be used to tell the story of the city's extensive links to empire. The museum worked with a group of co-curators – Sumaya Kassim, Abeera Kamran, Shaheen Kasmani and Aliyah Hasinah – all of whom identify as women of colour. The exhibition firmly situated the city's history within the framework of empire, clearly demonstrating the interdependency of the local and the global. Icons of Birmingham, including both the Cadbury family and Joseph Chamberlain, were reinterpreted so that the celebratory narrative of these local heroes was confronted by their more controversial involvement with empire. A quote from a speech by Chamberlain to the Imperial Institute in 1895 featured on the wall of the exhibition. The extract made clear his commitment to ideas of racial superiority. 'I believe', he opined, 'that the British race is the greatest of the governing races that the world has ever seen.' The fact that the museum itself is located on Chamberlain Square connected the institution, the man and the racial ideologies he espoused through the materiality and naming practices of the city space. In doing so the exhibition brought the Empire home by insisting that this was not simply something that occurred in distant and disconnected places but rather was an integrated part of the city's history and identity.

The exhibition engaged with some of the issues of provenance raised by Procter's tours. As Kassim has written, 'For many people of colour, collections symbolize historic and ongoing trauma and theft. Behind every beautiful object and historically important building or monument is trauma'.[24] This point was made powerfully through the inclusion of a letter from the museum's own curator dated 23 October 1964. The letter related to a possible new acquisition and read:

> I was telephoned by a Mr D. Cooper on Thursday who is offering to us, as a gift, one or two relics which he captured personally from members of Mau Mau during all that trouble, I suppose he was in the Army. They include one or two blood-stained knives and a home-made rifle. I thought they might make an amusing addition of a specialised sort to our African collection.[25]

The notion of the captured relic, still stained with the blood shed during colonial violence, as an 'amusing addition' to the collection is a devastating reminder of the colonial mindset and the ways in which it informed museum collecting and as a result public understanding of the imperial past. As Kassim has pointed out, 'To many white people, the collections are an enjoyable diversion, a nostalgic visit which conjures up a romanticised version of Empire.'[26]

The question of the relevance of empire was posed on the exhibition comments board. Visitors' replies reflected the deep divisions within British society which have crystallized around Brexit. Written in marker pen beneath the question were two very different responses. The first stated 'Proud to be British' and the second 'Brexit is imperial nostalgia'. As the comments board made clear, the representation and meaning of Britain's imperial past and its relationship to the present will continue to be contested precisely because there is no single unicultural interpretation that can speak to the many subjectivities of a diverse nation. Birmingham very narrowly voted to leave the European Union but the point the exhibition made clearly was that despite a very strong sense of local identity the city's history has always been bound up with places and people beyond its boundaries.

As Brexit is increasingly understood to be a question of culture rather than economics, the role that culture will play in its aftermath will be key. It is no surprise then that Prime Minister Theresa May proposed to earmark £120 million for a nationwide festival to mark Britain's departure from the European Union in 2022. The suggestion was quickly dubbed the 'Festival of Brexit' by cultural commentators. The parallels with UKIP's 'Best of Britain' exhibition demonstrate the degree to which the Conservative Party has drawn on its policies and rhetoric in recent years. Harking back to the Festival of Britain in 1951, the idea is embedded within a nostalgic cultural framework which continues to look to the past for a vision which will unite a divided nation. Similarly, supporters of the Leave campaign have also recognized the necessity of staking their claim to historical representation by announcing that they are collecting material for a Museum of Brexit. According to the website, the museum will tell 'the history of what we know today as Brexit. It's the story of how the UK – in official terms – "pooled" (or surrendered), and then reclaimed, our sovereignty'.[27] Both of these interventions underscore the centrality of the exhibitionary space in the configuration of collective memory and identity.

As the nation wrestles with competing versions of both the past and the present, museums can and should function as places in which to think through these questions. As the James Baldwin quote which is emblazoned on the walls of the hard-fought-for Smithsonian National Museum of African American History and Culture remind us, 'The great force of history comes from the fact that we carry it within us, are unconsciously controlled by it in many ways, and history is literally present in all that we do'. Both the history of empire and the issue of Brexit are deeply contested and fundamentally intertwined subjects that go to the heart of a sense of personal and national identity. How they are negotiated in the reformulation of the nation which is taking place in the wake of the referendum remains to be seen.

Notes

1. 'Andy Burnham sounds alarm at "very real prospect" of Brexit', *The Guardian* (10 June 2016), https://www.theguardian.com/politics/2016/jun/10/andy-burnham-warns-remain-is-failing-to-reach-labour-heartland
2. 'Theresa May's keynote speech at Tory conference in full', *The Independent* (5 October 2016), https://www.independent.co.uk/news/uk/politics/theresa-may-speech-tory-conference-2016-in-full-transcript-a7346171.html
3. David Olusoga, 'Statues are not the issue. These are "history wars", a battle over the past', *The Guardian* (27 August 2017), https://www.theguardian.com/commentisfree/2017/aug/26/statues-were-not-erected-to-teach-us-history-but-to-exert-power
4. David Smith, 'Trump paints himself as the real victim of Charlottesville in angry speech', *The Guardian* (23 August 2017), https://www.theguardian.com/us-news/2017/aug/23/donald-trump-arizona-rally-phoenix
5. Afua Hirsch, 'Toppling statues? Here's why Nelson's column should be next', *The Guardian* (22 August 2017), https://www.theguardian.com/commentisfree/2017/aug/22/toppling-statues-nelsons-column-should-be-next-slavery
6. Stephen Glover, 'Couldn't Afua Hirsch summon a smidgen of gratitude?', the *Daily Mail* (6 April 2018), https://www.dailymail.co.uk/news/article-5584069/STEPHEN-GLOVER-Afua-Hirsch-summon-smidgen-gratitude.html
7. John Chapman and Joey Millar, '"Tear down Nelson's column" British public OUTRAGED at monument "white supremacist" claim', *Daily Express* (24 August 2018), https://www.express.co.uk/news/uk/845245/Afua-Hirsch-nelsons-column-comment-london-monument-horatio-viscount-guardian
8. Michel-Rolph Trouillot, *Silencing the Past: Power and the Production of History* (Massachusetts: Beacon Press, 1997).
9. Gurminder Bhambra, 'Brexit, class and British "national" identity', *Discover Society* (5 July 2016), https://discoversociety.org/2016/07/05/viewpoint-brexit-class-and-british-national-identity/
10. John Harris, 'Sleaford's Brexit byelection: A people united by fear for the future – video', *The Guardian* (30 November 2016), 07:27-07:32, https://www.theguardian.com/commentisfree/video/2016/nov/30/sleaford-lincolnshire-brexitbyelection-young-video
11. Charlotte L. Riley, 'How a history of conquest shapes the present', *New Humanist* (3 July 2017), https://newhumanist.org.uk/articles/5204/how-a-history-of-conquest-shapes-the-present
12. Svetlana Boym, 'Nostalgia', *Atlas of Transformation*, http://monumenttotransformation.org/atlas-of-transformation/html/n/nostalgia/nostalgia-svetlana-boym.html
13. 'Restoring Britishness', January 2010, https://devolutionmatters.files.wordpress.com/2010/02/ukip-britishness.pdf

14 John G. Beech, 'The marketing of slavery heritage in the United Kingdom', in *Slavery, Contested Heritage and Thanotourism*, ed. G. M. Dann and A. V. Seaton (New York: Haworth Hospitality Press, 2001).

15 Kathleen Wilson, *The Island Race: Englishness, Empire and Identity in the Eighteenth Century* (London: Routledge, 2003), 15.

16 David Lammy, Speech on the Windrush crisis in Parliament, 30 April 2018, https://www.davidlammy.co.uk/single-post/2018/05/29/Speeches-on-the-Windrush-crisis-in- Parliament

17 'Slavery in the Cabinet of Curiosities: Hans Sloane's Atlantic World', *The British Museum*, https://www.britishmuseum.org/research/news/hans_sloanes_atlantic_world.aspx

18 Liam Deacon, 'History Rewritten: Museum Conducts Politically Correct Purge of Art', https://www.breitbart.com/europe/2015/12/14/history-rewritten-museum-conducts-politically-correct-purge-art/

19 Nina Siegal, 'Rijksmuseum Removing Racially Charged Terms From Artworks' Titles and Descriptions', *ArtsBeat, New York Times Blog*, 10 December 2015, https://artsbeat.blogs.nytimes.com/2015/12/10/rijksmuseum-removing-racially-charged-terms-from-artworks-titles-and-descriptions/

20 'Uncomfortable art tours', *the exhibitionist*, https://www.theexhibitionist.org/

21 Miles Dilworth, 'Art historian, 23, and museum guide is using sell-out tours to label Lord Nelson a "white supremacist" and brand Queen Victoria a "thief"', *Daily Mail* (23 April 2018), https://www.dailymail.co.uk/news/article-5645381/Museum-guide-using-sell-tours-label-Lord-Nelson-white-supremacist.html

22 Standing Committee of the SWIPM, 10 March 1786. Quoted in Catherine Hall, 'Edward Long and the work of re-remembering', in *Britain's History and Memory of Transatlantic Slavery: The Local Nuances of a 'National Sin'*, ed. Katie Donington, Ryan Hanley and Jessica Moody (Liverpool: Liverpool University Press, 2016), 140.

23 'Heritage Training Placements', Historic England, https://historicengland.org.uk/services-skills/training-skills/work-based-training/paid-training-placements/

24 'The museum will not be decolonised', *Media Diversified* (15 November 2017), https://mediadiversified.org/2017/11/15/the-museum-will-not-be-decolonised/

25 Letter from the Curator of Birmingham City Art Gallery and Museum, 23 October 1964. ARCH/O/T, Birmingham City Art Gallery and Museum.

26 'The museum will not be decolonised', *Media Diversified* (15 November 2017), https://mediadiversified.org/2017/11/15/the-museum-will-not-be-decolonised/

27 'The Plan', *The Museum of Brexit*, https://www.museumofbrexit.uk/the-plan

Chapter 13
The Guerrilla Arts in Brexit Bristol

Olivette Otele

In May 2018, the statue of former slave trader Edward Colston at the heart of Bristol was again thrust to the centre of controversy. Following a pattern of 'guerrilla arts' that challenge the representation of the past in the urban landscape, a woollen red ball and chain had been attached to the legs of one of the fathers of the city. The symbolism was unmistakable, employing a form of memorabilia designed to interrogate popular understandings of the history of colonialism and Empire. The episode was just one of many instances where Britain's colonial past impinged on everyday streetscapes. Not least in the post-Brexit context, the role and place of memorabilia of the past have become a contested terrain of Britain as a global power.

This chapter seeks to analyse how Bristol, an important port in the history of the British transatlantic slave trade for a short period in the eighteenth century, has become the locus for controversial histories articulated around memory politics. It looks at the way 'reluctant sites of memory' collide with urban memorialization processes. Beyond the recurring debates about the nation's colonial past, questions of identity and belonging have taken a new turn since Britain's decision to leave the European Union. What appeared to be a vote about an allegedly undemocratic European Union has proven to be a conduit for resentment-fuelled discussions about immigration in which the post-memory of colonialism has become entangled with the future political visions of the country's major parties. In the balance sheet approach that seems to have permeated debates about the past in Britain, the resurgence and vibrancy of once-dormant imperial memories highlights the intersection between popular feeling and contested historical facts. The past seems ever-present and has forced historians to engage variously with the emotional and political dimensions of Britain's colonial legacy. At the heart of it all, memory is an indispensable parameter that needs to be examined.

Bristol, like many European cities, has been trying to come to terms with the controversy raised by the memory and trauma of the slave trade era, and the debate has raised a number of questions. Can conflicting memories be conceived as collective? Could Bristol ever reach a stage where one can talk about reconciliation? One often thinks of collective memory as simply the sum of the various memories that a group of people have about certain events or certain periods, but that is accurate only to a certain extent. Witnesses of an accident may well provide completely conflicting accounts of the same incident – there may be agreement on a few cardinal facts based on the evidence, but the impact of the accident might elicit any number of rival, rational explanations, with the addition or suppression of certain details. Yet, what is considered mere detail by some can constitute deeper meaning for others. We naturally select and classify the information we have found or have been given, and our ability to sympathize or empathize plays a role in the interpretation of what we see and the way we transmit the information to others. Invariably, the interpretation of the event is directly linked to the social and political background of the beholder, and to the historical context of the event itself. Brexit was the context that furthered discussions about Bristol's imperial past and the city's memorialization strategies.

For decades in Bristol, the number of African captives transported across the Atlantic has been the detail that gave meaning to debates about the past. Logbooks, diaries, letters, investors and the Society of Merchant Venturers archives clearly established that the slave trade had been a vital part of Bristol's economy.[1] Compensation received by British slave owners was also clearly recorded and showed that British tax payers paid for wealthy planters to be compensated for the loss of their property (including the market value of enslaved men, women and children) after the abolition slavery in 1834. The controversy in Bristol today (and in many other cities in Britain, France, Spain and the United States) boils down to whether certain slave owners should be celebrated in the city's urban landscape or whether their statues and other forms of memorialization should be removed. I term these 'Reluctant Sites of Memory' – monuments, buildings, sculptures, street names that seem superficially innocuous, while evoking powerful mirrors of our past and present. Such signs of a contested past can elicit a profound reticence on the part of minority groups and majority communities alike. 'No British city is more wilfully blind to its history than Bristol', remarked the historian David Olusoga in 2017, adding that the city 'stands head and shoulders above the competition in its capacity to obscure its past and obfuscate its history.'[2] Yet such resistant cityscapes also furnish oblique but vivid reflections of our abilities to forget, harbouring latent potential to generate knowledge and understanding despite the social, cultural and economic divisions they symbolize.

In a war, it is not unusual to see the defeated faction attempt to write its own side of events, often by way of discrediting the myths of the opposing victorious faction. It is, however, interesting to note that the so-called victors also need to create their own, customized account of the event, reflecting not only the need to share the moment with others and future generations but also the desire to take ownership of the event itself. The group that tells the story is as important as the story itself. Thus for centuries, the history of transatlantic slavery was taught in schools in ways that highlighted the story of abolition rather than the dehumanizing experiences of enslaved people. Bristol, like many other port cities, posited itself as an adventurous and successful place that owed its victories over the oceans to pirates such as Blackbeard and privateers like Woodes Rogers. Little attention was paid to what these stories of conquest meant for those whose ancestors had been enslaved centuries ago.

Since the 1990s, however, a remarkable number of initiatives have been led by the city's museums in collaboration with historians, community members, activists and archivists. An extensive Slave Trail relating to that traumatic past and counting no less than 42 stops was set up.[3] In 1999 a bridge commemorating the life of a black servant called Pero was opened at the heart of the city. Located in the trendy area of the city that saw a number of regeneration initiatives, it links the animated sites with cafes and restaurant with the docks and the M Shed Museum, aiming at showcasing the story of the city across time including the involvement of Bristol in the history of enslavement. Nevertheless, very few passers-by seem aware that a plaque to Pero exists or that the bridge is related to the history of a black man in the eighteenth century. Equally forgotten has been the story of the Wills family that made their fortune through tobacco grown by enslaved people from North America. In 2017, a petition was launched to rename the Wills Memorial Building that the family donated to the University of Bristol in 1903 – failing to persuade the university management who stood firm on the building's original name.[4]

Much of the debate has crystallized around the figure of Edward Colston, the Bristol-born merchant and slave trader who endowed schools, hospitals and churches throughout the city in the early eighteenth century. The emotional value Bristolians attach to Colston is deeply rooted in what they perceive to be the city's glorious seafaring past, epitomized by the rise to prominence of the merchant classes. Colston emerged at a time when England was turning to the African trade dominated by the United Provinces, the Portuguese and the Spanish, becoming a shareholder of the Royal African Company in 1680. Colston's business was concentrated in London, and while continuing to invest in various ventures he became a Member of Parliament in 1710. By the time of his death in Surrey in 1721, he had become in many respects a stranger to Bristol, yet in later years the city chose to pay him homage and elevate him as one of the city's most distinguished sons. The bronze statue sculpted by John

Cassidy was erected in Bristol 1895, its grade II listing by English Heritage placing it among the city's most protected urban treasures.

So-called 'guerrilla artists' have been at the forefront of the controversy surrounding the Colston sculpture, building on Bristol's reputation as a vibrant centre for street arts and igniting passions among rival community factions.[5] An early example was the virtual installation of artist Hew Locke in 2006, who covered the statue with gold as a marker of the moral infamy of a wealth-creating industry that benefitted the city as a whole.[6] More recently in April 2017, the face of Colston's statue was daubed in white paint, causing outrage among certain sections of the community.[7] Described as the work of 'vandals' by the *Bristol Post*, no thought was given to interpreting the gesture as something more than wilful destruction; as a potentially constructive palimpsest that could provide new layers of meaning to the tormented history of the city.

Months later, sculptor Will Coles chose a different tack by attaching an 'Unauthorized Heritage' plaque to the base of the Colston statue in August 2017. It took council workers several months to notice and then remove the offending item, which again was aimed at drawing people's attention to the link between the city and the slave trade. Parodying the shape and format of an English Heritage 'blue plaque', the inscription read: 'Bristol, Capital of the Atlantic Slave Trade, 1730–1745. This commemorates the 12 000 000 enslaved of whom 6 000 000 died as captives.' Although the figures were historically accurate in terms of the slave trade as a whole, they were exaggerated as far the history of Bristol was concerned (which accounted for about half a million of the total traffic in enslaved Africans). While historians debated the veracity of the figures, their conflation forced the viewer to stop and engage with that history, whether to contest or to acknowledge it.

Similarly, a recurring discussion about the wording of the official plaque attached to Colston's statue has focused community energies in recent years. As an alternative to removing the statue completely, prominent Bristolians were asked to rewrite the plaque following a process of consultation with academics, educators, poets and school children, at the behest of an influential group of activists known as the Countering Colston Group. Historian Madge Dresser was chosen by Bristol City Council to gather these various ideas and produce a text, as follows:

> As a high official of the Royal African Company from 1680 to 1692, Edward Colston played an active role in the enslavement of over 84,000 Africans (including 12,000 children) of whom over 19,000 died en route to the Caribbean and America. Colston also invested in the Spanish slave trade and in slave-produced sugar. As Tory MP for Bristol (1710–1713), he defended the city's 'right' to trade in enslaved Africans. Bristolians who did not subscribe to his religious and political beliefs were not permitted to benefit from his charities.[8]

Despite the extensive consultative process, not all Bristolians were content with the wording. The Society of Merchant Venturers and right-wing Conservative councillor Richard Eddy argued that the words did not fairly reflect Colston's deeds as a benefactor, and thus a new round of discussion ensued that resulted in a revised text:

> Edward Colston (1636–1721) was a Bristol-born merchant, long honoured as the city's greatest benefactor. He made vast donations to restore churches, establish schools, almshouses and various charities in Bristol and across the country.
> Much of his wealth came from investments in slave trading, sugar and other slave-produced goods.
> When a high official of the Royal African Company (1680–1692) (which had the monopoly on the British slave trade until 1698), he played an active role in the trafficking of over 84,000 enslaved Africans (including 12,000 children) of whom over 19,000 died on their way across the Atlantic.
> As MP for Bristol (1710–1713) he worked to safeguard Bristol's slave-trading interests. His role in the exploitation of enslaved Africans and his opposition to any form of religious or political dissent, has in recent years made him the focus of increasing controversy.[9]

The debate highlights the tension that exists when memory and politics are so closely linked. Yet the speed with which the compromise was reached was remarkable, suggesting that memory, politics and memorialization in Bristol could combine in ways to produce mutually acceptable forms of reconciliation. Other recent developments also reflect a community willingness to revise Colston's hitherto untarnished legacy. Among the more prominent landmarks to bear his name was Bristol's most important concert venue, Colston Hall, which became the target of petitioners who succeeded in having the name changed in June 2017. Equally significant was the announcement a few months later in December 2017 that Colston's Primary School would change its name, opening its doors in September 2018 as Cotham Gardens Primary School. Further discussions have been taking place since July 2018 about renaming Colston Road running through one of the most multicultural parts of the city.[10]

Beyond renaming, residents and activists have explored ways to challenge colonial representations into seemingly post-colonial memoryscapes. As defined by Ziva Kodney, memoryscape is an 'exploration of the urban landscape [which] presents a dialectic tension between landscape perception as a collective production and as familiar and mundane phenomena. Both practices emphasize the landscape's unique role as an instrument of memory and reconciliation'.[11] In the case of Bristol, reconciliation was preceded by controversy and the reclaiming of the urban landscape by guerrilla artists and other activists. The landscape provided a social and political terrain for protest as much as a creative space for enhancing or de-escalating tensions.

David Andress describes these schizophrenic patterns of collective memory as a form of *Cultural Dementia*.[12] In an era of fake news, where new forms of social media enable dynamic and fast-moving forms of populist politics, documented historical facts can be more readily and widely contested. In that context, 'our recurrent dementia takes the form of particular kinds of forgetting, misremembering and mistaking the past'.[13] Andress goes on to explain that 'the dementia sufferer is denied the comfort of knowing they don't remember'.[14] The debates about Colston clearly show that the past is known, but the struggle is over whether the views of those who retain a positive view of the imperial past should be preserved. What is at stake is not the facts but the memorialization of the past. It is therefore necessary to understand what role memory plays in the memorialization process and how it shapes power structures.

According to Marie Claire Lavabre, the collective memory is a work of reduction between various actors, such as elected leaders, academics, state representatives and other entrepreneurs of memory.[15] This implies coming together to produce a narrative that is acceptable for a great number of people in order to reach a consensus about narrated events. Two main questions arise in that process. The first is about the individuals or groups who should be considered valid representatives for a community of people. The second pertains to how we should determine which aspects of the past should be placed under scrutiny. Although the memory and memorialization of the past can provide a sense of belonging and unify a community, difficulties emerge when the various protagonists of the same community attach different meanings to the same events. 'Historical memory' is both a conscious and unconscious process, which needs the various parties involved to interact in order to become a collective memory. Edward Colston was both a philanthropist and a slave trader who was responsible for the transportation of men, women and children from Africa to the Americas.[16] Focusing on his philanthropic deeds only obscures the city's contentious past, while guerrilla arts serve as both a marker of recognition of a common story as well as a tool for highlighting the need for a diversity of voices in public spaces. Often criticized for blurring the line between vandalism and art, guerrilla arts continue to divide opinion.

In the midst of these debates, the question of Brexit has never been far away, with Bristol voting to remain in the European Union by 62 per cent to 38 per cent. In tune with voting patterns elsewhere, the most affluent parts of Bristol wanted to remain while the more impoverished chose to leave. The race divide also played a role in the Remain vote, with a majority of minority ethnic people electing to Remain, including those residing in areas of social deprivation.[17] The results reflect a campaign led by black activists who pointed to the rise in hate crimes that targeted minority ethnic groups during the campaign itself, arguing that a

Brexit win would only further exacerbate racial tensions. There also seemed to be a misunderstanding about the concept of freedom of movement, with many believing that once EU citizens had departed, Black and minority ethnic communities would also be invited to leave.[18] Gurminder K. Bhambra notes that 'imperial nostalgia' played an important role in those misconceptions.[19]

Debates in Bristol were also clearly affected by the wider national and international context in which similar controversies were unfolding. The Rhodes Must Fall movement that was initiated in South Africa reached British shores in the polarized public campaign in Oxford aimed at removing the statue of Cecil Rhodes. In 2014, at the time of the Oxford Rhodes controversy, 59 per cent of British respondents stated that they were proud of the British Empire.[20] Evidently, the Empire was not just part of the past, but remained an integral component of Britain's identity. Identity, however, was more broadly defined by younger generations, for whom Englishness (for example) was not defined by skin colour or by religion. A YouGov survey conducted in 2018 showed that 8 people out of 10 surveyed stated that what made someone English was firstly whether they were born in England or not.[21] When linking these findings to Bristol's debate about the memorialization of the past, it seems that the city has navigated the tides of controversies about Empire on its own terms. In Bristol, the controversy is not about the Empire as a whole, so much as the specific history of transatlantic slavery. It is not only about toppling a statue but about creating a space for reframing the narratives about that history. It means removing, rewording and constantly challenging the accepted forms of memorialization through guerrilla arts and other forms of urban activism.

However, discrepancies remain. There is no denying the conspicuous gap between a visibly multicultural city that seems to have come to terms with its colonial past and examples of discrimination such as the low number of black teachers (26 out of 1300) working in secondary schools in the city.[22] Equally worrying are the number of racist incidents that have been plaguing the city despite high-profile gains such as the election of Lord Mayor Cleo Lake and the Mayor Marvin Rees, both of dual heritage.[23] As far as memorialization is concerned, Bristol's guerrilla arts seem to have become a conventional form of representation that sometimes fails to take into account the sensitivity of certain communities.

Noteworthy in this regard was the guerrilla art installation of October 2018 in which 100 mini-statues were laid out at the foot of the Colston monument, arranged in the pattern of human cargo chained to the bow of a slave ship. The link between modern-day slavery and the transatlantic slavery of centuries ago was depicted by the labels on the blocks forming the outline of the ship, signalling 'domestic servant', 'fruit picker', 'sex worker', 'car wash attendant', and other marginalized professions. Such imagery was once the mainstay of eighteenth-century abolitionists, who used the cargo inventory of the Brookes Slave Ship with its hundreds of bodies packed like sardines to highlight the inhumanity of the slave trade.[24] What posed a problem for a contemporary audience was the artistic redeployment of these faceless, voiceless anonymous enslaved people. Such imagery did not take into account black agency in the process of emancipation, nor did it necessarily provide the space for the wider white population to see enslaved people as anything other than debased human cargo. The example of Brexit Bristol suggests that even in mounting a challenge to the urban landscape of colonialism, the very terms of contestation can evoke the visual currency of the imperial past.

Notes

1 O. Otele, 'Mémoire et politique: l'enrichissement de Bristol par le commerce triangulaire, objet de polémique', unpublished PhD dissertation, Université La Sorbonne, 2005 and M. Dresser, *Slavery Obscured: The Social History of the Slave Trade in Bristol* (Bristol: Redcliffe Press, 2007).

2 David Olusoga, 'Bristol's Colston Hall is an affront to a multicultural city. Let's rename it now', *The Guardian* (26 February 2017).

3 Victoria County History, 'Bristol Slave Trail', https://www.victoriacountyhistory.ac.uk/explore/collection/bristol-slavery-trail

4 'Bristol University makes decision over renaming Wills Memorial Building after slavery debate', https://www.bristolpost.co.uk/news/bristol-news/bristol-university-makes-decision-over-163397

5 Renowned graffiti artist Banksy was born in Bristol and there are a few examples of his artworks in the city.

6 Hew Locke, commissioned work, http://www.hewlocke.net/restoration2.html

7 'Vandals paint face of Edward Colston white', https://www.bristolpost.co.uk/news/bristol-news/vandals-paint-face-edward-colston-30443

8 'Proposed Wording for New Plaque on Colston Statue Revealed', https://www.bristol247.com/news-and-features/news/proposed-wording-new-plaque-colston-statue-revealed/

9 'Rows breaks out as Merchant venture accused of "sanitizing" Edward Colston's involvement in slave trade', https://www.bristolpost.co.uk/news/bristol-news/row-breaks-out-merchant-venturer-1925896

10 'Now residents want to rename Colston Road', https://www.bristolpost.co.uk/news/bristol-news/now-residents-want-rename-colston-1751671

11 Z. Kolodney, 'Contested Urban Memoryscape Strategies and Tactics in Post-1948 Haifa' in *Representations of Israeli-Jewish – Israeli-Palestinian Memory and Historical Narratives of the 1948 War*, Israel Studies, vol. 21, no. 1 (Indiana University Press, 2016).

12 David Andress, *Cultural Dementia: How the West has Lost its History and Risks Losing Everything Else* (London: Head of Zeus, 2018). On 'Schizophrenic collective memory' see O. Otele, 'Bristol et le commerce triangulaire: schizophrenie et enjeux

de la memoire collective' in *Violence d'État, parole libératrice et colonialisme* ed. E. Hanquart-Turner (Ivry-sur-Seine : Editions A3, 2005), 69–84.

13 Ibid., 39.

14 Ibid., 42.

15 M.-C. Lavabre, 'Peut-on agir sur la mémoire' in Les Cahiers français, *La mémoire entre histoire et politique,* Numero 303 (Juillet-Aout 2001).

16 Bristol Radical History Group, 'Edward Colston Research paper 1', https://www.brh.org.uk/site/articles/edward-colston-research-paper-1/

17 'Full Brexit Results: What we learned', https://www.bristol247.com/news-and-features/features/full-bristol-brexit-results-what-we-learned/

18 TUC, *Challenging Racism After the Referendum*, https://www.tuc.org.uk/sites/default/files/ChallengingracismaftertheEUreferendum2.pdf

19 K. G. Bhambra, 'The imperial nostalgia of a "small Island"', http://ukandeu.ac.uk/the-imperial-nostalgia-of-a-small-island/

20 YouGov, 'The British Empire is something to be proud of', https://yougov.co.uk/topics/politics/articles-reports/2014/07/26/britain-proud-its-empire

21 BBC News, 'The English question: Young are less proud to be English', https://www.bbc.co.uk/news/uk-england-44142843

22 '"Shocking" Lack of Black teachers in Bristol Schools', *The Voice*, http://www.voice-online.co.uk/career-education-article/%E2%80%98shocking%E2%80%99-lack-black-teachers-bristol-schools

23 'Bristol, the slave trade and a reckoning with the past', https://www.ft.com/content/032fe4a0-9a96-11e8-ab77-f854c65a4465

24 British Library, 'Diagram of the Brookes Slave Ship', https://www.bl.uk/collection-items/diagram-of-the-brookes-slave-ship

Chapter 14
Biggar vs Little Britain
Richard Drayton

In his essay 'The Historiographical Operation', Michel de Certeau alerts us to seek out what he calls the significant deviation in history – 'deviation' to be understood, I think, in the mathematical sense – those slightly off-centre events or personalities which allow us to illuminate the normal distribution of cultural or social phenomena.[1] If we pursue what the Italian microhistorian Carlo Ginzburg called 'clues', and which his compatriot Edoardo Grendi called the 'exceptional typical', we may better understand larger social structures.[2]

Nigel Biggar was born in March 1955 in Castle Douglas in the west fringe of the Scottish borders, almost as close to Belfast, as the crow flies, as to Glasgow and Edinburgh. He was the youngest son of Francis Raymond Biggar (born 1913), who worked for the family firm Thomas Biggar and Sons, farmers, millers and dealers in grain and manure, founded by his great-great-grandfather in 1842.[3] It is not my aim to compare Nigel Biggar to Mennochio, the mad miller of Montereale, whose exceptionally typical mental world Carlo Ginzburg famously explored in *The Cheese and the Worms*. Biggar is rather an index point which, while eccentric, lies much closer to the mean in the standard distribution of ideology of his age than Mennochio. But as with the Italian miller, a journey into the mind-world of Biggar can help us to understand larger, and less articulate and visible cultural currents in late twentieth and twenty-first century Britain. It may provide insight into how some of the embers of empire continue to burn, and even to kindle obscure new flames.

If the Brexit moment is in many ways characterized by a kind of 'return of the repressed', as the psychoanalysts would put it, Nigel Biggar's strange career as a public intellectual is emblematic of it. He is unique in the striking portfolio of political positions for which he has proposed ethical arguments: against Irish republicanism and in defence of Northern Irish Unionism;[4] against Scottish independence and in defence of Scottish Unionism;[5] in support of 'just war' (within which he includes the Afghanistan, Iraq and Libyan Wars, while he excludes the Easter Rebellion of

1916 and military republicanism in Ireland, and implicitly the Afghan and Iraqi resistance fighters);[6] for the moral purpose of the First World War;[7] for intervention in Syria as Britain's 'moral duty';[8] for the arbitrary killing of Bin Laden;[9] for hereditary monarchy;[10] in defence of an unelected House of Lords;[11] against the disestablishment of the Anglican Church,[12] chiding the editors of *Charlie Hebdo* for their abuse of free speech while urging that of course they should not have been killed for it,[13] for Cecil Rhodes's statue to remain on Oriel's façade but against a statue to Mary Seacole at St Thomas's hospital;[14] against the European Court of Justice's extension of the right to benefits of EU migrant workers;[15] against the removal of Trident from Scotland;[16] in defence of the killing of wounded combatants on the battlefield as an ethical option (since the Afghan rebels have no modern medical care), but against euthanasia within the West, because here we have the means to cure and relieve pain;[17] in support of an ethical case for torture, or as he prefers to call it 'aggressive interrogation', in which he includes sleep deprivation, hooding, stress posture, deprivation of food and water, even waterboarding;[18] against giving transgender people civic status,[19] and for an ethically-justified imperialism. Biggar in March 2019 asserted, 'I voted Remain, just, but dislike most of the company I'm in'.[20] 'Remain' has strangely, however, not been among causes he has championed, indeed in 2017 he denounced the 'imperial ambitions' of the European Union, and in January 2019 lent his name in a letter which described Britain's relationship to Europe as 'political servitude' and argued that British universities would benefit from a 'No Deal'.[21] While perhaps alone in taking a public stand on this system of positions as a whole, it is clear that Biggar is fully representative of a powerful current within British public opinion, and has quite self-consciously sought to quicken this solidarity.

Biggar has sought out the sympathy of a mob of rightwards opinion, and not just in the content of his views, where he clearly reaches from his pulpit towards the pews. Biggar has cultivated an interesting querulous tone in his press and Twitter personae, like a kind of middlebrow Katie Hopkins, he presents himself, and is being marketed by others, as one of a majority whose rightwards views have been drowned out by a noisy bullying liberal but illiberal minority, a majority which at last will speak.[22]

In an article published in *The Conservative* of April 2017 under the title 'Outing yourself as a rightist isn't easy', he declared:

> The zealous certainty of a minority can tie the tongues of an uncertain majority. But when someone dares to stand up and out, others begin to find their voices, reassured that what they think can be said in public without risking social death.[23]

This, I would suggest, is part of the music of the Brexit moment, a passive aggressive lament of a denigrated traditionalism, a denigrated Conservatism, a

British patriotism, perhaps even a denigrated 'whiteness', which will now take back control. His strange career deserves our attention not just for what it represents now, or where it comes from, but where perhaps, with or without his control, it will go. For some of the ugly possible outcomes, one needs only look at how he, wittingly or unwittingly, directed the swarm of wasps of right-wing Twitter trolls and *Daily Mail* columnists to attack the Cambridge lecturer Priyamvada Gopal.[24] The Biggar phenomenon is a sign of the times to which we should pay attention.

Biggar took Dr Johnson's high road to England early as a teenager to Monkton Combe, a minor public school near Bath, a very muscular Christian Victorian foundation. Sir Richard Dearlove, best known as Tony Blair's head of MI6 during the production of the 'dodgy dossier', is another Old Monktonian. Since 2014 the school now has a 'Biggar Society' which meets once a term for a dinner and a lecture on theology.[25] He went up to Worcester College, Oxford, where he graduated in 1976 with a degree in modern history. He appears to have been pulled towards the Calvinist current in late-twentieth-century Anglican evangelical theology associated with J. I. Packer.[26] Packer went to teach at Regent College in Vancouver in 1979, and Biggar followed him, taking an MA in theology in 1981, going on to Chicago where he received his PhD in 1986. Biggar returned to Oxford and was fixed up with a post at the evangelical bastion Latimer House, which Packer had helped found during the 1960s.[27] There he made his first sign of his future direction in a coded attack on Archbishop Runcie and his liberal wing of the Church in a pamphlet called *Theological Politics* (1988). This was a broadside against Archbishop Runcie's *Faith in the City,* the famous 1985 Anglican Church report which blamed a material and spiritual crisis in the inner cities on Thatcherite policy, which Biggar found to be weak in its theology.[28] Two years later, to be fair, Biggar did offer a partial critique of Thatcherism, writing 'it is mistaken to suppose that the systematic contraction of state support will stimulate a recovery of relevant kinds of personal responsibility', essentially proposing the complementary argument to 'Render unto Caesar . . . .', which was that welfare provision should be the complement to an aggressive attempt by the Church to challenge a moral crisis.[29] A somewhat meteoric career unfolded. While only ordained as Deacon in 1990 and priest in 1991, he ascended to the rather snug billet of Chaplain of Oriel College, Oxford. In 1993 he published his most substantial scholarly work, a 190-page study of Karl Barth's ethics.[30] On this slender barque, he sailed to a chair at Leeds in 1999. In 2004 he moved to Trinity College, Dublin, to the Chair of Theology and Ethics, returning to Oxford to the Regius Chair of Moral and Pastoral Theology in 2007, the directorship in 2008 of the McDonald Centre for Theology, Ethics and Public Life, and the office of Canon of Christ Church Cathedral, Oxford.

A big fish in the Anglican pond, he would however probably have remained obscure to a wider public had he not made three key interventions on the question of empire: first, in the 'Rhodes Must Fall in Oxford' controversy from late 2015; second, in the late 2016 controversy over Bruce Gilley's notorious 'The case for colonialism' essay in *Third World Quarterly*; and, since late 2017, with his 'Ethics and Empire' project at his Macdonald Centre for Ethics at Oxford.[31] If one uses Lexis-Nexis to audit the presence of Nigel Biggar in the British press up to December 2018, some 262 of the 318 occurrences of his name in the press throughout his lifetime appeared after January 2015, with 186 after December 2017 alone.[32] The views of the poor bullied Regius Professor of Theology have become a touchstone for right-wing political commentary. 'Climate of fear at Oxford warns colonialism scholar Nigel Biggar', read a typical hysterical *Times* headline of 3 February 2018. Put to one side the extraordinary apotheosis of a commentator on a subject into a scholar of it, and sample the mood of paranoia and its uses. The strangeness in the career of Biggar does not lie in his views, but in the way in which he has used them in a deliberate way to seek out a public notoriety, and how in turn he has been picked up, packaged and retailed by figures like Rod Liddle, and the columnists of *The Telegraph* and the *Daily Mail*, the self-constructed lonely prophet calling from the wilderness of Christ Church High Table, with only the comment pages of *The Times* in which to share his views, turned into a commodity in high circulation.

Having now identified the Biggar nebula in the night sky, let us now explore the mysteries of this 'exceptionally typical' ideological constellation.

Biggar describes his growing up in the sixties and rejecting the change he saw around him: 'my Inner Edwardian refused to vacate my soul, . . . I found the cultural changes swirling around me painful and unsettling . . . But observing that the tide was against me, I went into inner exile'.[33] In his own narrative, he returned from that desert to prophesy, with the critical moment of his 'coming out' being his 2013 book *In Defence of War,* which ends with his rousing ethical case for the Iraq War.

But Unionism was much earlier the cause of this lowland Scot. His first public political interventions on non-theological questions were a sequence of letters to *The Times*, *The Independent* and *The Guardian* in the 1990s on the Irish question.[34] In 2002, he was happy to retail the paranoia of the Ulster unionists, offering the allegation that even after the Good Friday Agreement 'the evidence is that IRA continues to hunt for weapons in the global market'.[35] In his abundant public commentary on matters Irish, there is no editorial or letter to the press in which Biggar makes any disapproving comment about British army or Unionist paramilitary violence. When the question of Scottish independence became live, Biggar emerged as a vigorous Unionist campaigner. While other No campaigners urged mainly economic arguments, he sought to muster ethical ones, even going so far as to call Scottish independence 'a false god'.[36] In February 2018, as *The Times* announced in an article entitled 'Brainy Brits come out for Brexit',

Biggar joined 40 'leading intellectuals' in *These Islands*, a think-tank committed to providing the ideology for a twenty-first-century Unionism.[37]

Biggar's Unionism is not a collateral ideological commitment. Central to all Biggar's thought, indeed his theology and ethics is the idea that kinship and the forms of solidarity found among those most closely related to, and living in proximity to you, are the central ground of ethical life, and indeed of encounter with the divine. What Kierkegaard called the 'infinite qualitative distinction' between God and man, an idea enlarged by Karl Barth, Biggar's most important theological influence, as the inability of the created to know the Creator except through the creation, constitutes the ground on which for Biggar loyalty to tribe, nation, empire become ethical desiderata.[38] In a highbrow version of Ayn Rand's 'To say "I love you" one must first know how to say the "I"', Biggar believes morality must begin in a love which is grounded in one's kin, one's kind, one's immediate community. In 1993, he wrote:

> Note that it is our neighbour whom we are to love – the one nearby. That is to say, we are to love in the only way that creatures genuinely can: by caring for those who are given to cross our finite path. Being creatures, and not gods, we cannot love everyone; but we can love our neighbours . . . we may not avert our eyes from the battered body on the side of the road that we rush down in pursuit of . . . some Grand Humanitarian Cause. The charity of creatures really does begin at home, or somewhere close by, even if it eventually expands beyond its domestic matrix.[39]

His argument in 2016 for Britain leaving the European Union appeals to identical grounds: 'We are finite, not infinite; creatures, not gods . . . we should feel special affection for, loyalty toward, and gratitude to those communities, customs, and institutions that have benefitted us by inducting us into human goods . . . we owe [the nation state] our gratitude and loyalty.'[40]

Biggar's view on the British Empire, first offered in the last chapter of his short 2014 book *Between Kin and Cosmopolis*, derives from this idea that 'gratitude and loyalty' are owed to an imagined community of the Union's dead. The problem that empire 'comprises the imposition of rule by one people upon another' can be solved if 'the imposition of imperial rule can have the salutary effect of imposing a unifying, pacific, and law-abiding order on peoples otherwise inclined to war among themselves' (p. 91). Biggar does not seem to find it necessary to ask Tacitus's question of who gets to decide what is peace and order, and what is desolation and tyranny, for he knows that his kin's way is best. He is untroubled by the risk that a love of kin can become a kind of idolatry, particularly when supporting fantasies of violence and domination, even, or perhaps in particular, when those are adorned with an ethical surplice.

The collective identity and 'order' constituted by kinship licenses an ethical imperial violence. Biggar thus urged to an American readership a relaxed attitude to an empire dominating others by force:

> The problem arises, however, when [one assumes] that anything in the world that involves hierarchy or coercion – that is, one person dominating another – is necessarily an instance of 'domination' as stipulated and therefore immoral . . . Surely we *want* the police to *dominate* the mafia, don't we? And we *want* those fighting in a just cause to *dominate* those fighting in an unjust one?[41]

This culminates in an argument for how 'callousness' can even become a 'Christian virtue': we begin with kin, and those truths we know intimately on our own terms, and sometimes honouring them may require erecting a barrier of fibrous insensitivity to the ideas, the feelings, even the right to life of others who are non-kin. The waging of war, with all its collateral damage, becomes a moral obligation: Britain, if it is true to the God which it knows from within, must take up the world's fight, 'By all means let's have post-imperial modesty but let's refuse post-imperial sulking . . . We continue to have significant power, hard and soft, and we have a moral obligation to use that power to best effect.'[42]

We might note the affinity between this post-Calvinist constitution of kinship as the ground of imperial ethics and callousness, and the thought of another lowland Scot, born just 50 miles away in Ecclefechan, 150 years before Biggar. One hears an echo of Thomas Carlyle, who in his infamous *Occasional Discourse on the Nigger Question* (1853) argued the British should care for those close to them before cosmopolitan 'philanthropy' towards offshore suffering, who preferred a society organized by ancient hierarchies, loyalties and kinship, while celebrating the Empire's heroes.[43] Biggar's pro-empire, indeed pro-empire violence apologetics, and his closely linked 'just war' arguments and justifications for torture, are certainly in continuity with how Carlyle, Kingsley, Dickens and Froude found fine words to defend the brutal repression of the Morant Bay Rebellion in Jamaica in 1865 when British troops killed 439 people, flogged hundreds with cat-o-nine tails made up mostly of brass piano wire, killed pregnant women, even smashed babies' heads.[44]

As with Carlyle and Froude, there is an efficient logical circle which connects Biggar's taking of kinship as moral community to his justification of contemporary violence, to his pursuit of an edifying moral spectacle in the history of the British Empire. 'We' have the right to kill and rule others without their consent now, and even where we judge it necessary to torture, and we had it then. A certain anxiety about history arises from this glance backwards and forwards to different generations of killers and torturers with whom one identifies. It seems to be coped with either by averting the gaze from episodes of the inhumanity of one's imagined kin, or by applying positive stories to bandage over events which might provoke shame. This Whiggish insistence on the Empire's past as underpinning a national mission to be revived and extended, today Afghanistan tomorrow Syria, explains why almost every Oxford historian has run as quickly and far as he or she can from Biggar's 'Ethics and Empire' project.[45]

There are larger reasons than a Whiggish attitude for grave concern about Biggar's use of history. As one revelatory example, I recommend his essay 'Less Hegel, More History! Christian Ethics and Political Realities', in which he urges his theological colleagues to think less from theory and instead to turn to history (in particular war and high-political decision-making):

> Suppose, then, that one evening our ethicist lays down his copy of Augustine or Vitoria and takes up Barrie Pitt's history of the battle of El Alamein, when the British Commonwealth scored its first major victory on land over the Germans in the Second World War . . . History, then, teaches that a kind of certain professional callousness is a condition of military success.[46]

It is quite extraordinary: from a story told about Montgomery by a single historian, Biggar feels able to deduce a truth which can somehow affect ethical thinking in some enduring portable way.

Sir Christopher Clark once made the devastating quip that the problem with Max Hastings is he thinks anyone who writes about the past is a historian. Biggar takes this one step worse, it seems anyone who reads about the past, even in a single secondary source, can speak with the authority of the historian. His method consists of cherry-picking what he takes to be facts from books which reflect back to him the kin-ego in an attractive form, and keeping a scrupulous distance from anything which might contradict his intuitions. He doesn't seem inclined to read widely enough to get anything quite right. His website proposes as its first example of the positive ethical role of the British Empire how Britain 'suppressed the Atlantic and African slave-trades after 1833.'[47] The problem is not just the schoolboy error, which has been up on the website for over a year, of confusing the date of the Emancipation Act (1833) for that of the Abolition of the Slave Trade (1807, enforced south of the Equator only after 1850); more worrying is its ignorance of Britain's role long after 1834 as the key financier of, and trader with, the cotton and sugar plantations of the United States, Brazil and Cuba, where slavery persisted into the 1860s and 1880s.[48] In his apology for Cecil Rhodes, he takes a single account of Rhodes having Zulu friends as a child, and his will's intention that the Rhodes Scholarships be open to all South African races (by which the old rogue of course meant only Afrikaners as well as the English, not Khoisan, Xhosa, Zulu, Malays, Indians or Chinese), as evidence of Rhodes not being a racist.[49] In support of his take on the Irish War of Independence, he appeals repeatedly to Peter Hart's *The IRA and its Enemies: Violence and*

Community in Cork, 1916–1923 (1998), without noting the accusations of academic fraud raised by its critics, nor any alternative histories of that crisis.[50] It is enough that one view friendly to his political instincts has been published.

My own personal dealings with Biggar have been limited to the famous 'Must Rhodes Fall?' debate in the Oxford Union, in which his team was defeated. The event was clearly troubling enough for him to provoke him to write at length about it in his apologia about 'coming out as a rightist':

> [In] the opening sally of one of my opponents, Richard Drayton . . . [he] argued that, if he were to presume to offer his opinions on the theology of the eucharist, he, as an historian of Africa, wouldn't deserve to be taken seriously. Therefore, nor should mine on Rhodes, I being a mere theologian. Had there been time to respond, I'd have said that, had an Africanist shared his views on the eucharist, I'd have treated them on their merits, and that it was disappointing that he wouldn't extend the same justice to me.[51]

This is interesting on many levels. He has forgotten not just that my comment on this theme is not at the debut but actually 24 minutes and 50 seconds in, but that I said nothing about 'opinions' but was pointing out the 'appalling oversimplifications and errors' of history he had just made.[52] I can't help feeling, too, that his decision not to present me to that particular constituency of readers as Rhodes Professor of Imperial History but as 'an historian of Africa' had its own slippery rhetorical purpose. But most striking was the concluding suggestion that history was about 'views' and that his idea of the past, on whatever shallow basis it rested, should be taken seriously. Sadly, while the Lutheran doctrine of the priesthood of all believers may be a fine basis for spiritual life, neither in climate science nor in history does it provide a sound basis for thinking, nor standing in scholarly debate. The pride and dignity of history as a discipline is that it yields robust and measured knowledge of the past by the weighing of evidence and interpretations based on deep immersion in contemporary sources and traditions of scholarship. The price of admission to the history game is higher than simply having strong views about the past. Perhaps Biggar's lawyerly arguing of provocative views, with friendly 'facts' hastily mustered and hostile ones ignored or quarantined, is respectable in the world of Christian ethics? But there too, it seems, there are some who are troubled by oversimplifications and omissions in his theology.[53]

Neither Biggar nor his growing public seem to see, or at least to be troubled by, the lack of rigour and shallow learning which underpins his attempt to tell moralizing stories about the nation. This is because the actual truth of what happened in the past is probably secondary in importance to him and his audience. What matters is kinship, and what threads of possible truth might be harvested, by whatever means, and twined into a twenty-first-century rehearsal of that imagined identity. He is not 'post-truth', but pre-truth: knowing who you are, who are your kin, what their past and their projects are, precedes and organizes a moral and cognitive order. It is, in practice, a profoundly situationist ethics, in which the predicament of birth becomes the ground on which the world is commanded. It is an ethics and intellectual practice that begins and ends in narcissism, even an idolatry of the self. If there is a kind of urgency, even stridency, to Biggar's voice, that clearly has its basis in a sense of threat to that cherished idol of the self as it is experienced in history and memory. 'When an Anglo-Saxon puts together Japan, the Second World War and a locomotive, he arrives at one thing only: the Burma Railway', Biggar writes on a visit to Japan in 2016 when, ironically, he chided his hosts for their national lack of shame and repentance for their imperial crimes.[54] Perhaps, at least if that self-defined 'Anglo-Saxon' brings on holiday with him the childhood trauma of seeing whites reduced to slaves and coolies in *Bridge Over the River Kwai*.

The kin idol's face became painfully visible in Biggar's response to the Royal Historical Society's October 2018 report *Race, Ethnicity & Equality in UK History*. Declaring his scepticism about what he called the RHS's 'campaign to promote "Black History"', he declared that history teaching should instead prioritize how 'we British have come to be as we are'.[55] Quite apart from suggesting he hadn't actually read the report before shooting from the hip, he seems to think that 'we British' have a history to which 'Black History' is peripheral. Now, to be clear, Biggar is not a racist. As Chaplain of Oriel in 1995, after reading Colin Powell's autobiography, he urged the British Army to ensure its officers were not promoted on the basis of 'the colour of their skin, their private incomes, or their public-school manners'.[56] People of colour are clearly welcome to the commons of the kin, although perhaps only as supplements, as they agree to fit into the old order. It is not clear, though, judging from his response to the report, if Biggar has quite wrestled with the price of this idea of history, as explained in a jesting response to his letter in 1995: 'Mr Biggar could in turn cheer me up by telling me why he thinks so few people of General Colin Powell's background have achieved the distinction of, say, a bishopric, headship of an Oxbridge college or even the dizzy heights of a college chaplaincy?'[57] He has not understood, not least in the question of Rhodes statue in Oxford, how a backward-looking idea of dead kin distorts one's capacity to make kinship with the living in the present.

For Biggar and his secular congregation his practical theology of war and history fills a space of post-colonial loss. It compensates for a sense of personal diminishment premised on an earlier narcissistic identification with Britain's power, with an imagined past and future of a Greater Britain. That he and they generally favour Brexit is not coincidental. 'Take back control' was the theme of the politics of Brexit, given a libidinal twist, for example in Daniel Hannan's suggestion 'Let's dump the E.U. and rekindle our love affair with India'.[58]

Melancholy is combined with the pleasurable fiction of a repressed self claiming expression, with fantasies of agency, power, and virtue.[59] Were this just a solitary vice, we might allow its sharers their private pleasures, but it is linked with real-world violent projects which can never be satisfied, an imagined past that never can be restored, and a kinship, so passionately desired, which will only be whole in mourning. This is the pathos of the Brexit camp. In a decade or two, this whole mind-world will be gone, as foreign and strange to Britain as medieval crusaders. We may hope these embers of empire do not spark new destructive flames before, at last, they die.

Notes

1 Michel de Certeau, *The Writing of History*, trans. Tom Conley, (New York: Columbia University Press), 77–8.

2 Carlo Ginzburg and Anna Davin, 'Morelli, Freud and Sherlock Holmes: Clues and Scientific Method'. *History Workshop*, no. 9 (1980): 5–36; Edoardo Grendi, 'Microanalisi e Storia Sociale, SOCIALE.' *Quaderni Storici* 12, no. 35 (2) (1977): 506–20; Matti Peltonen, 'Clues, Margins, and Monads: The Micro-Macro Link in Historical Research'. *History and Theory* 40, no. 3 (2001): 347–59.

3 'Biggar, Rev. Canon Prof. Nigel John', *Who's Who*, http://www.ukwhoswho.com/view/10.1093/ww/9780199540884.001.0001/ww-9780199540884-e-245063. Biggar's family history may be pursued through https://www.genealogy.com/ftm/b/i/g/Kenneth-H-Biggar/WEBSITE-0001/UHP-0295.html

4 'How to define a united Ireland', *The Times,* 31 December 1993 and 'Overcoming "obstacles" to Anglo-Irish negotiations', *The Independent*, 18 July 1994.

5 'Independence will do nothing for Scots', *Standpoint Magazine*, May 2014, http://www.standpointmag.co.uk/features-may-14-independence-nothing-for-scots-nigel-biggar-referendumpage=0%2C0%2C0%2C0%2C0%2C0%2C0%2C0%2C0%2C4; 'Scottish independence seems like a false God', https://www.mcdonaldcentre.org.uk/news/scottish-independence-seems-false-god

6 Nigel Biggar, *In Defence of War* (Oxford: Oxford University Press, 2013); 'Don't be so sure that invading Iraq was immoral', *Financial Times* (10 February 2010); 'Saddam's evil regime had to go', *The Times* (27 August 2015). For his comment on the Easter Rebellion and the Anglo-Irish civil war of 1919–21 see his *Between Kin and Cosmopolis: An Ethic of the Nation* (London: James Clarke, 2014): 93–4.

7 'Was Britain Right to Go to War in 1914?', *Standpoint Magazine*, http://standpointmag.co.uk/features-september-13-was-britain-right-to-go-to-war-in-1914-nigel-biggar-first-world-war?page=0%2C0%2C0%2C0%2C0%2C0%2C0%2C0%2C0%2C0%2C4

8 'Intervention in Syria is Britain's moral duty', *The Times* (10 October 2015).

9 *The Times* (10 May 2011).

10 *The Times* (19 November 1999).

11 *The Times* (26 August 2011).

12 Nigel Biggar, 'What is the good of Establishment?', *Standpoint Magazine* (April 2011), http://www.standpointmag.co.uk/features-april-11-what-is-the-good-of-establishment-nigel-biggar-church-of-england-humanist-liberalism

13 *The Times* (9 January 2016).

14 Nigel Biggar, Opening speech in Oxford Union debate of 19 January 2016, which may be seen on https://www.youtube.com/watch?v=uPsQF91bZFA; on Seacole, *The Times* (20 June 2016).

15 'Europe's imperial ambitions led to Brexit', *The Times* (4 September 2017). For Biggar's pro-Brexit views his Twitter stream of retweets provides abundant further evidence.

16 'Agenda: Why we should learn to live with Trident', *The Herald* (18 July 2016), https://www.heraldscotland.com/news/14624940.agenda-why-we-should-learn-to-live-with-trident/

17 Nigel Biggar, 'In defence of killing the innocent, deliberately but not intentionally', *Public Discourse* (28 April 2014), https://www.thepublicdiscourse.com/2014/04/13050/; Nigel Biggar, *Aiming to Kill: The Ethics of Suicide and Euthanasia* (London: Darton, Longman & Todd, 2004).

18 Nigel Biggar, 'Individual Rights versus Common Security? Christian Moral Reasoning about Torture', *Studies in Christian Ethics* 27, no. 1 (2014): 13–14.

19 'The Obsession with gender identity has gone too far', *The Times* (2 August 2018).

20 https://twitter.com/NigelBiggar/status/1110252451070918657

21 'Europe's imperial ambitions lead to Brexit', *The Times*, 4 September 2017, and 'Universities needn't fear a No-Deal Brexit', *The Guardian*, 8 January 2019.

22 E.g. the equation of Biggar with the victims of Stalinism in *The Times* (8 October 2018).

23 Nigel Biggar, 'Outing yourself as a rightist isn't easy', *The Conservative Online*, http://theconservative.online/article/outing_yourself_as_a_rightist_isnt_easy

24 For his attempt to urge the University of Cambridge and/or Churchill College, Cambridge to discipline Gopal, and the use of Twitter to stoke the fire, see Nigel Biggar, 'Vile abuse is now tolerated in our universities', *The Times* (10 April 2018), and the retweet, https://twitter.com/nigelbiggar/status/984346457686839296 . As an example of what followed see Guy Adams, 'How can Cambridge allow this Don to spit out her hate-filled bile', *Daily Mail*, https://www.pressreader.com/uk/daily-mail/20180412/281861529084026, or read the thread on tweets such as https://twitter.com/alexvtunzelmann/status/984366969762795520. For a discussion of the episode see https://thetab.com/uk/cambridge/2018/04/12/cambridge-academic-faces-racist-daily-mail-smear-campaign-110185

25 'Societies @ Monkton', https://www.monktoncombeschool.com/assets/files/seniorschooldocs/SocietiesIndex2014-2015.pdf

26 On Packer's influential career see Timothy F. George (ed.), *J. I. Packer and the Evangelical Future: The Impact of His Life and Thought* (Grand Rapids, MI: Baker Academic, 2009) and Leland Ryken, *J. I. Packer: An Evangelical Life* (Wheaton, IL: Crossway, 2015).

27 It seems, however, that tensions had opened up between Packer and Biggar by the late 1980s; see his review of J. I. Packer et al., *Here we Stand: Justification by Faith Today* (London: Hodder & Stoughton, 1986) in *The Churchman*, vol. 100(4), 365–7, https://biblicalstudies.org.uk/pdf/churchman/100-04_346.pdf

28 *Theological Politics: A Critique of 'Faith in the City'*. Latimer Studies 29/30 (Oxford: Latimer House, 1988).

29 'Mrs. Thatcher's Moral Reformation', *Latimer Comment* 30 (Spring 1990). I am grateful to the Librarian of Latimer House for providing me with a copy.

30 Nigel Biggar, *The Hastening that Waits: Karl Barth's Ethics* (Oxford: Clarendon, 1993).

31 The introductory page of the 'Ethics and Empire' website helpfully collects, and provides digital links to, all of these interventions: https://www.mcdonaldcentre.org.uk/ethics-and-empire

32 https://www.lexisnexis.com/uk/legal/api/version1/sr?sr–igel+Biggar&csi=139185&oc =00240&shr=t&scl=t&hac=f&hct=f&nonLatin1Chars=true&elb=t&apiFlaps=All+Result s%3BNews%3B&crth=off&secondRedirectIndicator=true#0|1|BOOLEAN||||

33 Biggar, 'Outing yourself as a Rightist isn't easy'.

34 *The Times* (31 December 1993); *The Independent* (18 July 1994); *The Guardian* (3 September 1994).

35 *The Guardian* (27 September 2002).

36 Biggar, 'Scottish Independence Seems like a False God', *Church Times* (8 September 2014), http://www.mcdonaldcentre.org.uk/news/scottish-independence-seems-false-god; Nigel Biggar, 'Unionists Don't Despair, Scotland is not Lost – Yet', *Standpoint* (September 2015), http://standpointmag.co.uk/features-september-2015-nigel-biggar-scotland-is-not-lost-snp

37 *The Times* (18 February 2018).

38 Nigel Biggar, *Between Kin and Cosmopolis* (Eugene, OR: Cascade Books, 2014).

39 'Faith and Reason: The lightness of a half real liberty', *The Independent* (17 April 1993).

40 Nigel Biggar, 'The nation state and the case for remaining in the EU', http://www.reimagingeurope.co.uk/nation-state-case-remaining-eu/

41 Nigel Biggar, 'Less Hegel, More History! Christian Ethics and Political Realities', *Providence Magazine* (March 2016), https://providencemag.com/2016/05/less-hegel-history-christian-ethics-political-realities/

42 Nigel Biggar, 'What the United Kingdom is Good For', *These Islands* (24 October 2017), http://www.these-islands.co.uk/publications/i260/what_the_united_kingdom_is_good_for.aspx; and see *The Times* (1 February 2017).

43 Thomas Carlyle, *Occasional Discourse on the Nigger Question* (London, 1853).

44 *Report of the Jamaica Royal Commission* (London, 1866), especially 77, 334; Bernard Semmel, *The Governor Eyre Controversy* (London: MacGibbon & Kee, 1962).

45 Of the army of Oxford historians, the only loyal participant is Alexander Morrison of New College.

46 Biggar, 'Less Hegel, More History! Christian Ethics and Political Realities'.

47 See https://www.mcdonaldcentre.org.uk/ethics-and-empire

48 See Marika Sherwood, *After Abolition: Britain and the Slave Trade since 1807* (London: I. B. Tauris, 2007).

49 E.g. Nigel Biggar, 'Rhodes, Race and the Abuse of History', *Standpoint Magazine* (March 2016), http://www.standpointmag.co.uk/node/6388/full

50 Biggar, *In Defence of War*, 46 n.141 and *Between Kin and Cosmopolis*, 94–5. On the controversy see Ian McBride, 'The Peter Hart Affair in Perspective: History, Ideology and the Irish Revolution *The Historical Journal* 61, no. 1 (2018): 249–71.

51 Biggar, 'Outing yourself as a Rightist isn't easy'.

52 See 'Must Rhodes Fall? | Full Debate | Oxford Union', *YouTube* (21 January 2016), https://www.youtube.com/watch?v=y3aBDBdDIgU

53 Richard B. Hays's complains about Biggar brushing aside and ignoring counter-examples, and offering large claims on flimsy evidence in 'Narrate and Embody: A response to Nigel Biggar's "Specify and Distinguish"', *Studies in Christian Ethics* 22, no. 2 (2009): 185–19, especially 187, 191 and 192; Andrew Torrance charges that 'Biggar's presentation of Barth is superficial', in 'Karl Barth on the Irresistible Nature of Grace', *Journal of Reformed Theology* 10, no. 2 (2016): 19; and Alistair McIntosh describes the 'straw man feel' of *In Defence of War* in his review in *Third Way* 36, no. 10 (2013): 40, http://www.alastairmcintosh.com/articles/2013-ThirdWay-Defence-War-Biggar.pdf

54 *The Times* (16 February 2016).

55 *The Times* (19 October 2018).

56 *The Times* (7 October 1995).

57 Harry Holt, Letter, *The Times* (17 October 1995).

58 *The Telegraph* (9 November 2015).

59 See Paul Gilroy, *Postcolonial Melancholia* (New York: Columbia University Press, 2005) and Fintan O'Toole, *Heroic Failure: Brexit and the Politics of Pain* (London: Head of Zeus, 2018).

Chapter 15
Visions of China
Robert Bickers

I am doing what the British people want, which is delivering on Brexit, but also getting out around the world, ensuring that we bring jobs back to Britain. Companies will be selling more Great British products to China as a result of this trip. There will be more people in jobs in the UK as a result of this trip. That's Global Britain in action.

Prime Minister Theresa May, on her return from China, 2 February 2018[1]

Ah yes, there is always China, but then this is an old, fond, foolish dream. 'Before leaving England', wrote a British naval officer in his memoirs,

> I made a tour of our principal building yards, especially those on the Clyde, to find the cost of building [a cruiser], and I was surprised and shocked to find vast machine rooms standing idle, long queues of un-employed men and general poverty. I had had no idea things were so bad. This was in January 1931. I resolved there and then to do my best to get Chinese ships to be built in the United Kingdom.[2]

The writer, Harold Baillie-Grohman, then a recently-appointed captain, was a career naval officer, who in November 1930 was appointed to head the British Naval Mission to China. His military experience aside, Baillie-Grohman's qualifications for this task were slight. Like most Royal Navy officers, he had completed a tour on the China Station, serving from April 1912 to January 1914 as a Lieutenant on the armoured cruiser HMS *Monmouth*. This was not generally an experience that taught men much about China. And the land of 1912–14, in the immediate aftermath of the revolution that led to the fall of the Qing Dynasty and the replacement of the imperial system with a republic, was not the China of 1931. While Baillie-Grohman toured shipyards, China's National Government, which was dominated by the Guomindang – the National People's Party – which had seized power in 1926–28 in what was known as the Nationalist Revolution – was consolidating its authority after resisting the challenges posed by large-scale revolts by militarist power-holders in the north and south-east. These had been defeated on the battlefield and through palavers, and by the end of 1930 the Nationalist leader Chiang Kai-shek was firmly in control.

The Naval Mission resulted from a Sino-British agreement signed in Nanjing in June 1929 that had been developed at the initiative of China's naval chief. Its aim was to support the modernization of the Chinese navy, and its key activities were the training of naval cadets in Britain, the despatch of an advisory mission to China, and the upgrading of the fleet, partly through 'substantial orders' to be placed in Britain or Northern Ireland.[3] The relationship with Britain on naval matters was a long-standing one, although it had never been smooth, but its maritime forces had never been prioritized by the Chinese state.[4] Its first experience of deploying a modern fleet in battle had lasted about twelve furious minutes when French warships sprang a surprise attack on its southern squadron in Fuzhou harbour on 23 August 1884 and largely destroyed it. The 1929 agreement fell more firmly into a history of the jockeying for political influence and potential commercial advantage by foreign powers in China, whose diplomats there sought advisory posts for their nationals in national and provincial governments. It was also squarely in a tradition of manoeuvring Chinese power-holders into agreements that committed them to contracting for goods or services provided by agents of one nationality in preference to another.

Baillie-Grohman's papers provide much by way of evidence for his careful attempts to bring himself up to speed. He corresponded with retired China hands, pulled together a reading list, and tried to prepare himself for dealing with the Nationalists and their new dispensation. The Guomindang was a revolutionary anti-imperialist party that had capitalized on a wave of nationalist protest across China in 1925–27 sparked by bloody encounters between foreign forces and Chinese demonstrators or militaries. Although it had viciously suppressed its former communist allies and its own left-wing, the Guomindang remained committed to terminating what were characterized as the 'unequal treaties' that buttressed foreign privilege in China. It aimed to remake the state, and to remake its foreign relations. By late 1930 it had made significant progress with this, not least in regaining sovereignty over its tariffs and pushing weaker foreign states to renegotiate their treaties. Nationalist diplomats were talented, highly educated and cosmopolitan. Their British interlocutors, largely trained in and for an older world, found it difficult to adjust.

Baillie-Grohman's other concern was to try to understand China and the Chinese (and the 'Chinese mind') in a more general sense. He needed to know how to negotiate, how to interact, and what to expect. His informants were retired British members of the Chinese Maritime Customs Service, naval officers with more recent experience in the country, and consuls. This continued when he arrived. As he was based in Nanjing, the Nationalist capital, he even sought out the China-born American author, Pearl Buck, who lived in the city, and whose novel of Chinese rural life, *The Good Earth*, had recently been published to widespread acclaim. His correspondents fired back their thoughts on the Chinese character, Chinese society and culture, adding to the notes he took on his discussion with Buck: 'Be firm', they are 'too adaptable', 'lack a sense of proportion', and so on.[5]

Despite all this preparation, the British Naval Mission was a failure. Baillie-Grohman did not secure the orders he hoped to get for British yards. He did not lack support from the diplomats, but his dream of a Chinese rescue for the Clydeside unemployed was quickly disillusioned. The mission was a 'farce' he told the British Minister to China in August 1931. Although the British shipbuilders Vickers-Armstrong had quickly come to Whitehall in the autumn of 1929 to seek support for a tender to construct a cruiser, other British interests objected, for the resources would come from a charge on China's Customs revenue, and that was already steeply hypothecated to servicing long-standing debts. Although the British cabinet had approved the initiative, and Vickers-Armstrong had spent almost a year pursuing the deal, the contract had gone to a Japanese yard with the keel laid down in the Harima Shipyard just as Baillie-Grohman arrived in China, a prospect a paper presented to cabinet had described as 'regrettable from the point of view of unemployment in this country'.[6] Persisting nonetheless, to the end, Baillie-Grohman used a meeting he managed to secure with the Chinese Minister of Finance, Song Ziwen, to lobby for a building programme that would deliver six destroyers, seaplanes and flying boats. He produced a paper arguing for the 'primary importance of sea power' to China, outlining why it could not afford not to develop this capacity. Since his arrival the Japanese Kwantung Army had precipitated the invasion of Manchuria by Imperial forces, a short, bloody, Sino-Japanese war in Shanghai in the early spring of 1932, and the establishment of the puppet state of Manzhouguo. China faced an existential threat, but it now lay within its borders, and no fleets could protect it from that. Song promised to give the 'suggestions his earnest consideration', and changed the subject. Baillie-Grohman went home, empty-handed.[7]

Hope springs eternal in the British heart when thoughts turn to China. It always has, and not only British hearts of course. A vast country surely promises a vast market. Merchants, boosters and wideboys have long looked east to secure themselves a comfortable future. From time to time it has promised the 'El Dorado of commercial men' (1864), 'Four Hundred Million Customers' (1937), the largest market in the world, quick fortunes or steady profits for foreign producers.[8] But any assessment of the course of commerce in the nineteenth and twentieth centuries shows how a resilient and adaptable economy again and again and again undermined the position of Western traders. Any and all advantages they held soon turned to dust, even when the treaties held, and warships like the *Monmouth* rocked in Chinese harbours.[9] Baillie-Grohman was no fool, and meant well, but he was singularly ill-equipped for the role he tried to play. He knew little more than he had learned from wardroom talk on the *Monmouth* back in the days after the fall of the Qing, and then from those he sought advice from as he prepared to travel east. His notes are a fantastic pottage of old saws and clichés, archaic characterization and redundant guidance. With this messy matter he framed his work in China.

This episode prompts a threefold reflection on structural weaknesses and imbalances in Sino-British relations, hopes and dreams. These coalesce around, first, issues of knowledge capacity in Britain; second, its own historic record in China; and third, its place in China's own imaginary. We might additionally note the fact that Baillie-Grohman was so shocked when he made his visits to shipyards, when British shipbuilding was in the midst of a major depression, which suggests how disconnected this intelligent, inquisitive man was from the economic realities of his country's life. In 1929 unemployment in Scotland was 12 per cent; by 1932 it reached almost 28 per cent.[10] To his credit, he thought he saw a direct way he could try to help. Armed with clause 54 of the 1929 agreement, he argued that the National Government should honour its commitment and place its orders. But like many supplicants before and since, he failed. And what are treaties and agreements if policy and pragmatism suggest a partner take a different course?

Baillie-Grohman's homespun repertoire of China knowledge hardly served him well. But for all that the British had had a significant presence in China for nearly a century, knowledge about the country, its cultures and peoples, was grossly deficient. China was barely taught in the universities, and barely recognized as a locus of subjects of any intrinsic worth, its languages were only sparsely taught, and most of what was discussed by British Sinologists dwelt on the deeper past. Even in the specialist commercial sector focusing on China, acquiring a knowledge of its language was given little more than symbolic importance. A young man heading east who had acquired any useful grounding in Chinese was rare, even those who had taken targeted courses in 'Practical Chinese' in London before they sailed.[11] Despite the odd initiative to upgrade the skills of the British business community in China, notably during the First World War, as part of a wider economic warfare strategy, few Britons working in or with China spoke any of its languages. Most of what Britons heading out to China learned they imbibed through representations of China and Chinese in popular culture, or from older 'hands' who spoke from experience. Briton handed on ignorance to Briton, and it largely deepened in the process.

There were a few exceptions, but there was no resource from which the British could draw when they needed to engage effectively with China. This was not without its critics, who pointed to German and Japanese initiatives. The most impressive was the Japanese Tōa Dōbun Shoin (East Asia Common Culture Academy), that from a campus in Shanghai sent out over 5,000 graduates between 1900 and 1945 who found employment in China and Japan, in government, business, education and other sectors. They were trained in Chinese languages, and conducted extensive research fieldwork, investigating Chinese political, commercial and social conditions, and producing (sometimes to commission) an extensive body of reports and assessments. Of course, Japan's distinct advantages in terms of its knowledge of China utterly failed to prevent its militaries embroiling it in a catastrophic war of imperialist aggression: knowledge alone is no asset.[12] Historians' accounts of the sophistication and quality of British intelligence and knowledge of China are more influenced by models of the relationship between power and knowledge than the realities of British practice.[13] The China consular service was to a limited extent an exception, but most men who joined that service were not high-flyers. They had failed in London, and their examination rankings saw them allotted to the east.[14] And in 1930, despite the Royal Navy's own ninety-year presence in Chinese waters, and despite most of its officer corps spending a year or two there, it could not send out as naval adviser a man who spoke a single word of Chinese.

The naïve discussions that pepper Baillie-Grohman's papers show that he and his correspondents were unable to grasp the realities of Chinese politics and the fact that Chinese political actors had their own objectives. Even as he prepared to leave the country, this well-meaning man presented a plan that explained to its Minister of Finance, one of the regime's longest-lasting and most powerful figures, an analysis of what should be its priorities and ambitions. The expert from the Senior Service knew what was best for China. He seemed also to lack any sense of the legacy of British violence in China in the recent past, a roster of 'incidents' and clashes all within the five years prior to his arrival (some instigated by his Navy colleagues), which had placed the British at the forefront of the enemies of the Nationalist Revolution, and he seemed unaware of the continuing impact of the remaining British presence. British businessmen with American and Japanese collaborators, and a token (and outnumbered) group of Chinese councillors, governed the heart of Shanghai. There were British-controlled concessions in Tianjin, Xiamen, and Guangzhou, their streets, like Shanghai's, patrolled by British men and British Indian recruits to concession police forces. A British Supreme Court sat in Shanghai and exercised jurisdiction alongside British consuls over British subjects. The Royal Navy patrolled the Yangzi and coast, and the Guangdong and Guangxi province river systems, protecting British vessels that dominated China's shipping sphere, and it held summer exercises at its base at Weihaiwei. Hong Kong remained a British Crown

Colony. The Guomindang's political objectives included dismantling all this apparatus of control and influence. The British were their political enemies, and in their Southeast Asian colonies combatted the rise in influence of the Guomindang among their Chinese colonial subjects. But, exercising as ever the sweet privilege of British envoys before and since, Baillie-Grohman thought all this was past matter.

Even setting aside this bitter legacy, Chinese elites did not look to Britain as they planned the rehabilitation and development of their country, nor later its defence. They turned to Germany for technological and military advice and assistance; they looked to Japan, despite the conflict, in an ambiguous relationship that drew on geographical proximity and the model it provided of development and re-establishment of sovereignty and autonomy. They looked to assert China's place in international organizations and networks, such as the League of Nations, arguing that these should recognize the integrity and value of the cultures and civilizations that were excluded from these, except as voiceless colonial subjects. Most of all they looked to the United States, where large numbers of them had been educated, and from which came an increasingly influential body of ideas, and philanthropic and other initiatives. The world looked different from Nanjing: London was far away, the British confused, conservative and wedded to their concessions and privileges, their symbols and past glories, to the Union Jack flying high in Chinese cities. Ultimately this new Chinese leadership looked to themselves, for they aimed to re-establish China's position as a dominant regional power, reclaiming in a way the role of the Qing, and one that would play a leading role in reshaping the global order. In the midst of the Second World War, when finally allied with the British and Americans against the Japanese, those ideas found articulate presentation in Chiang Kai-shek's manifesto, *China's Destiny* (*Zhongguo de mingyun*, 1943). The vision of China presented shocked Allied observers, for here was no gratitude or humility, but a paean to nationalism as a supreme virtue, and claim for the re-establishment of greatness and, it seemed, influence far across its borders.

So what has changed? When latter-day Baillie-Grohmans step off their planes at Shanghai's Pudong Airport, or Beijing Capital, fresh to China, hoping to sell their 'Great British products', or come to join networking events organized by the Foreign & Commonwealth Office and UK's Department of International Trade under the 'Great' marketing banner, having been inspired by analysis presented online or at events in Bristol, London, or Manchester by the China-Britain Business Council or British Chamber of Commerce, are they better prepared? After all, the former body argues that the British 'are ideal partners for the Chinese economy and for Chinese firms' and endorses the view that 'the UK has a history of global trading engagement stretching across centuries'.[15] Are they more fully briefed in terms of their knowledge of China; are they better placed in terms of the historic relationship and its legacies; will they find there willing partners who share their global vision and whose strategic objectives are aligned with their own? The answers are simple: no, no, and no.

For a start British capacity in terms of critically understanding China, its politics, culture and society, and in terms of language training and cultural familiarization, remains disproportionate to the challenges the country faces, the opportunities that exist, and clear crying need. Universities have certainly seen a substantial increase in provision of language programmes, and the appointment to disciplinary departments of those trained in the history, politics, sociology or economics of China, for example. China as a field of study is much more solidly within the mainstream repertoire that an undergraduate in many disciplines might choose from. China has moved out of the hands of Sinology into social sciences, arts and humanities disciplines, and out of a small set of universities and across the British higher education landscape. But this is limited (only 35 out of 106 HEIs have a dedicated Chinese studies programme of any sort), and it is uneven, and this growth has largely been outsourced: Germany, the Netherlands, the United States and of course China, have in large measure provided the trained researchers who have filled these posts. An internationalized academic culture is to be welcomed and defended, but the surrender of a national capacity in this (and other) specialist area studies sectors ought to be a matter of some concern. The growth in specialist centres and programmes has had its setbacks, with closures of programmes in prominent universities. Between 2012/13 and 2014/15 numbers of students enrolled full-time in Chinese studies courses actually declined by 10 per cent, and postgraduate numbers by 30 per cent.[16] Only 210 British nationals commenced study of a single-honours Chinese programme in 2016/17; 190 began Japanese.[17] Specific capacity-building initiatives have come and gone, answering the clarion calls of reports from the Higher Education Funding Council and others about capacity in 'strategically important and vulnerable subjects' – defined as 'recognizably specialist knowledge, skills and competencies [that] will be required by the economy, society or Government in future'. But if sustainability remains an urgent issue, the potential for actual growth to engage with the new challenges and opportunities of a Global Britain engaging China is simply a chimera.[18] Even without the potential steep challenges of renegotiating a global presence after Brexit, this is a lamentable state of affairs; with it, it's a crisis.

Even setting aside the lack of any sustainable capacity in Chinese specialisms that might, for example, help trade deal negotiations and build the bigger cadre of China-expertise across national life that will be needed, there is a wider public lack of understanding about China, about the nature, strategies and objectives of the Chinese party-state, and about the history of the bilateral relationship. There never was a 'golden age' in China–Britain relations to renew, of course (this phrase decorates recent public statements from London and from Beijing), unless that world of concessions, gunboats and, before Baillie-Grohman's time, opium, is elided. Empire itself is barely yesterday. Britain only abandoned its last enclave in China just over two decades ago, when in 1997 it surrendered the Crown Colony at Hong Kong. In the run-up to the transfer, Chinese party-state research institutes looked closely to see what hidden constitutional legacies 156 years of British rule might have left behind in a system that was, by treaty, to persist for an agreed 50 years after 1997. But the critical tensions have come instead from Hong Kong's young, sparking the pro-democracy Umbrella Movement in 2015, and continuing contestation of the increasingly hard line adopted by the Special Administrative Region's leadership, their tone and actions set by Beijing. Any notion that Britain had any post-handover duty of care, or responsibility to audit the implementation of the agreement it had been co-signatory to, has been rejected by China. The line adopted is simple: Britain has no right to interfere in China's internal affairs. This has its contemporary but also its historic facets. Britain's past record in China remains little known and less discussed in Britain. Try asking any group, of any age, of women and men who studied in the British education system whether they learned anything of China during their schooling. Almost without exception the answer will be no.

This is no lament from a historian who feels his discipline ignored or overlooked in public life. But it needs to be understood how the past is deployed regularly in China's foreign relations and its domestic politics. Japan, largely, has borne the brunt of this (and Japanese politics has not helped this at times). It is a weapon in the armoury. Out it comes when needed. There, for example, was a British Secretary of State 'resurrecting the Cold War and gunboat diplomacy', as China's Ambassador wrote in February 2019, when Gavin Williamson talked of sending Britain's lone aircraft carrier to the South China Sea, soft echoes of Harold Baillie-Grohman's old China Station beat.[19] And seemingly simple matters from the deeper past can inflame Chinese public opinion, such as antiquities looted in times of war, which resurface in auction houses, or which grace national museums and galleries. The British role in the opium trade, in Hong Kong, and in Tibet, and on the Sino-Indian border in general, all have the capacity to be used in contemporary politics. The Chinese people's 'bitter memory of history' was referred to in the Chinese Embassy's bullish riposte to public protests in Britain about the execution of a British subject convicted of drug smuggling in 2009: that 'bitter memory', of urbane Mr William Jardine, and affable Mr James Matheson, and their partners and collaborators in the opium trade, is kept alive in an ongoing Patriotic Education Campaign that runs through the entire educational system. On the day Xi Jinping formally assumed power in November 2012, the Chinese Communist Party's General Secretary, and so China's President, went with leading colleagues to visit the National Museum of China's permanent exhibition, 'The Road to Rejuvenation', which surveys in detail the century of 'National Humiliation', and the brighter path of development under

Communist Party rule. The past was a lesson, and the objective Xi said, was 'the great rejuvenation of the Chinese nation', with 'nationalism at the core'. The underlying issue is that the Chinese party-state secures its legitimacy today on the twin pillars of prosperity and a nationalism forged out of anti-imperialism. In its popular forms this nationalism can be raucous, and it can be violent, and its reference points are the past: yesterday's humiliations, yesterday's weaknesses, yesterday's defeats and subordination.

That nationalism also has another strand. The China resurgent dreams of Chiang Kai-shek in the darkest days of the Second World War have their modern parallel in the 'China Dream' of a 'Great Rejuvenation of the Chinese nation' in Xi Jinping's authoritarian state. If Chiang Kai-shek had had the navy Baillie-Grohman urged his minister to purchase, he too would have staked out an exclusive claim, as the Chinese state now has done, on the Spratly Islands, Paracels, and other contested shoals and archipelagos. China's investment globally in a new infrastructure beyond its borders, in harbours, canals, railways and roads, the so-called 'One Belt One Road' initiative, is a clear statement of its bid for influence and recognition. The first time a modern state initiated, rather more fitfully and slowly, a global infrastructure to facilitate trade, communications, and national defence, and to project its power softly, and bluntly, involving at least in part a rhetoric of disinterestedness ('civilizing mission'), was in the nineteenth century and it was headquartered from London. We call it empire. China's place within that new global system was subordinate, whatever the sweet talk otherwise of ambassadors and envoys.

Those sketching their visions of 'Global Britain' have argued, for example, that 'people around the world are looking for a lead from Britain', that 'the emerging balance of power system in Asia needs the influence of friendly countries', that a rising power like China, in short, 'needs' a British helping hand, that London is ready 'to encourage and support' Beijing as it takes its place in the world.[20] But there is no place in this new Chinese vision of its role in Asia, for Global Britain. Global China does not need a British helping hand, and will not reach for one; it does not offer any partnership of equals; it does not provide a future.

Notes

1 HC780 House of Commons Foreign Affairs Committee, *Global Britain: Sixth Report of Session 2017–19* (London: House of Commons, 2018), 9.

2 Vice-Admiral Harold Baillie-Grohman, 'Flashlights on the Past', volume two: National Maritime Museum Harold Baillie-Grohman papers, GRO 33. Unless otherwise cited below, this essay draws in large part from my book *Out of China: How the Chinese Ended the Era of Western Domination* (London: Penguin, 2017).

3 Clause 54, 'Contract for British Naval Assistance to China', 20 June 1929, copy in Admiralty to Foreign Office, 12 July 1929, F3511/825/10, FO 371/13941.

4 The most notable episodes were those involving H. N. Lay and Captain Sherard Osborne (in the early 1860s), and William Lang (1882–90): neither ended well. See Jack J. Gerson, *Horatio Nelson Lay and Sino-British Relations, 1854–1864* (Harvard University Asia Center, 1972); Chia-chen Wang, 'Li Hungchang and the Peiyang Navy', in Samuel C. Chu, and Kwang-Ching Liu (eds), *Li Hung-chang and China's Early Modernization* (Armonk, NY: M. E. Sharpe, 1994), 248–62.

5 'Training of Chinese Officers in Royal Navy', National Maritime Museum Harold Baillie-Grohman papers, GRO 14.

6 See papers in F825/10, FO 371/13941, especially Sir John Pratt, Foreign Office Minute, 'Supply of Cruisers to Chinese Government', 18 November 1929, F5959/825/10, FO 371/13941; *China Press* (4 May 1931): 2.

7 'Interview between Mr T. V. Soong, and Commodore Baillie-Grohman on Naval Policy, 1 December 1932, in F946/349/10, FO 371/17109. The cruiser, the *Ning Hai*, sailed in 1932, and was sunk by the Japanese in September 1937.

8 Carl Crow, *Four Hundred Million Customers* (London: Hamish Hamilton, 1937).

9 For one assessment see: Paul A. Varg, 'The Myth of the China Market, 1890–1914', *American Historical Review* 73, no. 3 (1968), 742–58; for a modern take see Joe Studwell, *The China Dream: the quest for the last great untapped market on earth* (London: Profile, 2002); for a fable of failure see Tim Collins, *Mr China* (New York: Collins, 2009).

10 Neil K. Buxton, 'Economic Growth in Scotland between the Wars: The Role of Production Structure and Rationalization', *Economic History Review*, N.S., 33, no. 4 (1980): 541.

11 See my articles '"Coolie work": Sir Reginald Johnston at the School of Oriental and African Studies, 1931–1937', *Journal of the Royal Asiatic Society* 3rd series. 5, no. 3 (1995): 385–401, and 'New Light on Lao She, London, and the London Missionary Society, 1921–1929', *Modern Chinese Literature* 8 (1994): 21–39.

12 Douglas R. Reynolds, 'Training Young China Hands: Tōa Dōbun Shoin and its Precursors, 1886–1945', in Peter Duus, Ramon H. Myers, and Mark R. Peattie (eds), *The Japanese Informal Empire in China, 1895–1937* (Princeton, NJ: Princeton University Press, 1989), 210–71.

13 For example, James L. Hevia, *English Lessons: The Pedagogy of Imperialism in Nineteenth-Century China* (Duke University Press, 2003).

14 P. D. Coates, *The China Consuls: British Consular Officers, 1843–1943* (Hong Kong: Oxford University Press, 1988).

15 Nicholas Beale, 'Opportunities in China for a Global Britain', in CBBC, *China Business Handbook 2017/18*, http://handbook.cbbc.org/handbook#chinabusinesshandbook201718/1_5_opportunities_in_china_for_a_global_britain

16 British Association for Chinese Studies, *Report on the Present State of China-related Studies in the UK*, August 2016, http://bacsuk.org.uk/wp-content/uploads/2015/05/BACS-report-on-China-Studies-2016.pdf. More problematic still is the abdication of responsibility for providing a more tangible infrastructure for developing capacity by British universities in favour of Chinese-funded Confucian Institutes. For a reasoned critique see Marshall Sahlins, *Confucius Institutes: Academic Malware* (Chicago: Prickly Paradigm Press, 2015).

17 Source: HESA data, https://www.hesa.ac.uk/data-and-analysis/students/what-study

18 The key recent report was chaired by Geoffrey Roberts, *Strategically important and vulnerable subjects: Final Report of the advisory group* (HEFCE, 2005/24).

19 Liu Xiaoming, 'Gunboat diplomacy can only harm Britain's relationship with China', *The Guardian* (26 February 2019).

20 Quotations from Boris Johnson's first major speech as Foreign Secretary: 'Beyond Brexit: A Global Britain', 2 December 2016, https://www.gov.uk/government/speeches/beyond-brexit-a-global-britain

Chapter 16
Afterword: The Ongoing Imperial History Wars

Dane Kennedy

We can get so caught up in the daily psychodrama that surrounds Brexit – will it happen? what form will it take? how will it alter Britain and its place in the world? – that it's easy to overlook the historical forces that set the stage for this crisis and shape the parameters of its possible outcomes. Hence the importance of these essays. They remind us of the manifold ways Brexit has a history; a history that's inextricably bound up with the British Empire and the lingering effects of its loss on modern Britons – or, more accurately, on modern English, Scottish, Northern Irish, and other inhabitants of an increasingly dis-United Kingdom.

This volume does not, it should be emphasized, reiterate the now tired and doubtful claim, so popular among some members of the commentariat, that Brexit is simply a manifestation of some deeply rooted nostalgia for empire.[1] Were that the case, we would need to explain, as Stuart Ward and Astrid Rasch astutely observe, the long delay between the end of empire and the enthusiasm for Brexit. Imperial nostalgia is too elusive and ephemeral a sentiment to carry serious explanatory weight for a phenomenon as disruptive and puzzling as Brexit. Rather than giving voice to feelings of nostalgia, which suggests a certain fondness – however misplaced – for the past, a more pertinent feature of the present crisis is what Bill Schwarz diagnoses as 'forgetfulness' and Neal Ascherson as 'amnesia'. This lack of awareness about the past by much of the public and its manipulation by pro-Brexit politicians are essential to an understanding of these unprecedented events.

It's crucial, then, that we distinguish between the intent of those who voted to leave the EU and those who articulated the vision and crafted the policies designed to implement that decision. Postmortems on the referendum have shown that Brexit voters had various concerns, including fear of the loss of national sovereignty, frustration with EU regulations, and objections to the influx of eastern Europeans. Underlying factors included the economic and social repercussions of the 2008 financial crash and the Syrian refugee crisis. While evocations of imperial glory occasionally surfaced in the pro-Brexit campaign, there's little evidence they influenced many voters. As Yasmin Khan notes, even Britons of South Asian origins – not the most receptive audience for such appeals – voted to leave.

For leading Brexiteers, on the other hand, the prospect that Britain could regain some of the greatness they associated with its imperial past was a powerful source of inspiration. Their emotional attachment to this half-remembered, half-invented past served an important practical purpose as well: it provided a convenient placeholder for the otherwise disparate and inchoate aspirations they had for a post-EU Britain. Once they won the referendum and confronted the challenge of exiting the EU, they found it useful, perhaps even necessary, to frame their plans for Britain's future in terms that evoked an idealized version of its past. It's at this point that the language of empire and its euphemisms began to proliferate among government leaders – from Theresa May's faux-visionary call for a new 'Global Britain' through Liam Fox's cynical promotion of the Commonwealth as a substitute for the EU and various other Brexiteers' starry-eyed infatuation with the 'Anglosphere' and 'CANZUK' to Boris Johnson's boorish recitation of Kipling's 'Mandalay' in a Buddhist temple in Myanmar, all of it summed up in that Foreign Office wag's clever coinage, 'Empire 2.0.'

A particularly noteworthy example of this calculated use of imperial rhetoric was recently sacked Defence Secretary Gavin Williamson's speech, 'Defence of Global Britain,' which detailed his vision for Britain's strategic role in the world after Brexit.[2] Embracing what he regarded as the 'greatest opportunity in 50 years to redefine our role,' he described a future for Britain that sounded eerily like its past. 'In an era of "Great Power" competition,' he declared in one passage, 'we cannot be satisfied simply protecting our own backyard. The UK is a global power with truly global interests . . . And since the new Global Great Game will be played on a global playing field, we must be prepared to compete for our interests and our values far, far from home.' Here the various euphemisms of empire – 'Great Power,' 'global power,' 'global interests,' 'Global Great Game,' and 'global playing field,' capped off by that ominous phrase, 'far, far from home' – are strung together to send the unmistakable message that post-Brexit Britain intends to reclaim the glory days of Pax Britannica. Reassuring his audience that 'Britain still matters on the global stage,' Williamson concluded by insisting that 'Brexit has brought us to a moment . . . when we must strengthen our global presence, enhance our lethality, and increase our mass' in order to 'project and maximise our influence around the world'. Whether one regards this speech as magical thinking or mere bluster, it does not shy away from the truth that 'lethality' lies at the heart of empire.

As David Thackery and Richard Toye point out in their essay, May and her colleagues probably don't actually have their sights set on a post-Brexit empire 2.0, or at least not one that resembles the original version. Instead, their evocations of empire are motivated, at least in part, by what Olivette Otele characterizes as 'memory politics,' which are meant to mobilize constituencies around historically charged conceptions of identity and belonging. The essays by Otele, Saul Dubow, and Katie Donington remind us that different parties have engaged in 'memory politics' about Britain's imperial heritage for different purposes. The growing number, visibility and influence of people of colour in British society have given rise to their own 'memory politics', for example. It's worth recalling in this context that all three of the prime ministers who preceded May sought to placate domestic as well as foreign constituencies by issuing apologies or expressions of regret for some of the shameful acts that occurred in the course of empire – Tony Blair for Britain's role in the slave trade and the Irish famine; Gordon Brown for the dominion child migrant scandal; David Cameron for the Bloody Sunday massacre in Northern Ireland and the Amritsar massacre in India. These gestures of contrition were condemned by the political right, however, as attacks on British pride and patriotism. When Blair referred to British colonialism in Africa as a 'blot on our conscience', then journalist Boris Johnson responded by asserting that the 'continent [of Africa] may be a blot, but it is not a blot upon our conscience. The problem is not that we were once in charge, but that we are not in charge any more.'[3] As Richard Drayton shows, it's a sentiment echoed today by that Oxford provocateur, Nigel Biggar. The Biggars of Britain regard campaigns to remove Rhodes' statue from its perch in Oriel College, to 'decolonize' museums and to otherwise call into question the imperial past as efforts to undermine the ethnic nationalism that their own politics celebrates.

The problem is that these politics have reignited the smouldering embers of empire while providing no coherent or viable strategy for Britain after it leaves the EU. No wonder Brexit has become such a psychodrama. It has reaggravated the festering wounds of Irish partition. It has revived the long-harboured resentments of Scottish nationalists. It has stirred up an increasingly volatile English nationalism. It has even placed the fate of Gibraltar, perhaps the most loyal of Britain's remaining colonial dependencies, in doubt. And to what end? While Brexiteers are fond of drawing inspiration for Britain's future from its imperial past, that past is so vast and varied that it confronts them with multiple, mutually incompatible and largely improbable options. Will it be a buccaneering empire of free trade? A closed Commonwealth trading zone? An ethnic alliance of CANZUK countries? An Anglosphere that includes the United States and, as some have suggested, even India? Or perhaps a renewed commitment to the white man's burden in Africa and elsewhere? Each of these options has its advocates. Yet the fact that none of them has any real prospects for success can be attributed, as this book makes abundantly clear, to the Brexiteers' failure to appreciate the complications and contradictions of the imperial past they so eagerly invoke.

As an American, I'm acutely aware that similar politics have been playing out in my country, where Donald Trump's appeals to ethnic nationalism and an idealized past won him the presidency. His campaign catchphrase, 'Make America Great Again,' touched much the same populist nerve as the Brexit slogan, 'Let's Take Back Control.' Camila Schofield demonstrates that Trump's bromance with Nigel Farage is rooted in a longer, deeper and more complex connection between far-right activists in the two countries. Let's not forget, however, that the sordid history of this 'special relationship' between the US and the UK extends beyond the fevered dreams of the populist right; it spurred an earlier, equally disastrous bout of enthusiasm for empire in the aftermath of al-Qaeda's 9/11 attacks. The historically framed arguments that were advanced then in support of the invasion and occupation of Afghanistan and Iraq were no less dubious than those now offered for Brexit. The time had come, we were told, for the United States to accept its responsibilities as Britain's heir and embrace its imperial destiny. We were assured that our countries' shared liberal heritage made our intentions benign, our interventions beneficial. We were informed by one celebrant of empire – writing before globalization had lost its glow – that the imperial baton being passed by the British into American hands was the magic wand of 'anglobalization,' and that it would bring freedom and opportunity to the peoples whose lands we invaded. If only.

Elsewhere I've referred to contending parties' uses and abuses of the imperial past for contemporary purposes as the imperial history wars.[4] Few of these wars have been as politically and morally consequential as the one that arose over this historical prescription for Afghanistan and Iraq – though the war over Brexit's Britannic promises may come close. Most of the imperial history wars have occurred within the confines of the academy, and to many outsiders they may seem mere turf wars. But none of these wars has been entirely about the past – they have always been about how the past informs the present, which is why they have stirred such strong passions. Historians are no more immune from the preoccupations of their own time and place than other members of society, nor should they be.

This book is, in fact, a testament to the insights that historians can bring to a subject as contentious and important as Brexit. I am struck in particular by two qualities that distinguish the perspectives fleshed out in the preceding pages. The first is a shared conviction that a knowledge of the past can help us make sense of the present, but that it cannot provide a model for the future – that is a mirage. And the second is a collective commitment to marshal this knowledge to expose and debunk those who would make politically deceptive, specious, or tendentious appeals to the past. Both of these qualities are essential if Britain is to escape its current impasse.

Notes

1 Examples include David Olugosa, 'Empire 2.0 is dangerous nostalgia for something that never existed', *The Guardian* (18 March 2017) and Ishaan Tharoor, 'Britain clings to imperial nostalgia as Brexit looms', *The Washington Post* (9 January 2019).
2 Gavin Williamson, 'Defence in Global Britain' speech (11 February 2019), https://www.gov.uk/government/speeches/defence-in-global-britain
3 Boris Johnson, 'Cancel the Guilt Trip', *The Spectator* (2 September 2002): 14.
4 Dane Kennedy, *The Imperial History Wars: Debating the British Empire* (London: Bloomsbury Academic, 2018).

Index

Abbott, Tony, 26, 28, 88
Afghanistan, 172
Africa, 1
African free trade zone, 15
agriculture standards, 31
AIDS, 114
Andress, David, 138
Anglo-Irish relations, 63, 66
Anglosphere, the, 25–34, 88–9, 95, 170
    appeal, 32
    definition, 22, 25
    extent, 29
    free market, 30–2
    influence, 29–32
    Initiative for Free Trade (IFT), 28
    lineage, 25–7
    and mutual recognition, 30–1
    outlook, 29
    resurgence of, 26, 28, 33
    role, 27, 33–4
    trade deals, 21
anti-European sentiments, 44–5
anti-immigrant populism, 91–3
Any Questions (TV programme), 56
Arendt, Hannah, 57
art galleries, 125–9
Ascherson, Neal, 4, 169
Atlanticism, 43–4
Attlee, Clement, 7
austerity, 2010, 4
Australia, 17, 19–20, 21, 28, 38, 88, 105
Australia–New Zealand Closer Economic Relations Trade Agreement, 30
authoritarian populism, 56
Aznar, Jose Maria, 83

backstop, the, 32
Baillie-Grohman, Harold, 157–60, 161, 163–4

Baker, Herbert, 111
Baldwin, James, 50, 129
Banks, Aaron, 118
Bannon, Steve, 93, 97
Barnier, Michel, 58n6
Barth, Karl, 147
Beech, John, 124
belated recall, process of, 7–8
Belfast Agreement, 1998, 32, 61, 67–8
Belgium, 41, 42, 77
Bell, Duncan, 88–9
Bell, Tim, 116, 117
Bell Pottinger, 116–17, 118
Benn, Tony, 16
Bennett, James C., 89
Bhambra, Gurminder, 40–1, 123, 139
Biggar, Nigel, 13–4n25, 143–52, 171
    on the British Empire, 147–9
    critique of Thatcherism, 145
    In Defence of War, 146
    'Ethics and Empire' project, 146, 149
    and Gilley controversy, 146
    Between Kin and Cosmopolis, 147
    and kinship, 147–8, 150–1
    'Less Hegel, More History! Christian Ethics and Political Realities', 149
    media presence, 146
    'Outing yourself as a rightist isn't easy', 144
    and Rhodes Must Fall movement, 146, 150
    Theological Politics, 145
    Unionism, 146–7
    use of history, 149–52
Biko, Steve, 113
Birmingham City Art Gallery and Museum, 'The Past Is Now' exhibition, 128–9

Black Consciousness movement, 113
black history, 76
Blair, Tony, 171
Blake, William, 50
Bokhari, Allum, 88
Boles, Nick, 31
Bonar Law, Andrew, 53
Boym, Svetlana, 123–4
Brazil, 17
Breitbart, 126
Breitbart News, 88
Brexit
    as collective neurological affliction, 3–4
    debate, 16
    ideology, 16
    promise of, 64–5
Brexit Ideologues, 51
Brexit imagination, the, 65–6
Brexit negotiations, 49, 58n6
Brexit referendum, 2, 3, 17, 18, 20, 39, 57, 67, 89
    Bristol results, 138–9
    Gibraltarian vote, 79
    Leave vote, 52–3
    manipulation, 117
    postmortems, 169–70
    regional variations, 71
    relentless focus on sovereignty, 28, 170
    Scotland and, 71–3, 75
Brexit: The Movie, 17–18, 18
Brexiteers, 5–6, 7, 170
    conviction, 22
    discontents, 27
    failure, 171–2
    as globalists, 17
    motivation, 123
    relentless focus on sovereignty, 28, 170
    rhetorical strategies, 18, 22
    trade priorities, 20–1
Bristol, 133–40
Bristol, University of, 135
Britain, 74–5
British Museum, 126
British Nationality Act, 1948, 106
British passport, 63
British prestige, 16
Britishness, 16, 63, 82, 101, 123–4
Brooke, Peter, 67

Buck, Pearl, 159
Buckley, William F., Jr, 92–3
Burnham, Andy, 121
Burton, Antoinette, 90–1, 97

Cambridge Analytica, 116, 117, 118
Cameron, David, 49, 57, 71, 104
Canada, 19–20, 21, 28, 30, 88, 105
Canadian–EU free trade agreement (CETA), 28
CANZUK cooperation, 21, 30, 170
Cape Town, University of, Rhodes Must Fall movement, 111–15, 118–19
Carlson, Tucker, 96–7, 115
Carlyle, Thomas, 148
Carson, Sir Edward, 55
Cassidy, John, 135–6
Catholic Church, power of, 66
Central African Federation, 57
Ceuta, 40
Chamberlain, Joseph, 20, 26
Channel 4, 117
Channel 4 Survation study, 2018, 62
Charlie Hebdo, 144
Charlottesville, 113, 121–2
Chiang Kai-shek, 162, 165
China, 17, 31–2
    bitter memory of history, 164
    British Naval Mission, 157–60
    Communist Party rule, 164–5
    foreign relations, 164
    and Hong Kong, 164
    and Japan, 161, 162, 164
    lack of academic capacity on, 163–4
    nationalism, 165
    Nationalist Revolution, 158, 161
    One Belt One Road initiative, 165
    relations with, 157–65
    rise of, 33
Chirac, Jacques, 92
chlorinated chicken, 31
Churchill, Winston, 38, 59, 60, 63, 106, 122
circles of interest, 33, 38–9, 43, 45
circuits of knowledge, 114–18
citizenship, 105, 106, 108
civil service, 52
Clark, Christopher, 149
Cold War, 41
Coles, Will, 136

collective identity, 148
collective memory, 134, 138
colonial mindset, 128–9
colonialism, 39–41, 171
    of the object, 125–6
coloniality, 113
Colston, Edward, 122, 133, 135–7, 138
Commonwealth, 7, 15, 17, 19, 21, 22, 26, 27, 29, 38, 106, 170
Commonwealth Chambers of Commerce, 19
Commonwealth Games, 2014, 76–7
Commonwealth Institute, 124
Commonwealth Prime Ministers Meetings, 19
community co-curation, 128
ConHome website, 26
Conservative, The, 144
Conservative Party, 67
    and the Anglosphere, 26–7
    European Research Group faction, 31
    fragmentation, 32
    modernizing MPs, 31
    in Scotland, 32
Conservative Political Action Conference, 2018, 87–8
cooperation, imperial, 19
Corn Laws, 18
Countering Colston, 122
Countering Colston Group, 136
Cox, Jo, murder of, 102
Crace, John, 51
cultural dementia, 138
cultural identity, 121–30
culture, role of, 129
culture wars, 121–30
Cummings, Dominic, 28
Curtis, Lionel, 7

Daddow, Oliver, 8
Daily Express, 102–3, 122
Daily Mail, 102–3, 107, 122, 126–7, 146
Daily Maverick, 117
Daily Telegraph, 2, 107, 146
David Horowitz Freedom Centre, 94
Davidson, Ruth, 32
Davis, David, 15, 17, 17–18, 30, 33, 62
de Certeau, Michel, 143
de Gaulle, Charles, 38, 40
De Klerk, F. W., 117

Deacon, Liam, 126
Dearlove, Sir Richard, 145
declinist studies, 19
decoloniality, 118
decolonization, 42, 44, 93
    of the curriculum, 114
    of the environment, 111–15, 118–19
dehumanization, 113
Deighton, Anne, 39
Democratic Unionist Party, 57, 63
Denmark, empire complex, 41–2
deregulation, 31
deserving migrants, 107
Dilke, Charles, 6, 8
discrimination, 107
dis-United Kingdom, 169
dog-whistle, 105
domestic issues, 27
dominion, 7
Dominions, the, 18, 18–19, 19, 26
Donington, Katie, 171
Drayton, Richard, 74, 150, 171
Dresser, Madge, 136–7
Dubow, Saul, 171
Durkin, Martin, 17–18

Economic Freedom Fighters, 112
economic individualism, 88
economic migrants, 102
Economists for Brexit, 31
Economists for Free Trade group, 28
Eddy, Richard, 137
education curricula, 4
EEC referendum, 1975, 16, 20
EFTA, 49
Elizabeth II, Queen, 66
Elton, Lord, 93
emigration, 106
emotional attachment, 170
Empire
    afterlives of, 4
    disregard of, 16–17
    feelings about, 5–6
    semantic tensions, 5–7
Empire 2.0, 6, 15–22, 25, 27, 38, 170, 171
empire complex, 37–45
    Belgium, 41
    Britain, 37–9, 42–5
    Denmark, 41–2

France, 40, 44
   the Netherlands, 39–40, 41
   Portugal, 41, 43
Empire Marketing Board, 19
empires of the mind, 3
England, 64–5, 74, 75
English fundamentalism, 52
English nationalism, 63, 68
English Unionism, 53–5
ethnic populism, 55, 56–7
Eurafrique, 39–40
Europe
   death narrative, 94
   hostility towards, 15–16
   turn towards, 19–20
European citizenship, 68
European Commission, 27
European Common Market, 20
European Court of Justice, 30
European Economic Community, 38–9, 39, 43
European integration
   British attitudes to, 38–9, 44
   and colonialism, 40–1
   turn against, 33
European Research Group, 28, 31
European single market, 20
European Union, 144
Europeanness, 40
Euroscepticism, 15, 27, 28, 33, 44–5
exclusion, 108–9
exports, 17, 20–1

fake news, 138
Falkland Islands, 4
Farage, Nigel, 51, 55, 66, 87–8, 90, 94, 97, 103–4, 172
faux histories, 51
Federation of British Industries, 18–19
First World War, 160
Five Eyes intelligence partnership, 31
Foreign Affairs Committee, 6
Foreign and Commonwealth Office, 28
foreign markets, engagement with, 18–21
Foreign Office, 21
foreigners, humiliation/subordination, 16
forgetfulness, 123, 169
   definition, 50–1
   historical, 49–57
Fortress Europe, 40

Fox, Liam, 22, 28, 33, 170
Fox News, 88, 94, 96–7, 115
France, 40, 42, 44, 18, 77
free trade, 17, 18, 30
   Anglosphere, 28–9, 30–2
   ideals, 29–30
freedom of movement, 102
Freeman, George, 31
freshies, 108
functionalism, 56
Future of England study, 2018, 61–2

General Agreement on Tariffs and Trade (GATT), 19
general election, 2015, 104
general election, 2017, 28
Gentleman, Amelia, 105
Geoghegan, Chris, 116
geopolitical thinking, 38–9
Germany, 18, 45, 77, 102
Gibraltar, 4, 79–85, 171
   Brexit referendum vote, 79
   Britishness, 82, 83
   Constitution, 2006, 80, 81–2
   co-sovereignty with Spain, 79–80, 83
   geopolitical baggage, 82–3
   relationship with Spain, 82–3
   relationship with the UK, 80–2, 84–5
   Spanish border, 82, 84
   Spanish claims on, 80
   status, 79, 83, 84–5
Gibraltar Protocol, 81, 85n4
Gilley, Bruce, 146
Ginzburg, Carlo, 143
Glasgow, 76
Glasgow, University of, 77
Global Britain, 1–4, 6, 7, 8, 25, 28, 74, 89, 119, 122, 165, 170
global grandeur, fantasies of regaining, 77
global nationhood, 2
global pre-eminence, Britain's history of, 37
global trade role, 18–21
Global UK, 74
globalization, 121, 172
Glover, Stephen, 122
Good Friday Agreement *see* Belfast Agreement, 1998
Gopal, Priyamvada, 145
Gove, Michael, 28, 57, 104

Index

Graham, Robert, 77
Great Power status, 16–17
Greater Belgium, 41
Greater Britain, 6–9, 25
Greenland, 41–2
Grendi, Edoardo, 143
Grob-Fitzgibbon, Benjamin, 15–16
Guardian, 84, 90, 105, 146
guerrilla artists, 136, 139–40

Hammond Perry, Kennetta, 107
Hannan, Daniel, 13n37, 26, 29, 30–1, 66, 151
Hansen, Peo, 39–40
Harper, Stephen, 26
Harris, John, 123
Hart, Peter, 149–50
Hastings, Max, 149
hate crimes, 101
Haynes, Douglas M., 89
Henderson, James, 117, 118
Heyer, Heather, 121–2
Hirsch, Afua, 122
historians, 5
　insights, 172
historic precedent, 3
historical amnesia, 5
historical baggage, 4
historical change, pattern of, 18–20
historical consciousness, absence of, 51
historical forgetfulness, 49–57
　definition, 50–1
historical memory, crisis in, 50
historical past, disappearance of, 51–2
historical perspective, lack of, 52
histories, multiplicity of, 5
history
　deviation in, 143
　escaping from, 65–6
　insights from, 172
history wars, 121–2, 169–72
Homo Britannicus, 74–5
Hong Kong, 19, 29, 164
Hoon, Jeff, 81–2
Hopkins, Katie, 94–7, 115, 144
Horowitz, David, 94, 97
Hyde, Marina, 51

Iceland, 41
identity, 139
　collective, 148
　cultural, 121
　Irish, 67–8
　national, 124
illegal immigrants, 105–6
immigration, 33, 91–3, 101–9, 109n1, 133
immigration policy, 4
imperial afterlives, plurality of, 5
imperial amnesia, 123
imperial belonging, 57
imperial business, unfinished, 42
Imperial Conference, 1949, 7
Imperial Economic Committee, 19
imperial eminence, fall from, 1
imperial exception, ghost of, 4
imperial imagination, 66–7
imperial mindsets, 16
imperial nostalgia, 17–18, 22, 122–3, 127, 139, 169
imperial past, lingering presence of, 4
imperial paternalism, 108
imperial preferences, 19
imperialism
　negative connotations, 5
　zombie, 16
imports, from EU, 20
Independent, The, 146
India, 19, 22
industrial decline, 4
Initiative for Free Trade (IFT), 28
Institute of Economic Affairs, 28, 31
intra-imperial tariff preferences, 19
Iraq, 172
Ireland, 59–69, 75–6
　ambivalence on, 61
　border crossing-points, 64
　border problem, 60, 62–3, 67, 69
　Britishness, 63
　Churchill on, 59, 60, 63
　economy, 66–7
　the English problem, 61–6
　identity, 67–8
　Johnson on, 61, 62
　May on, 63
　nationalism, 64, 66–9
　power of the Catholic Church, 66
Ireland, Republic of, 61
Irish crisis,1912–14, 53–5
Irish Question, the, 59–61, 63, 146
Irish Times, 83–4

Islamophobia, 105
Italy, 19, 45

Jameson, Leander Starr, 111
Japan, 161, 162, 164
Jardine, William, 164
Javid, Sajid, 108
Jenkins, Simon, 84
Jensen, Kristian, 37, 38, 41
Johnson, Boris, 2–3, 13n37, 28, 51, 57, 104, 170, 171
   and the Anglosphere, 26
   defensive tone, 16
   and Gibraltar, 81
   on Ireland, 61, 62
Jonsson, Stefan, 39–40
Joyce, James, *Ulysses*, 63–4, 68–9

Kassam, Raheem, 87–8, 89, 90, 97
Kassim, Sumaya, 128, 129
Kay, Jackie, 76
Kelly, Robin D. G., 89
Kenny, Michael, 75, 88
Kenya, 1
key tropes, 16
Khan, Sadiq, 87–8, 96, 97
Khan, Yasmin, 170
Kierkegaard, S., 147
kinship, 147–8, 150–1
Kipling, Rudyard, 54–5
knowledge, of the past, 172
knowledge systems, interactions between, 115
Knox, John, 74
Kodney, Ziva, 137–8
Kwarteng, Kwasi, 56, 127

Labour Party, *European Unity* manifesto, 1950, 38
Lammy, David, 125
Lancaster House, 1–2
Laurier, Wilfred, 7
Lavabre, Marie Claire, 138
League of British Covenanters, 53–4
League of Nations, 162
Leave campaign, 3, 17
Lee, Robert E., 113, 121–2
Legatum Institute, 28
legislature, assertion of authority, 49
liberal fascism, 96

liberal multiculturalism, 88
Lilico, Andrew, 60
Lives Matter movement, 113
Locke, Hew, 136
London riots, 2011, 4

Mac, 103
Malayan Independence, 1
Malcolm X, 91
Malema, Julius, 112
Malik, Nesrine, 90
Mangcu, Xolela, 114
Mankind Quarterly, 115–16
Marshall plan, 43
Matheson, James, 164
Mau Mau High Court case, 4
Maxwele, Chumani, 112
May, Theresa, 3, 6, 8, 15, 28, 129, 170, 171
   cabinet, 51
   and Gibraltar, 80
   and Ireland, 62, 63
   lack of wisdom, 49
   Lancaster House speech, 1–2
   public persona, 52
   and Scotland, 74
Mbeki, Thabo, 114
Mbembe, Achille, 113, 114
Melilla, 40
memorialization, of the past, 133–40
memory
   collective, 134, 138
   and politics, 137
   reluctant sites of, 133–40
memory politics, 133–40, 171
memoryscapes, 137–8
Mennochio, the mad miller of Montereale, 143
metonyms, 5
Mignolo, Walter, 114
migrants, 102–5
migration, 45, 106
military deployments, overseas, 4, 8
Minford, Patrick, 28
misremembered past narrative, 16
Molyneaux, Stefan, 96
Monnet, Jean, 43
Montgomerie, Tim, 26
moral categories, 5
Mordaunt, Penny, 104

Movement for Colonial Freedom, 16
multiculturalism, 89, 121, 126
Murray, Douglas, 93, 94, 97
Museum Detox, 127–8
Museum of Brexit, 129
Museum of London, 125
Museum of Scottish History, 76
museums, 125–9, 129, 135
mutual recognition, 30–1
myth-making, 51

Nairn, Tom, 58n12
Napoleonic wars, 41
National Audit Office, 106
national disintegration, 4
national figures, iconic, 127
national identity, 124
National Museum of China, 164–5
national narrative, 121–30
national pride, 16
national self-belief, 22
nationalism, 64, 108–9
    Chinese, 165
    English, 63, 68
    Irish, 64, 66–9
    populist, 45
    Scottish, 75, 77
nationhood, global, 2
NATO, 41, 43
Nelson, Horatio, 122
neo-Conservatives, 28
neo-imperial vision, 3
net migration, 106
Netherlands, the, 39–40, 41, 42, 43, 45
networks of influence, 115–18
New Statesman, 75
New Zealand, 17, 19–20, 21, 28, 30, 38, 88
NHS, 31
Nigeria, 1
nineteenth-century legacy, 17
Nix, Alexander, 117, 118
Northern Ireland, 61, 62, 67, 67–8
Northern Ireland backstop, 32
nostalgia, 52–3, 57
    imperial, 17–18, 22, 122–3, 127, 139, 169
    post-imperial, 15–16
    restorative, 123–4
Nunes, Devin, 97

Olusoga, David, 15, 107, 121, 134
Olympic Games, Rio, 2016, 3–4
opium trade, 164
Otele, Olivette, 171
otherness, 108–9
O'Toole, Fintan, 2, 16, 83–4, 84
Ottawa Conference, 1932, 19
outsiders, fear of, 103–4
Oxford, University of, 113

Packer, J. I., 145, 154n27
Panorama (newspaper), 84
passports, 63
past, the
    memorialization of, 133–40;
      see also Rhodes Must Fall movement
    value of knowledge of, 172
'The Past Is Now' exhibition, 128–9
Patel, Priti, 104, 108
paternalism, 108
patriotism, 124
Pax Britannica, 170
Pearce, Nick, 75, 88
'Plan for Britain', 1–4
political correctness, 126
political representation, crisis of, 49–50
populism, 56
    authoritarian, 56
    ethnic, 55, 56–7
populist nationalism, 45
populist revolt, from below, 53
Portugal, 41, 43, 45, 77
post-Brexit Britain, vision for, 1
post-colonial guilt, 93–4
post-colonial theory, 4
post-imperial angst, 25
post-imperial nostalgia, 15–16
post-truth, 50
Powell, Colin, 151
Powell, Enoch, 54, 55, 75, 89, 90, 91–2, 93, 97
Powellite rupture, the, 55
Power Grab, the, 73–4
pride, 16
Procter, Alice, 126–7
Pryor, James, 117
public history, importance of, 124

Quijano, Aníbal, 114

Race, Ethnicity & Equality in UK History (Royal Historical Society), 151
race and racism, 101–9, 139
racial hierarchies, 126
racial justice, 93–4
radical right, the, 115–18
Rahman, Tunku Abdul, 1
Rand, Ayn, 147
Randlords, 118–19
Rasch, Astrid, 169
Raspail, Jean, 92–3, 97
rediscovery, voyage of, 2
Rees-Mogg, Jacob, 3, 51, 88
refugees, 102–5
Remain campaign, 121
Remainers, 5, 15
restorative nostalgia, 123–4
'Restoring Britishness' (UKIP), 123–4
Reyes, Brian, 81
Rhodes, Cecil, 111–12, 118, 122, 149
Rhodes Must Fall movement, 4, 111–15, 118–19, 122, 139, 144, 146, 150, 171
Rhodesia, 57, 92
Rhodesia-Zimbabwe civil war, 1
right, the, 56
right-wing activism, women's, 96
Rijksmuseum, 126
Riley, Charlotte, 123
Rio Olympics, 2016, 3–4
Robertson, James, 77
Robinson, Tommy, 96, 115
Roche, Simon, 115
Rome, Treaty of, 39
Rotten, Johnny, 69
Round Table movement, 7
Royal Historical Society, *Race, Ethnicity & Equality in UK History*, 151
Runcie, Archbishop, 145
Rupert, Johann, 116
Russia, 117, 118

Salmond, Alex, 73
Sanchez, Mark, 83
Sandys, Duncan, 16
Saunders, Robert, 16
Savage, Michael, 115
Schofield, Camila, 172
Schwarz, Bill, 91–2, 169

Scotland, 68, 71–7
　attitude to Brexit, 71–3, 75, 77
　Conservatism in, 32
　devolution settlement, 72, 73
　European funds, 72
　imperial entanglements, 75–7
　independence, 4, 71–2
　national consciousness, 77
　nationalism, 75, 77
　nationhood, 74, 75
　remain vote, 71
Scottish Parliament, 73
second referendum, 49
Second World War, 19, 42–3, 74, 165
Seeley, J. R., 6–7
semantic tensions, 5–7
settler colonial tradition, 88
shared sovereignty, 32
Singapore, 29
single market, the, 30
Sino-British relations, 157–65
slavery and the slave trade, 76, 77, 107, 133–40, 149, 171
Sloane, Hans, 125
Smuts, Jan, 7
SNP, 32, 71, 73
social media, 116, 138
Society of Merchant Venturers, 134, 137
Song Ziwen, 159
South Africa
　Cambridge Analytica connection, 116, 117
　Rhodes Must Fall movement, 111–15, 118–19
　state capture, 116–17, 118
　white genocide, 96, 115
sovereignty, 27, 28–9, 31, 44, 81, 129
　and mutual recognition, 30
　relentless focus on, 28, 170
　shared, 32
Spain, 40, 41, 79, 79–80, 80, 82
Stirling, David, 118
streetscapes, and the colonial past, 133–40
Stuart, Gisela, 104
stupidity, acme of, 51
Sturgeon, Nicola, 71
Suez crisis, 44
Switzerland, 18
Syria, 102

take back control, 9, 28, 62, 101, 103, 104, 151, 172
tariffs, 18
Thackery, David, 171
Thamm, Marianne, 117
Thatcher, Margaret, 33, 117
Thatcher, Mark, 118
Thatcherism, 55, 93, 145
Third World Quarterly, 146
The Times, 15, 146
Tomkins, Adam, 32
totalitarian state, the, 57
Toye, Richard, 171
trade, gravity models, 29
trade deals, 15, 17
    Anglosphere, 21, 30
Trident, 4
Trouillot, Michel-Rolph, 122
Trump, Donald, 31–2, 56, 87, 90, 115, 121–2
    electoral victory, 117
    Make America Great Again, 123, 172
    support for Brexit, 31
TTIP negotiations, 31
Tuck, Stephen, 89
Turkey, 104
Turnbull, Mark, 117

Uganda, 1
UKIP
    cultural manifesto, 123–5
    refugee campaign poster, 103–4
    'Restoring Britishness', 123–4
    Turkish accession claim, 104
UK–US Free Trade Agreement, 28, 31
Umbrella Movement, 164
'Uncomfortable Art' tours, 126–7
uniculturalism, 124–5
Union, the, 32
Unionism, 53–5
United Kingdom
    breakup of, 71
    national identities, 68
United Nations, Special Committee of Decolonization, 80, 83
United States of America, 18, 44, 50, 105
    agri-products, 31
    Conservative Political Action Conference, 2018, 87–8

culture wars, 121–2
hegemonic position, 25–6
historical myth of independence, 88
Lives Matter movement, 113
new conservatism, 90
populism, 56
racial politics, 90–1
special relationship with, 39, 43, 87–97, 172
Trump electoral victory, 117
Trump presidency, 31–2, 56, 90, 172
white supremacy, 89, 93–4, 121–2
Utrecht, Treaty of, 80, 83, 85

vassalage, 51
Victoria and Albert Museum, 125, 126
Victorian era, , 3, 16–17 26
Vucetic, Srdjan, 88–9

Wales, 68, 74, 75
Ward, Stuart, 169
Welsh, Louise, 77
Welsh Assembly, 73
West Germany, 19
Wheeler, Heather, 3–4
white genocide, South Africa, 96, 115
white supremacy, 89–90, 93–4, 102, 115–16, 121–2
Williamson, Gavin, 8, 164
    'Defence of Global Britain' speech, 170
Wilson, Jason, 115
Wilson, Kathleen, 124
Windrush scandal, 105–7, 109, 125
Withdrawal Agreement, 27, 30
    Gibraltar Protocol, 81, 85n4
    Northern Ireland backstop, 32

xenophobia, 101–9
Xi Jinping, 164–5

Yiannopoulus, Milo, 88
YouGov, 139
Younge, Gary, 89

Zimbabwe, 1
zombie imperialism, 16
Zuma, Jacob, 116